HADDON HALL

WHEN DAVID INVENTED BOWIE

NÉJIB

HADDON HALL

WHEN DAVID INVENTED BOWIE

SELF MADE HERO

To Luce, Joseph
and Julie,
my prettiest stars.

First published in English in 2017
by SelfMadeHero
139-141 Pancras Road
London NW1 1UN
www.selfmadehero.com

Written and illustrated by Néjib
Translated from the French by Edward Gauvin

© Gallimard, 2012

English edition
Publishing Director: Emma Hayley
Sales & Marketing Manager: Sam Humphrey
Publishing Assistant: Guillaume Rater
UK Publicist: Paul Smith
US Publicist: Maya Bradford
Designer: Txabi Jones
With thanks to: Dan Lockwood

A CIP record for this book is available from the British Library

ISBN: 9781910593264

10 9 8 7 6 5 4 3 2 1

Printed and bound in Slovenia

It was the end of
the Swinging Sixties.

That day, like so many others,
the London sky was sad
like a cold cup of tea.

The nasty rain rattled tediously
at my windowpane.

I was waiting for my new
tenants to show up and
inhabit me.

They called me Haddon Hall.

I was an old-fashioned villa on the outskirts of London. I was rented out furnished.

The wicked wind blew down my long hallways.

My furniture was dated and my too-large rooms seemed too empty.

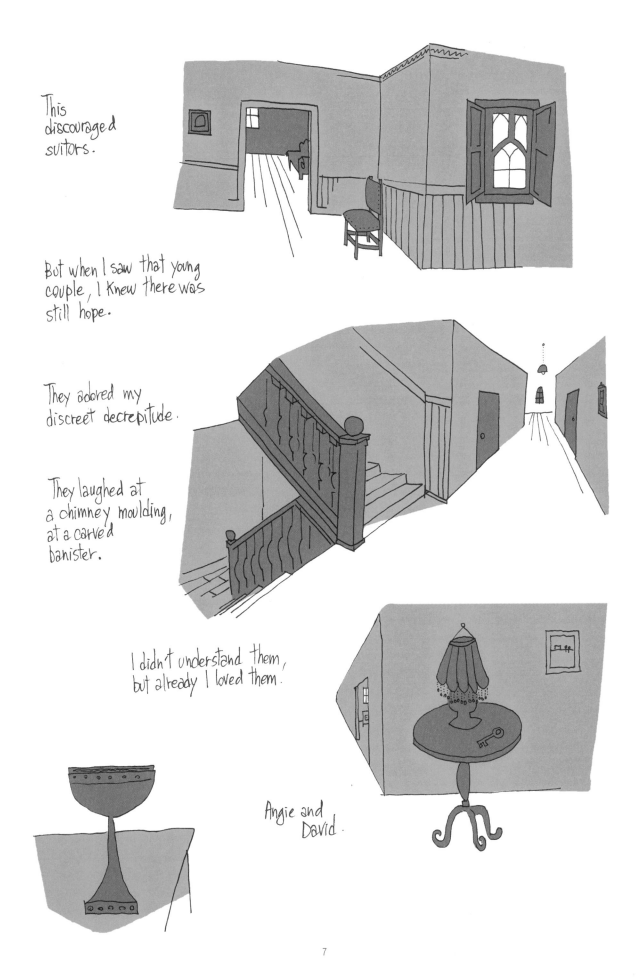

This discouraged suitors.

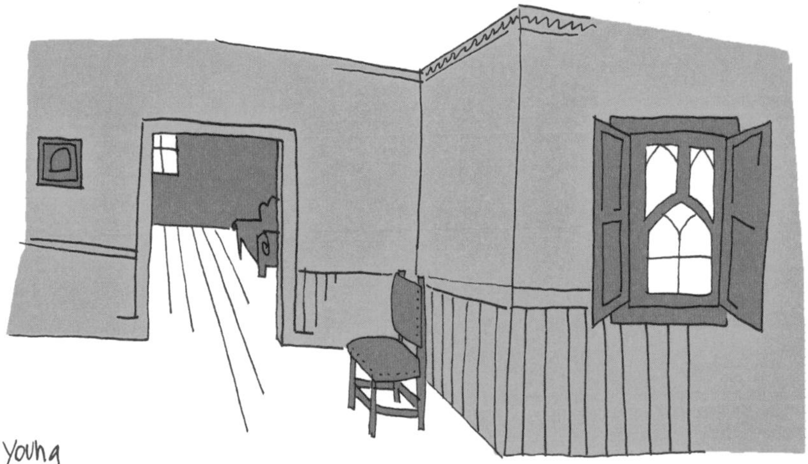

But when I saw that young couple, I knew there was still hope.

They adored my discreet decrepitude.

They laughed at a chimney moulding, at a carved banister.

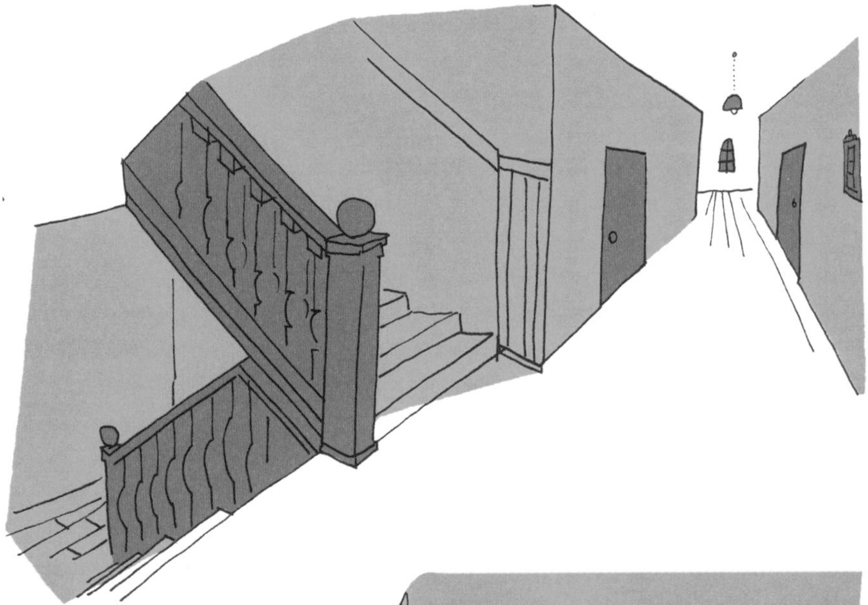

I didn't understand them, but already I loved them.

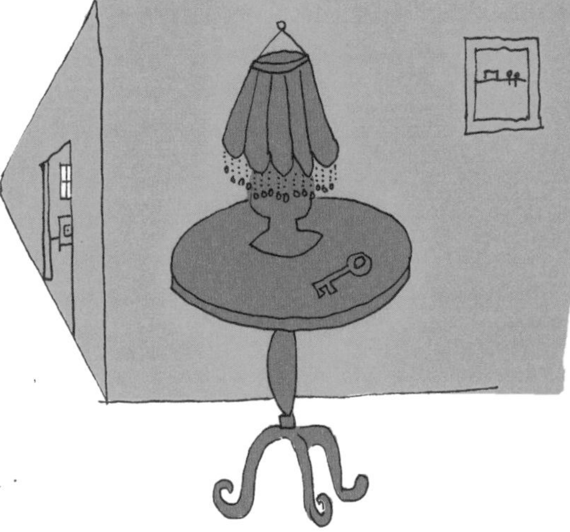

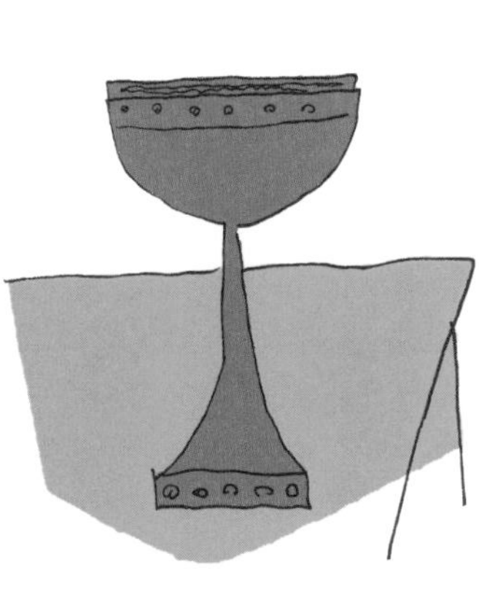

Angie and David.

When they said yes to the estate agent,
a delicious shiver ran the length of my roofbeams!

Welcome to Haddon Hall,
my friends!

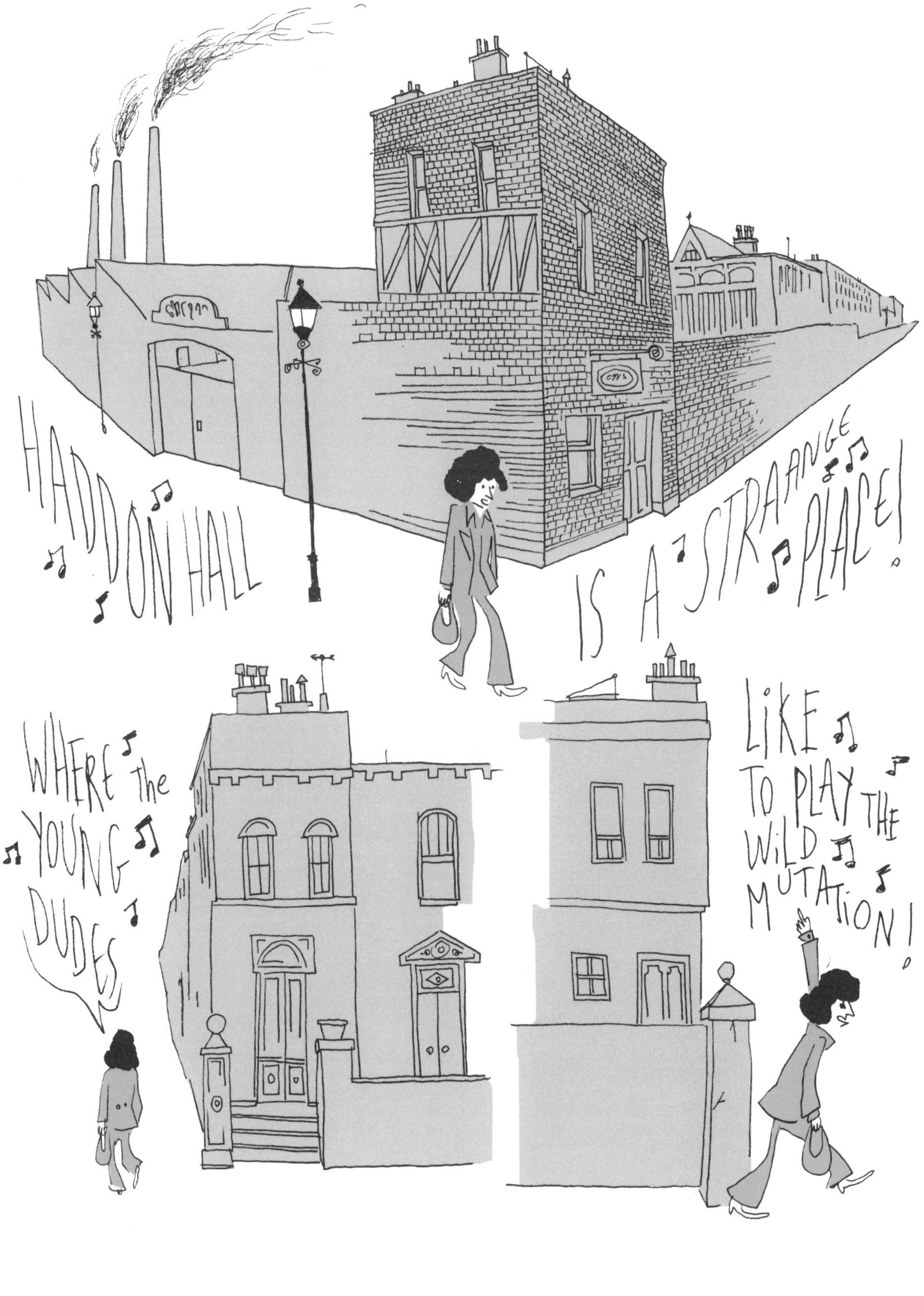
HADDON HALL
IS A STRAAANGE PLACE!
WHERE the YOUNG DUDES
LIKE TO PLAY THE WILD MUTATION!

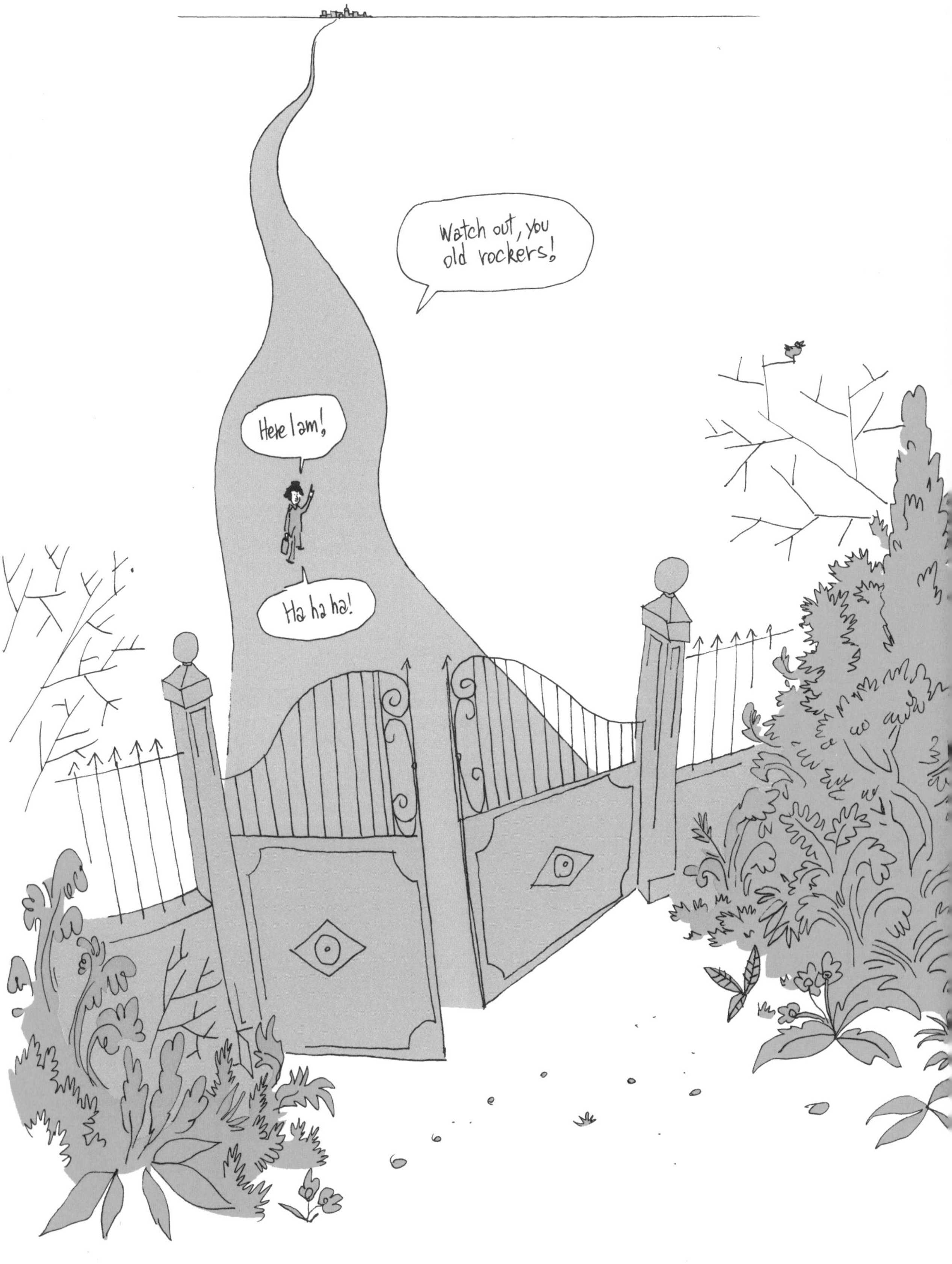
Watch out, you old rockers!
Here I am!
Ha ha ha!

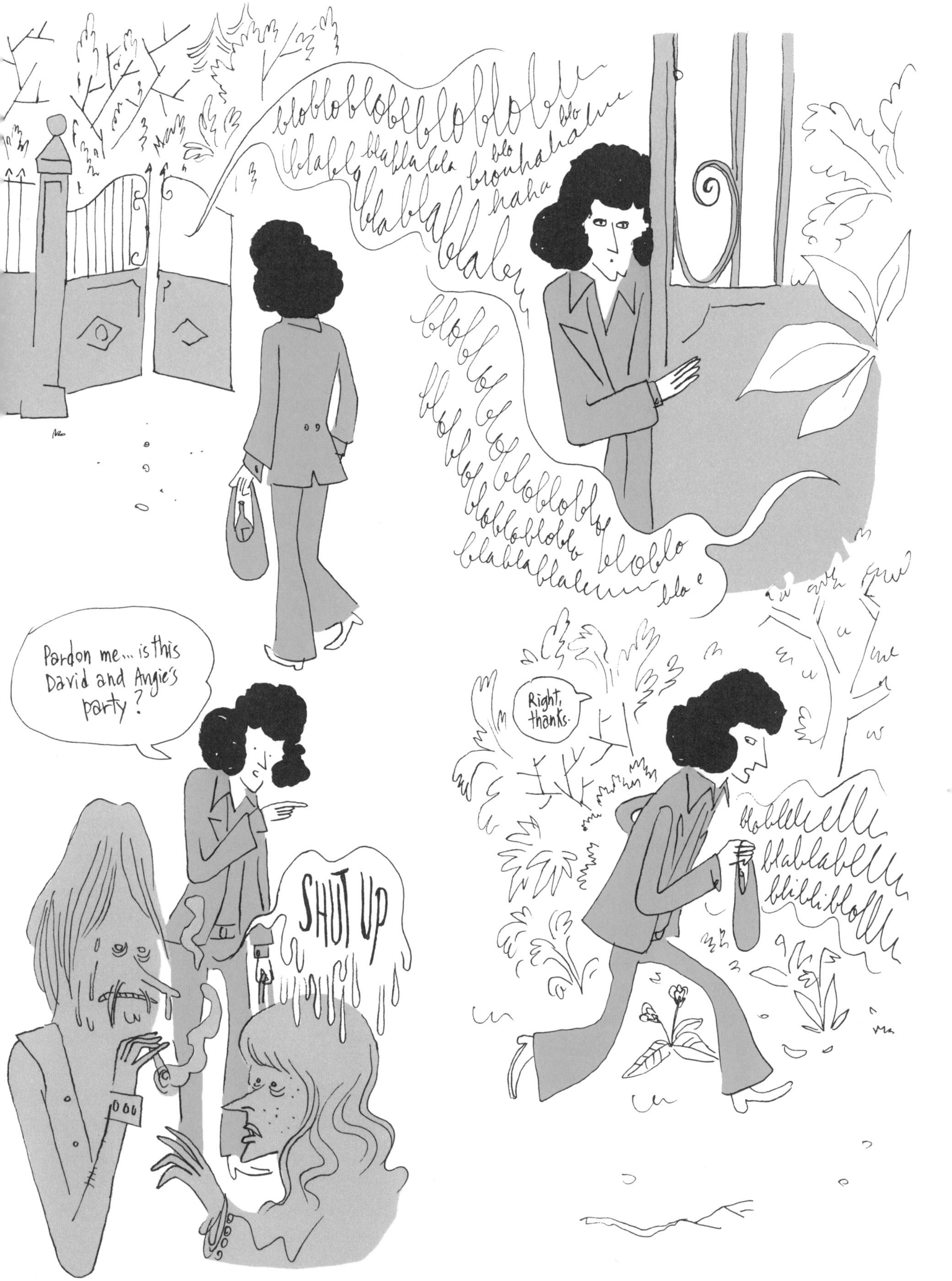
Pardon me... is this David and Angie's party?
SHUT UP
Right, thanks.

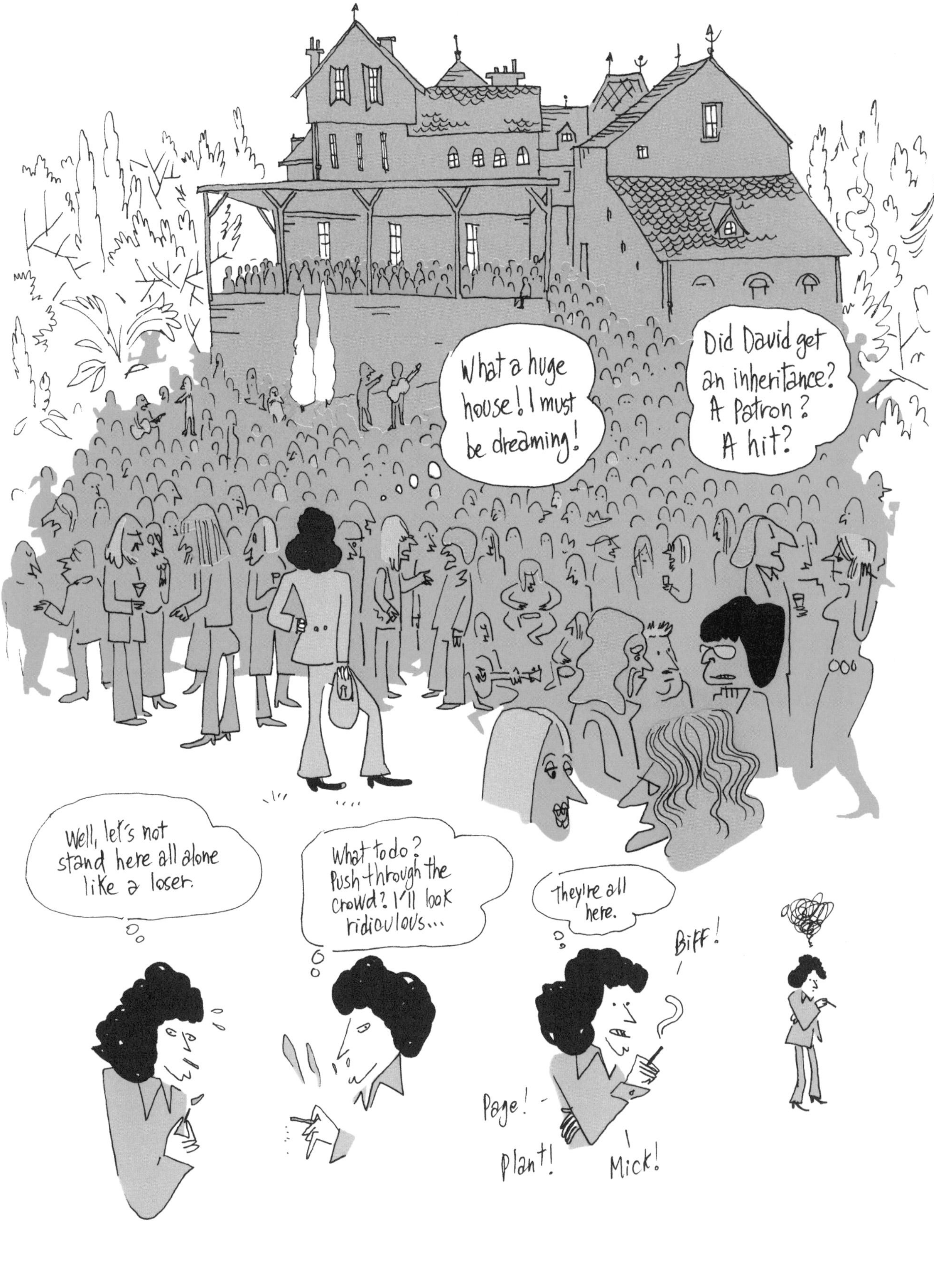
What a huge house! I must be dreaming!
Did David get an inheritance? A Patron? A hit?
Well, let's not stand here all alone like a loser.
What to do? Push through the crowd? I'll look ridiculous...
They're all here.
Biff!
Page!
Plant!
Mick!

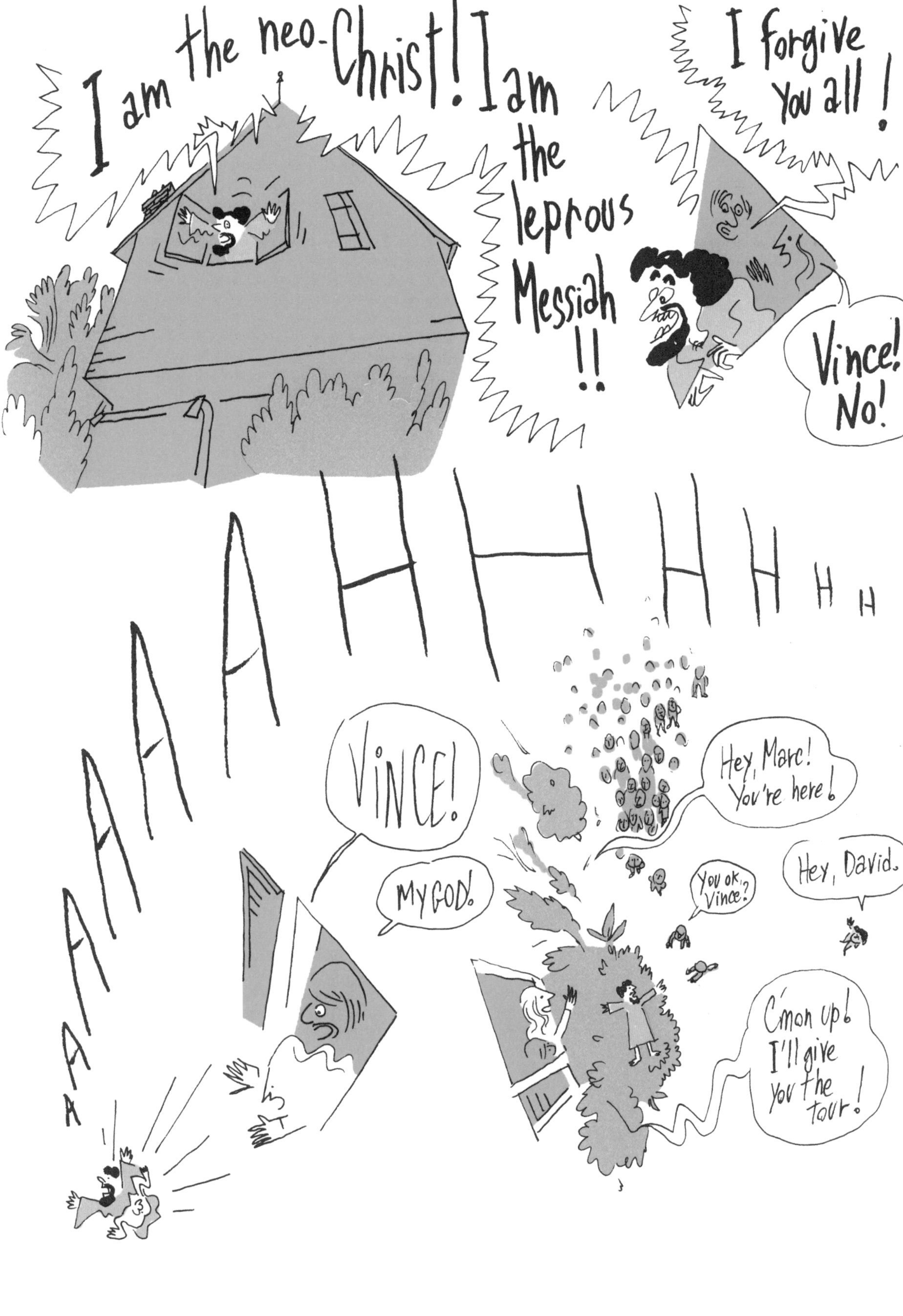
I am the neo-Christ! I am the leprous Messiah !!
I forgive you all !
Vince! No!
AAAAAAHHHHHHHH
VINCE!
MY GOD!
Hey, Marc! You're here!
You ok, Vince?
Hey, David.
C'mon up! I'll give you the tour!

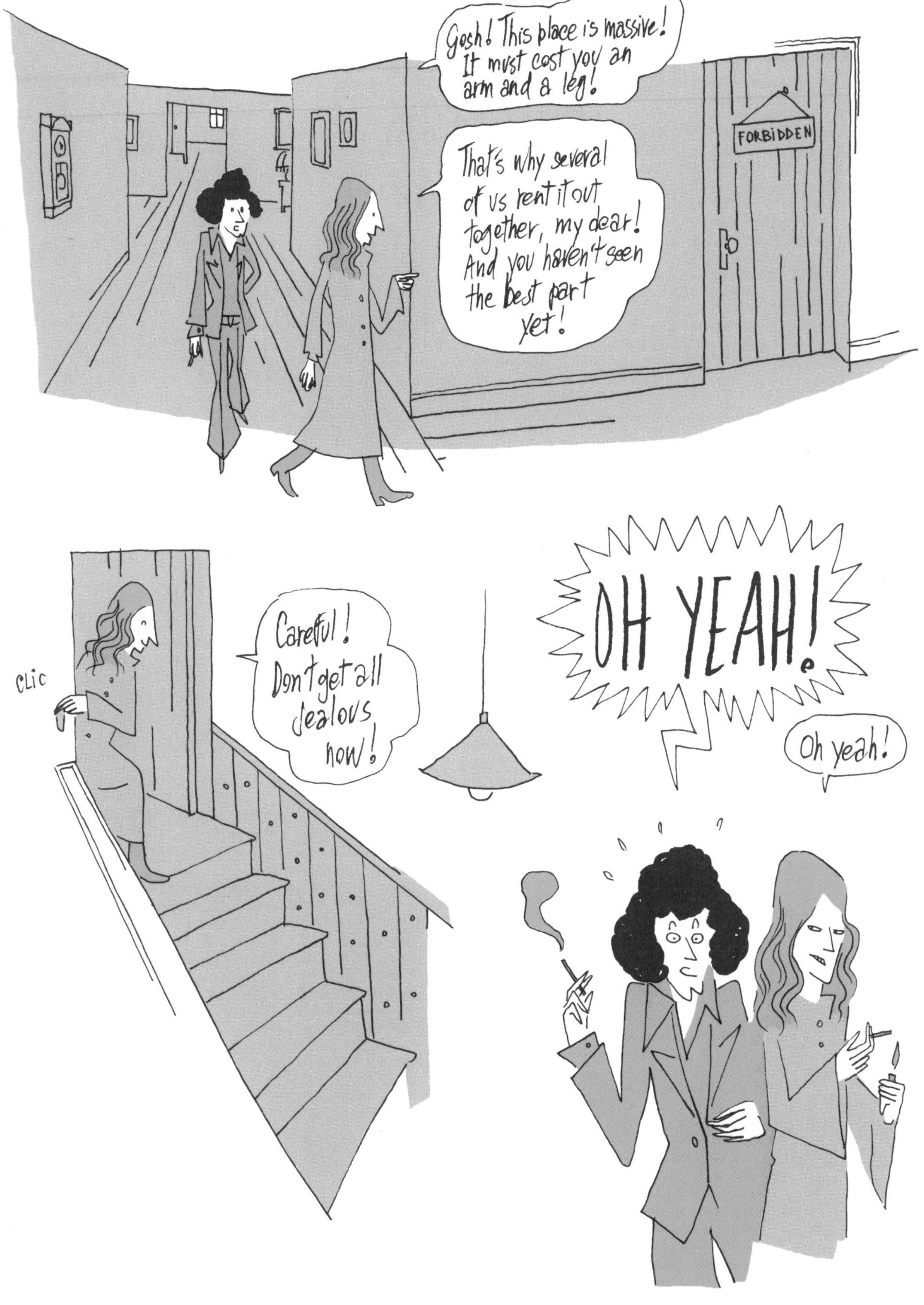
Gosh! This place is massive! It must cost you an arm and a leg!
FORBIDDEN
That's why several of us rent it out together, my dear! And you haven't seen the best part yet!
CLIC
Careful! Don't get all jealous now!
OH YEAH!
Oh yeah!

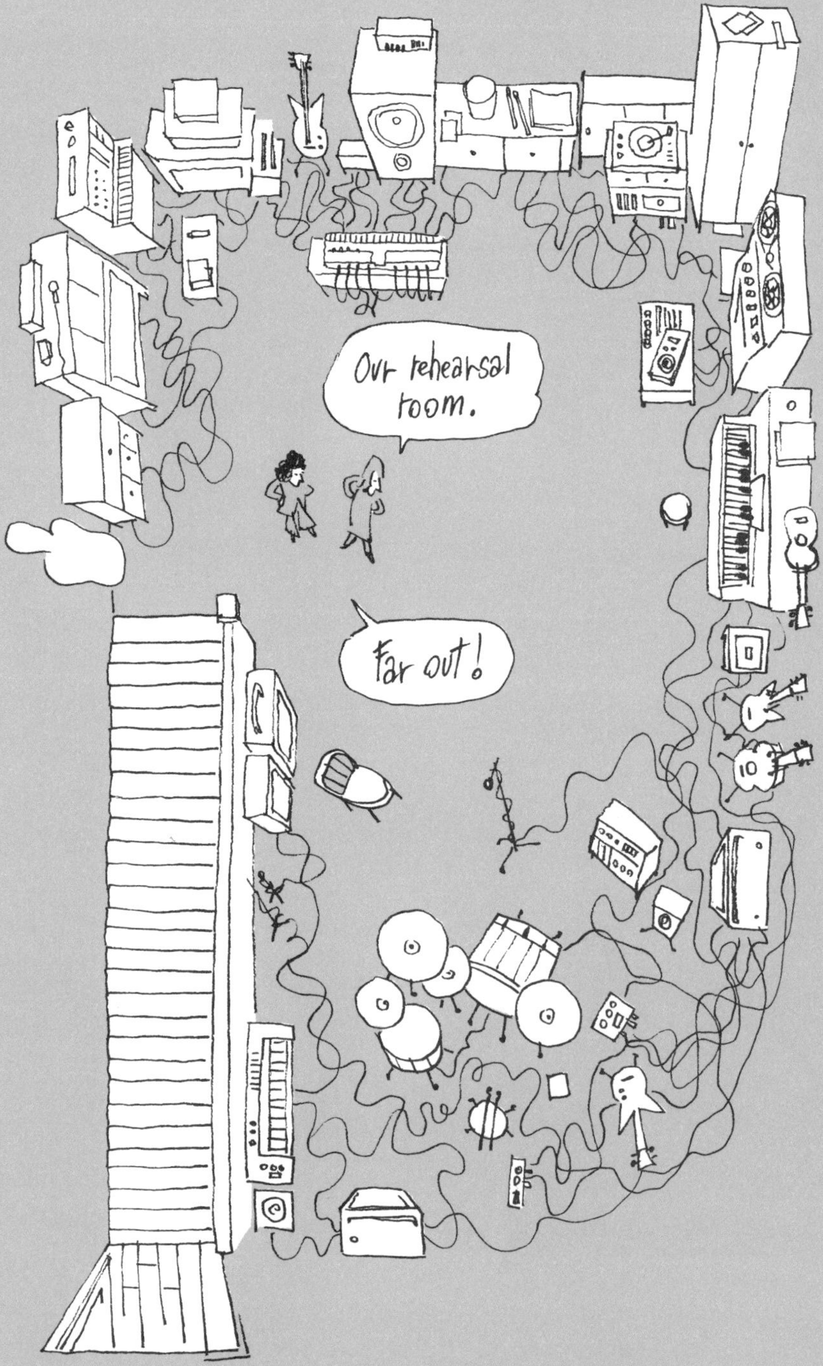
Our rehearsal room.
Far out!

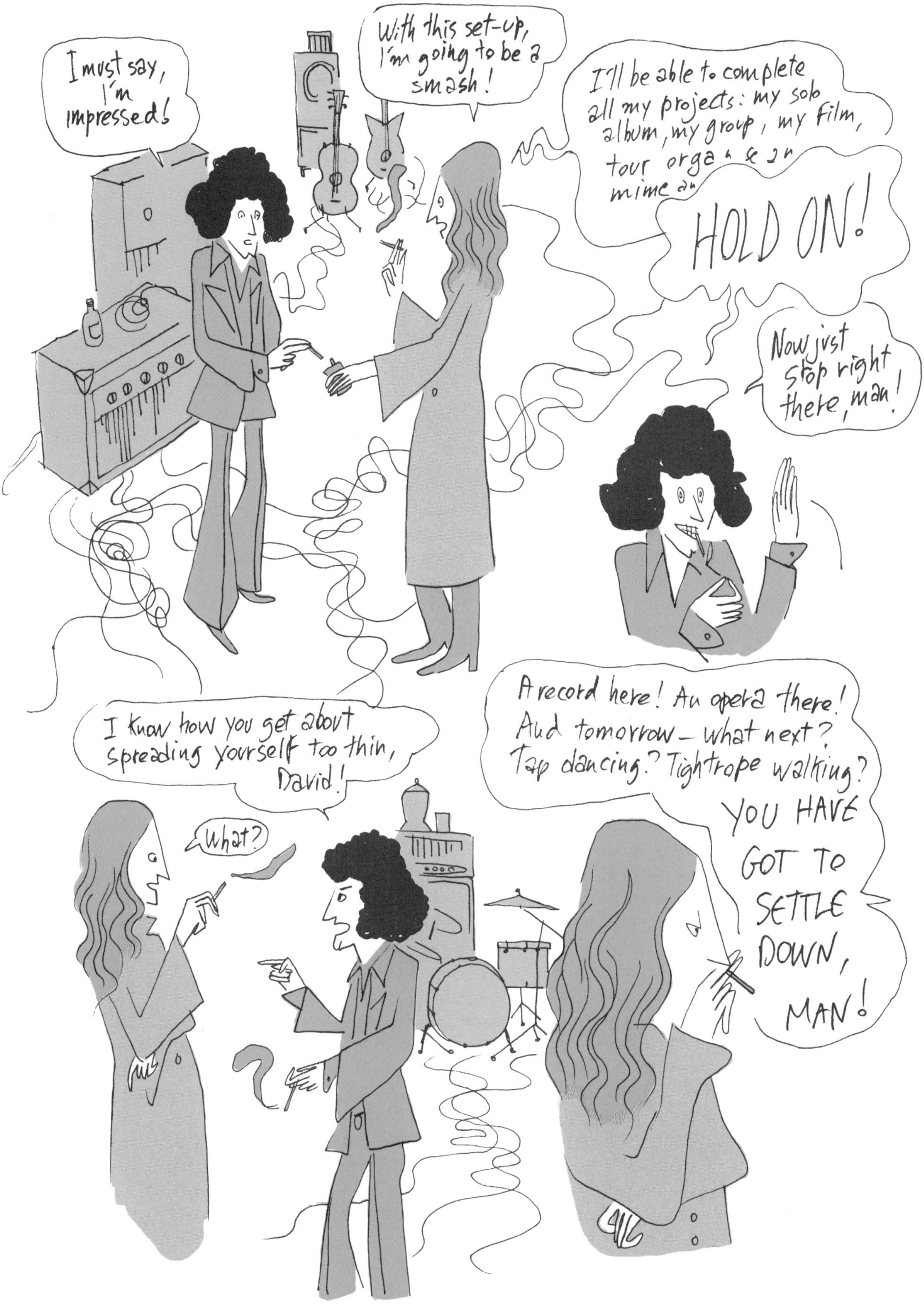
I must say, I'm impressed!
With this set-up, I'm going to be a smash!
I'll be able to complete all my projects: my solo album, my group, my film, tour orga
mime
HOLD ON!
Now just stop right there, man!
I know how you get about spreading yourself too thin, David!
What?
A record here! An opera there! And tomorrow – what next? Tap dancing? Tightrope walking?
YOU HAVE GOT TO SETTLE DOWN, MAN!

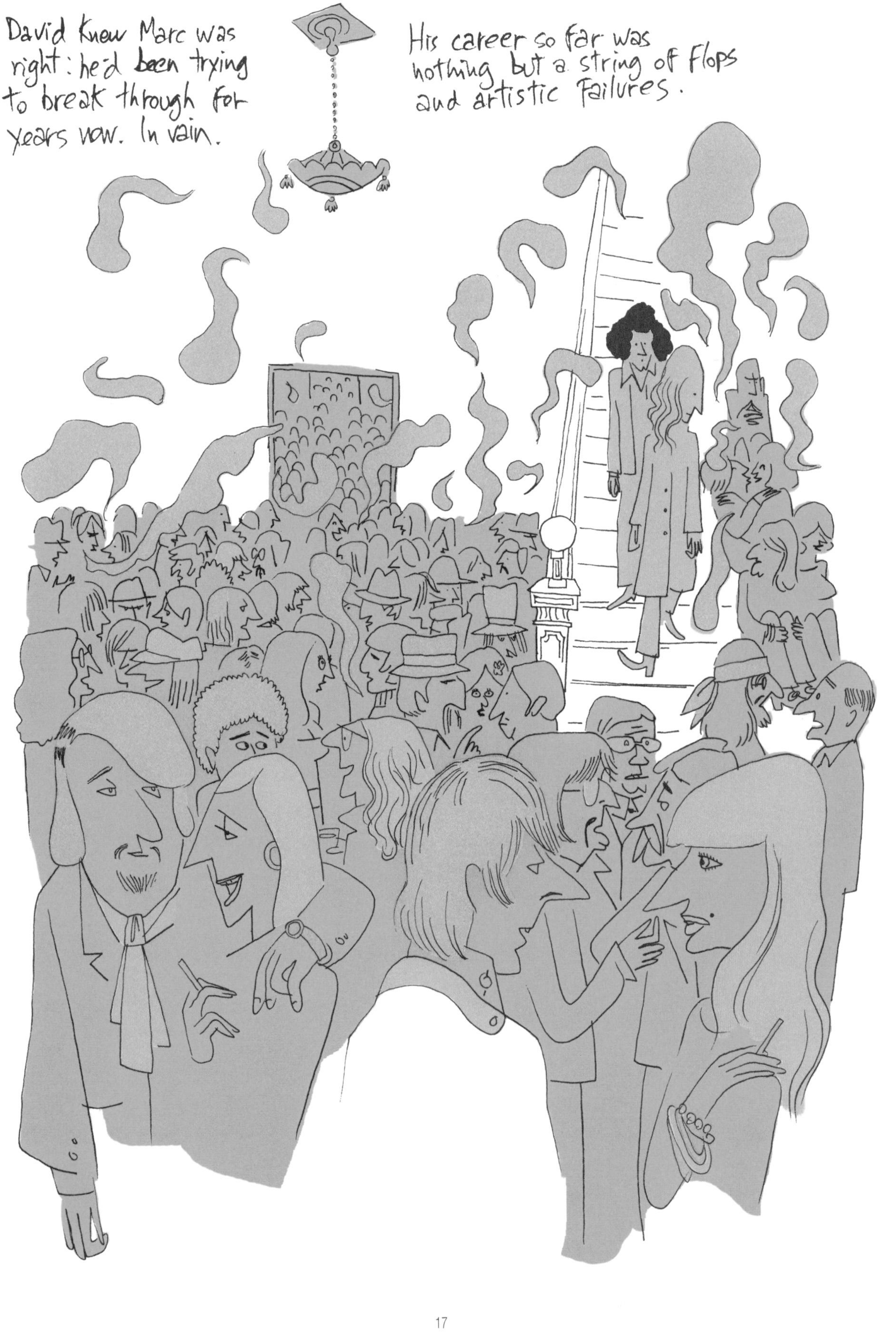
David knew Marc was right: he'd been trying to break through for years now. In vain.
His career so far was nothing but a string of flops and artistic failures.

Then our two friends turned to their favourite activity: putting on a show.

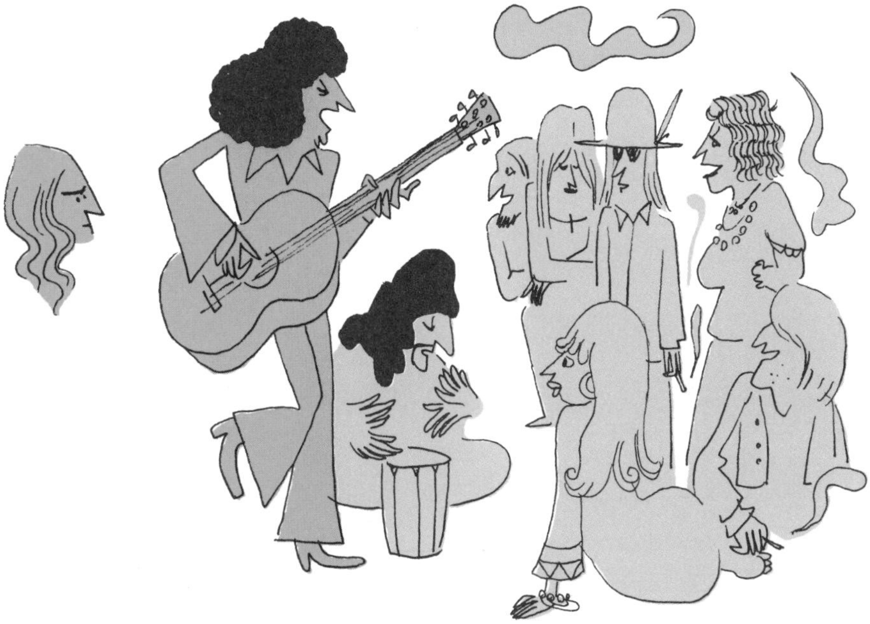

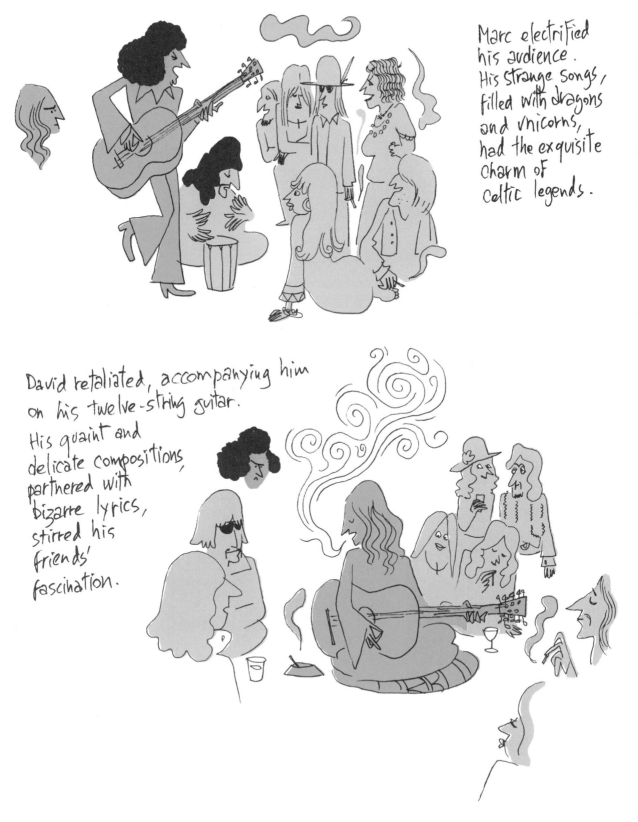

Marc electrified his audience. His strange songs, filled with dragons and unicorns, had the exquisite charm of Celtic legends.

David retaliated, accompanying him on his twelve-string guitar. His quaint and delicate compositions, partnered with bizarre lyrics, stirred his friends' fascination.

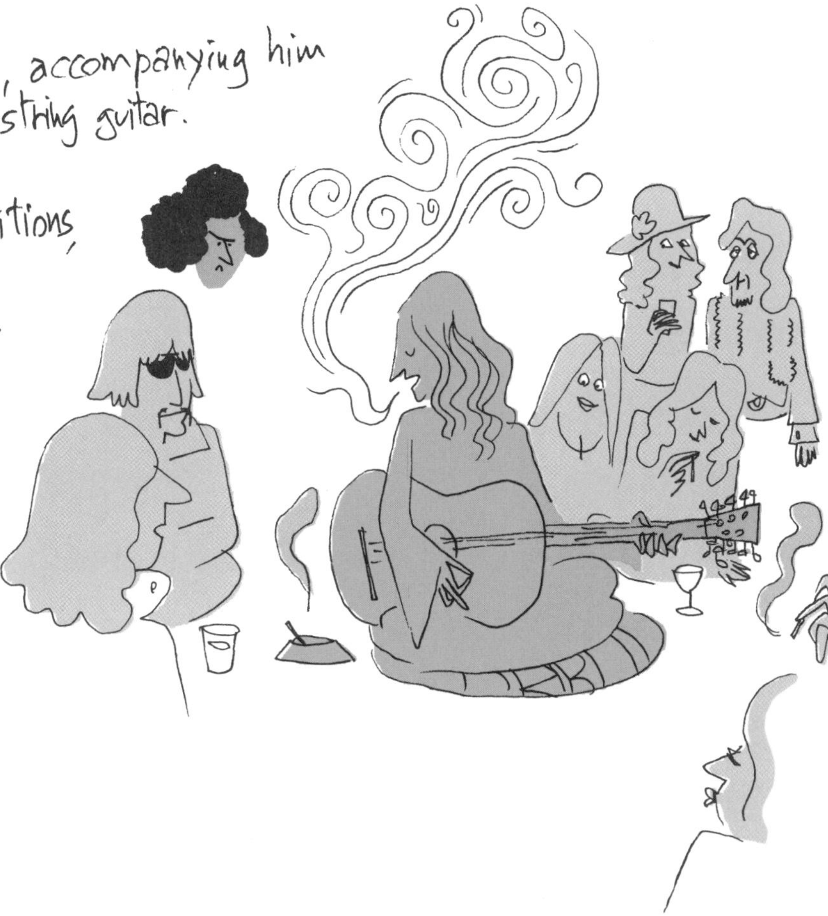

But when the Last Judgement comes around for pop stars,
I shall willingly testify in favour of our two wild blokes,
for behind their outsized egos hid two true lovers of music.
They could talk shop till they were blue in the face.
Only Tony Visconti, an American friend, could keep up.

Mornings after are always the same, with their overflowing ashtrays, the stale smell of cheap wine...

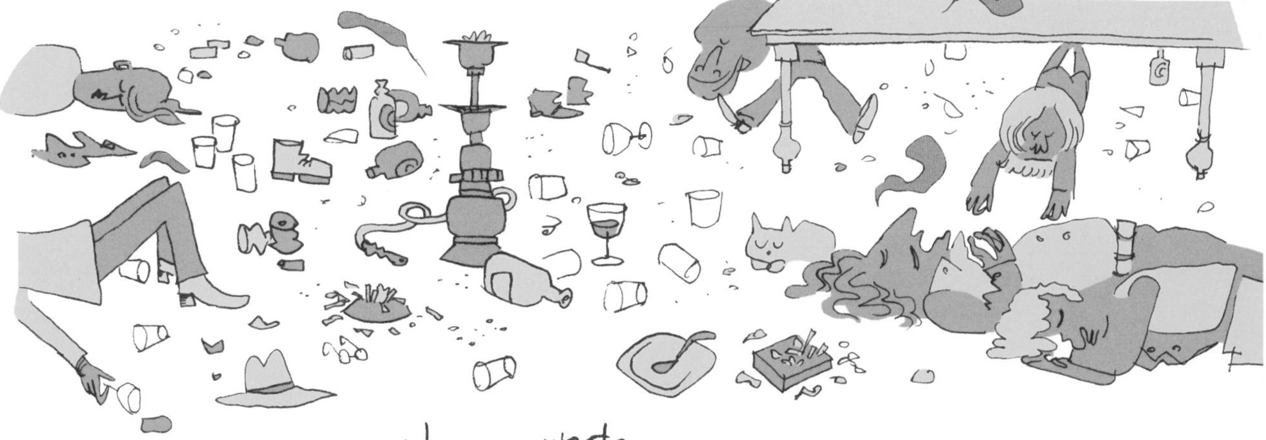

And unwelcome guests.

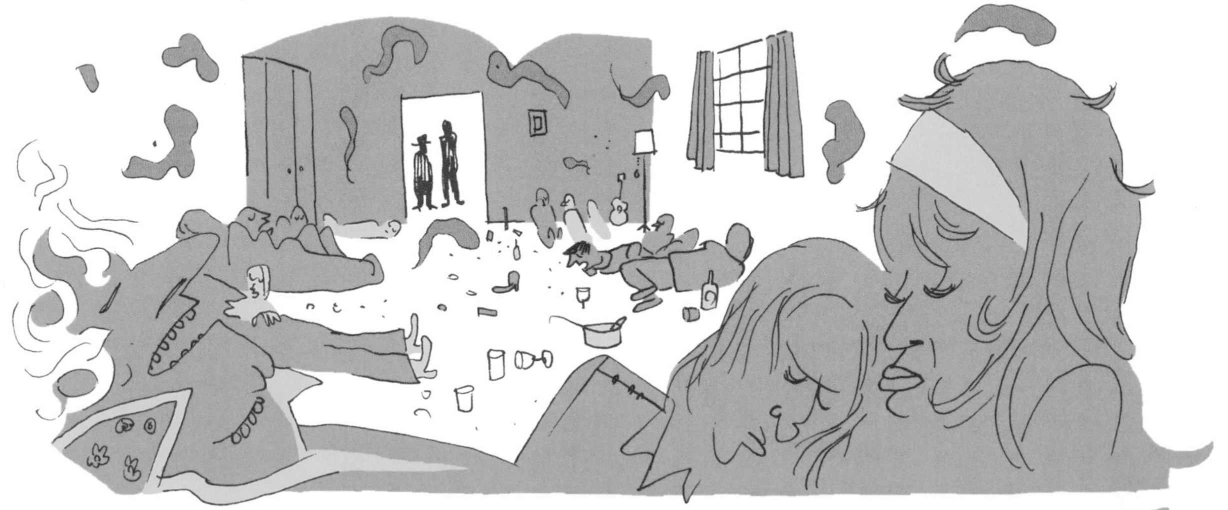

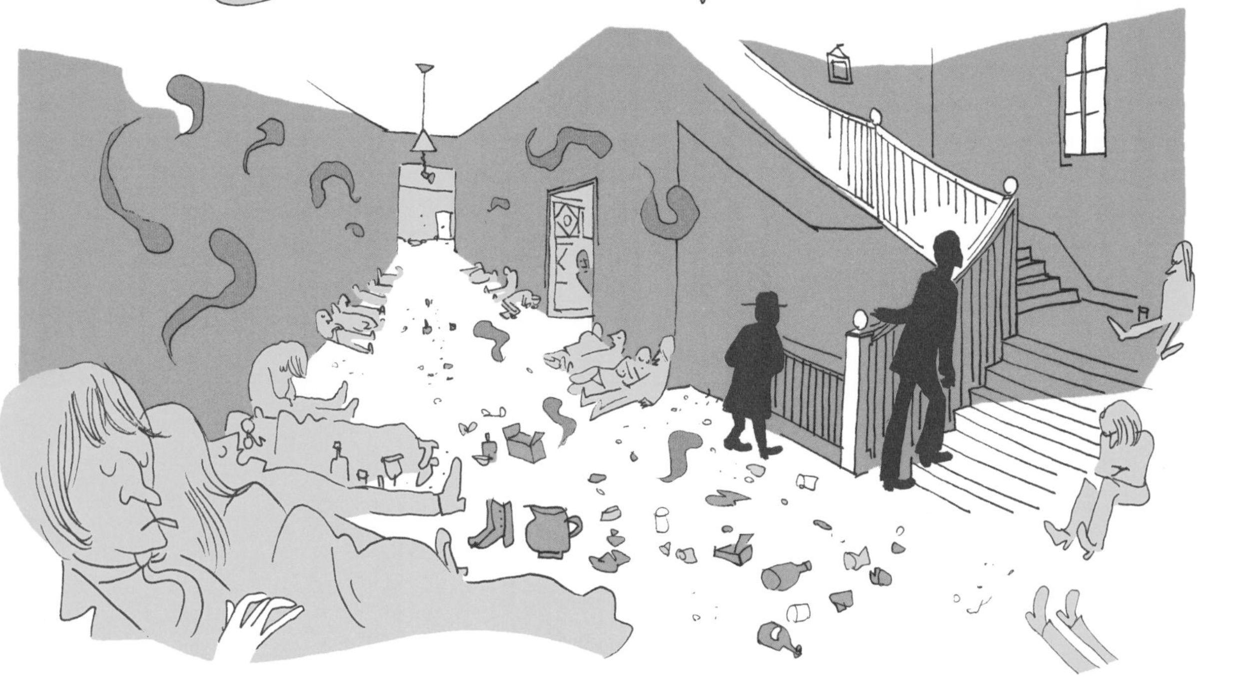

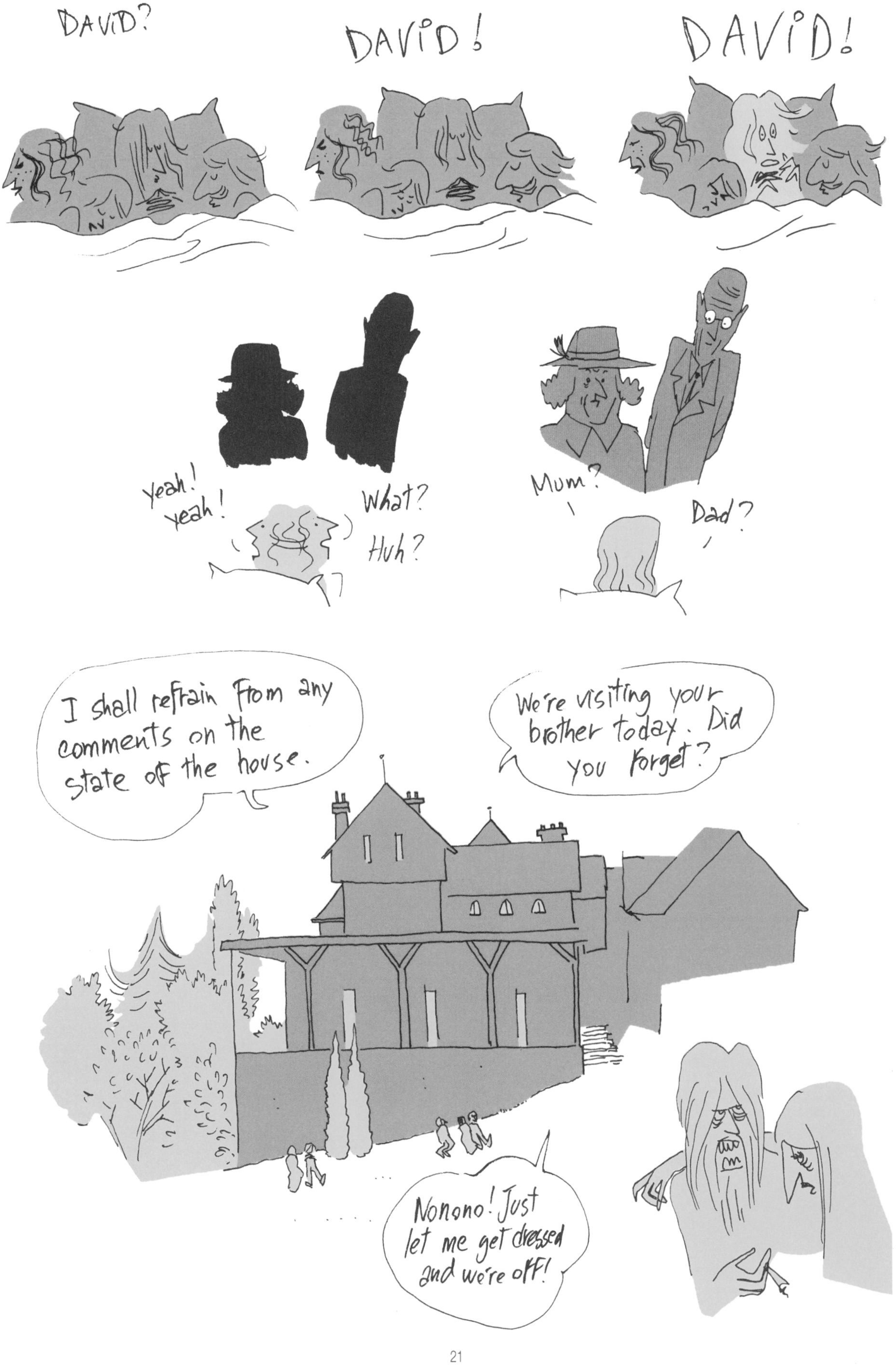
DAVID?
DAVID!
DAVID!
Yeah! yeah!
What?
Huh?
Mum?
Dad?
I shall refrain from any comments on the state of the house.
We're visiting your brother today. Did you forget?
Nonono! Just let me get dressed and we're off!

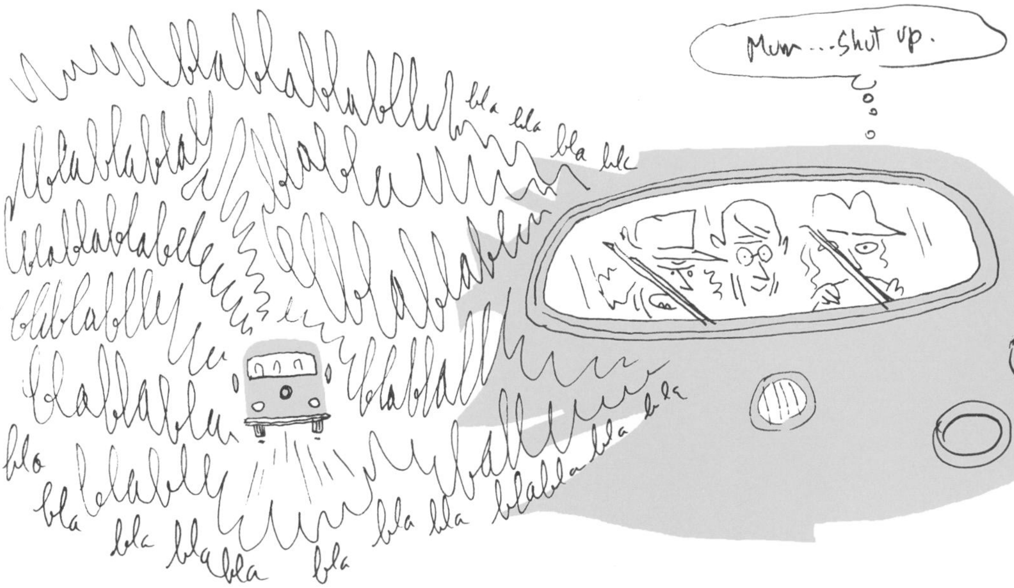
Mum... shut up.

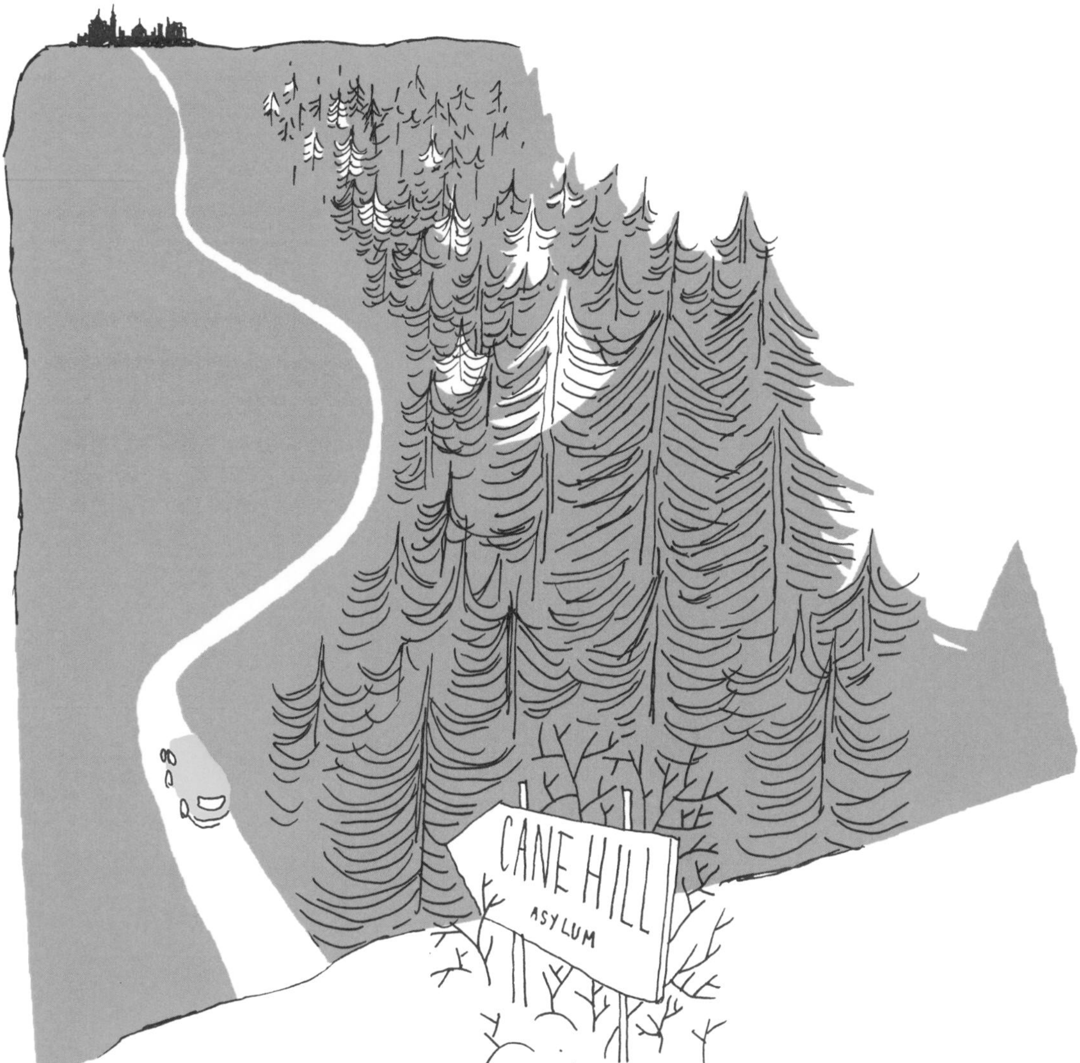
CANE HILL
ASYLUM

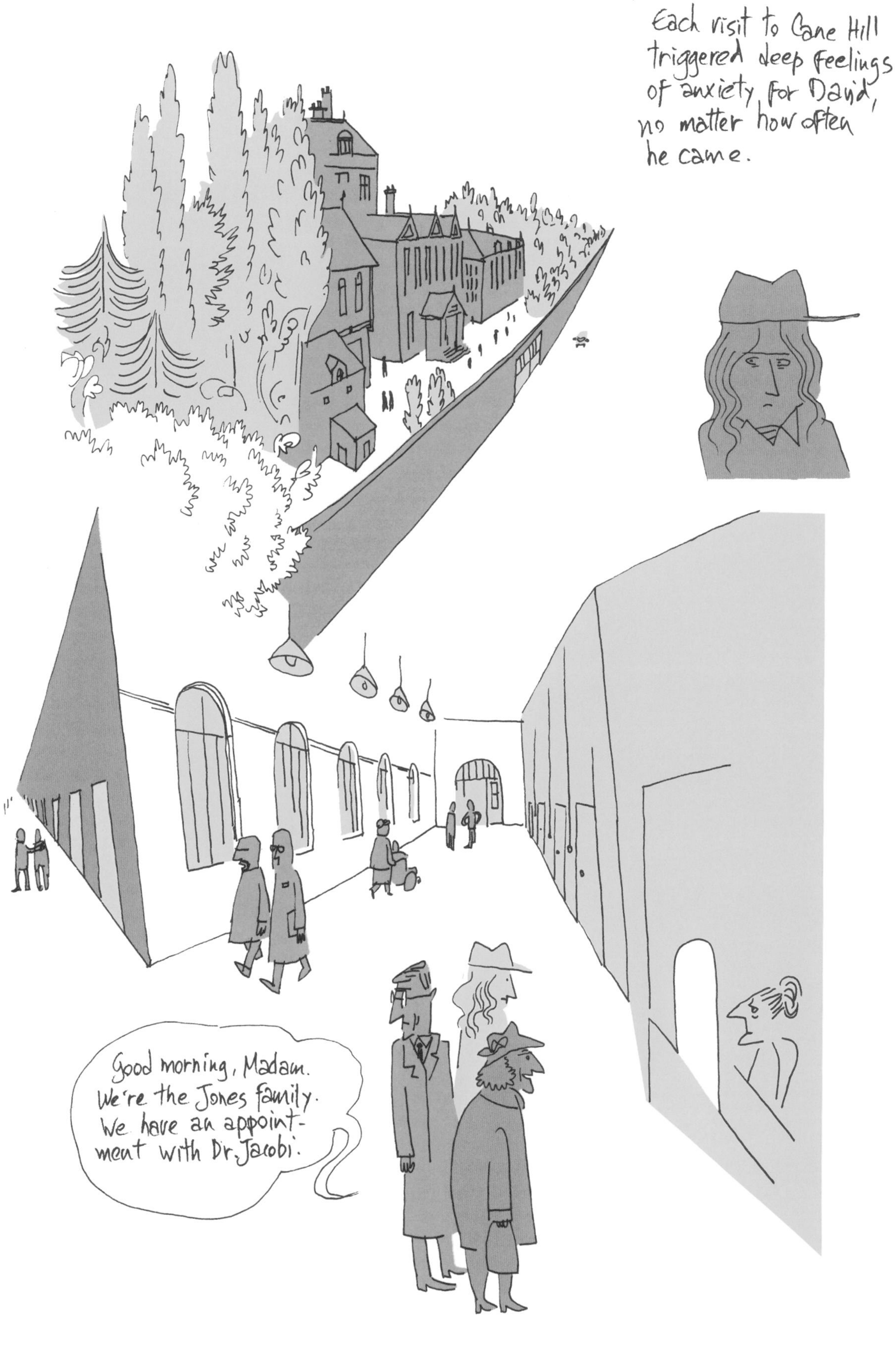
Each visit to Cane Hill triggered deep feelings of anxiety for David, no matter how often he came.
Good morning, Madam. We're the Jones family. We have an appointment with Dr. Jacobi.

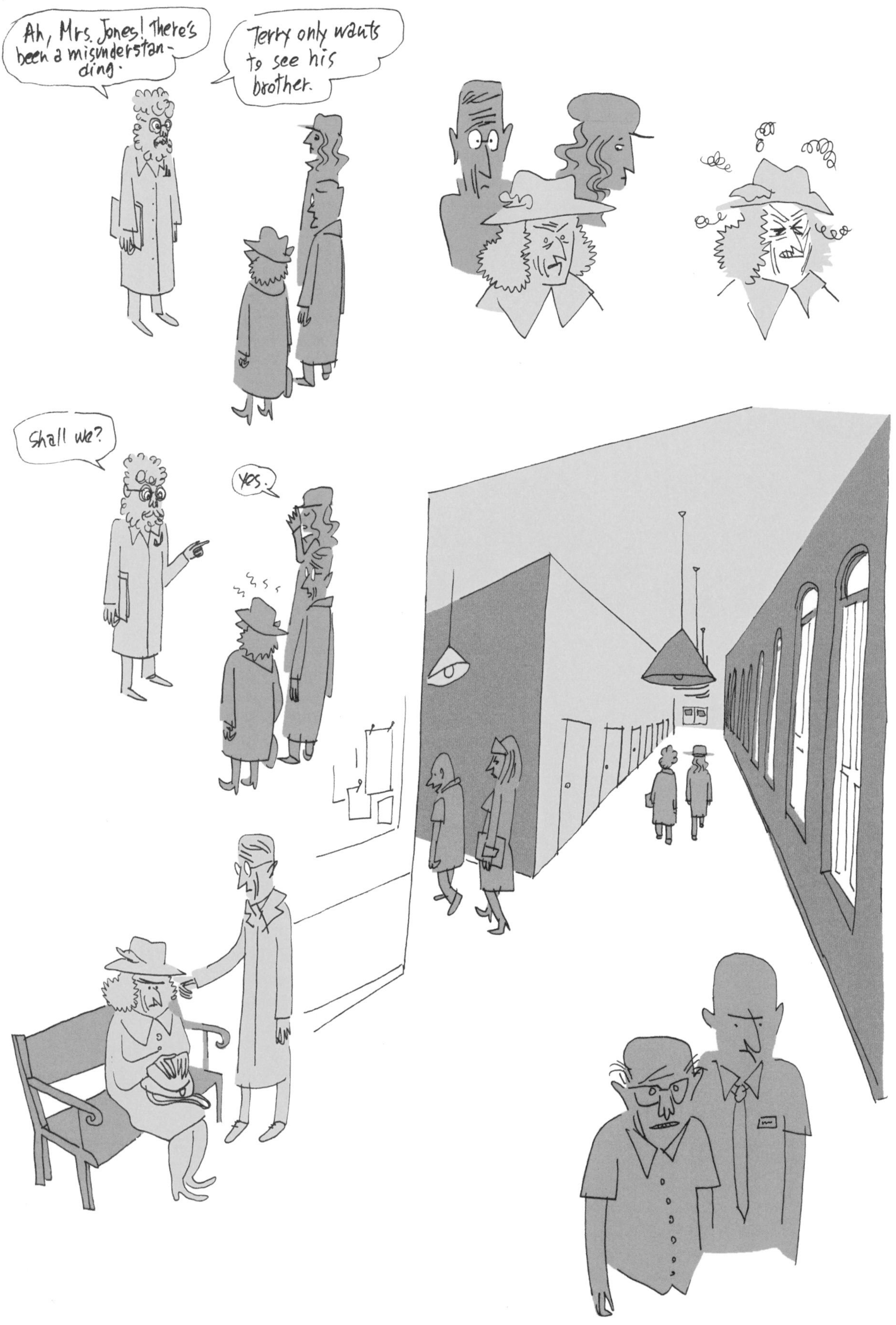
Ah, Mrs. Jones! There's been a misunderstanding.
Terry only wants to see his brother.
Shall we?
Yes.

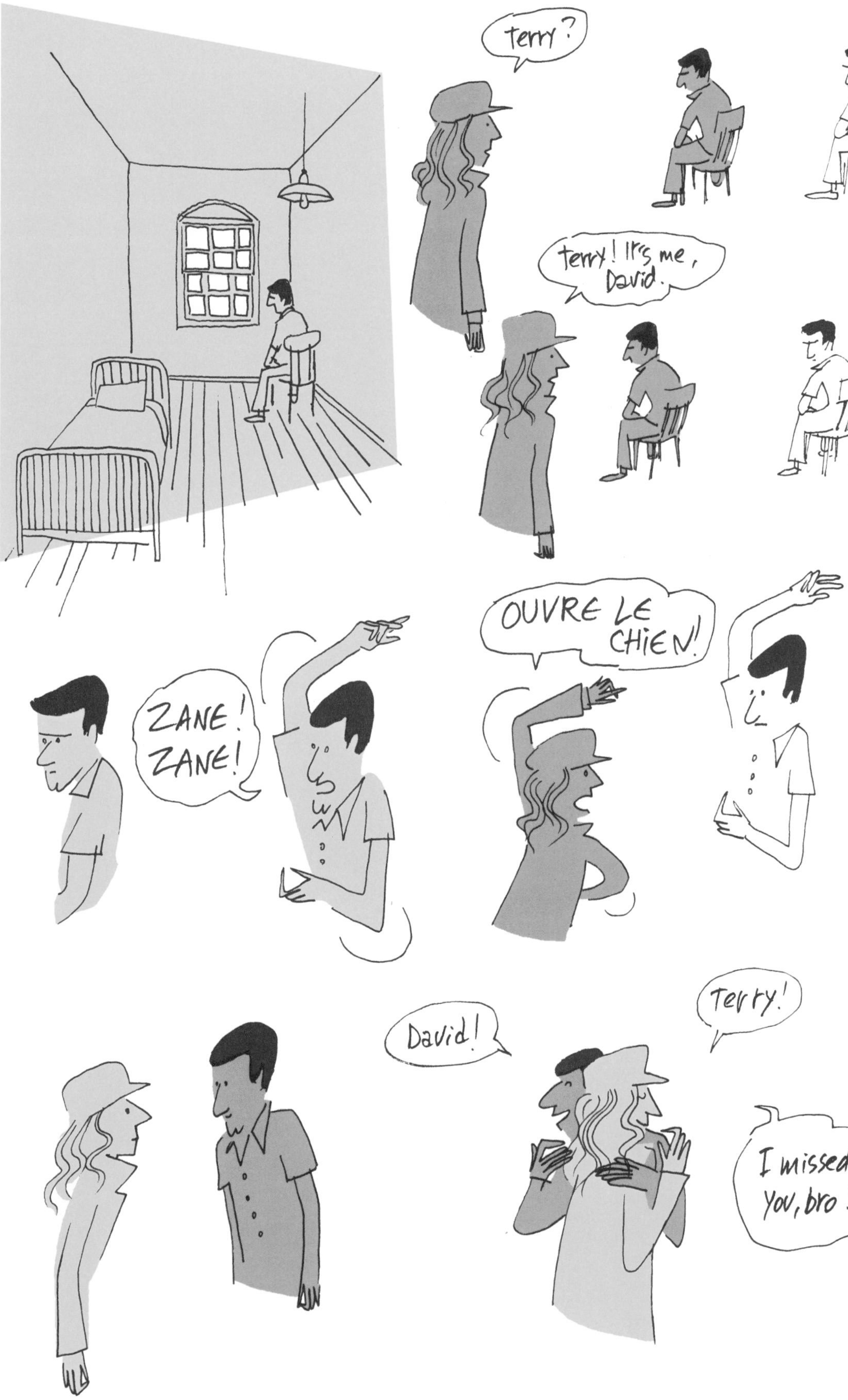
Terry?
Terry! It's me, David.
ZANE! ZANE!
OUVRE LE CHIEN!
David!
Terry!
I missed you, bro!

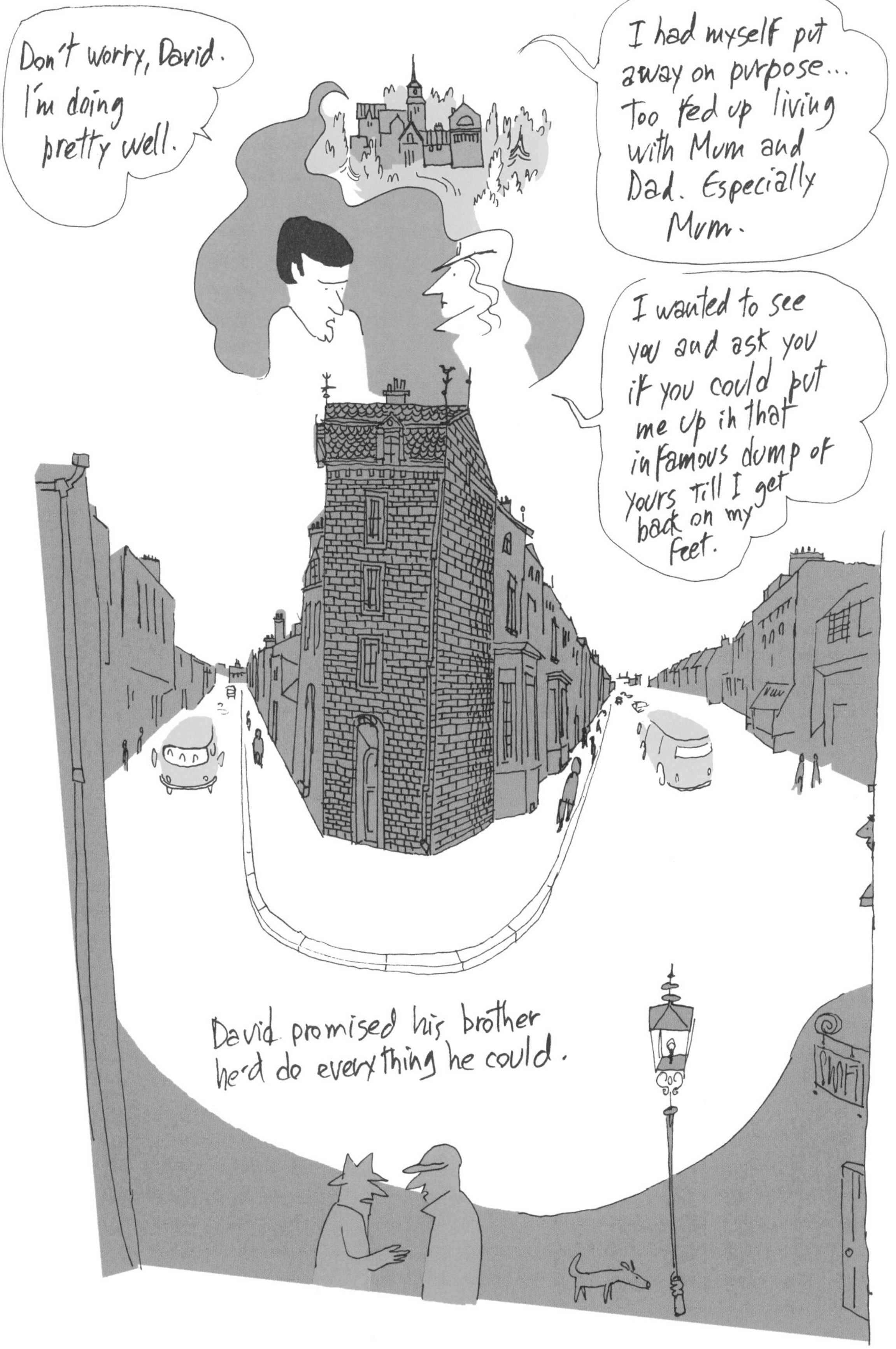
Don't worry, David. I'm doing pretty well.
I had myself put away on purpose... Too fed up living with Mum and Dad. Especially Mum.
I wanted to see you and ask you if you could put me up in that infamous dump of yours till I get back on my feet.
David promised his brother he'd do everything he could.
SHOP

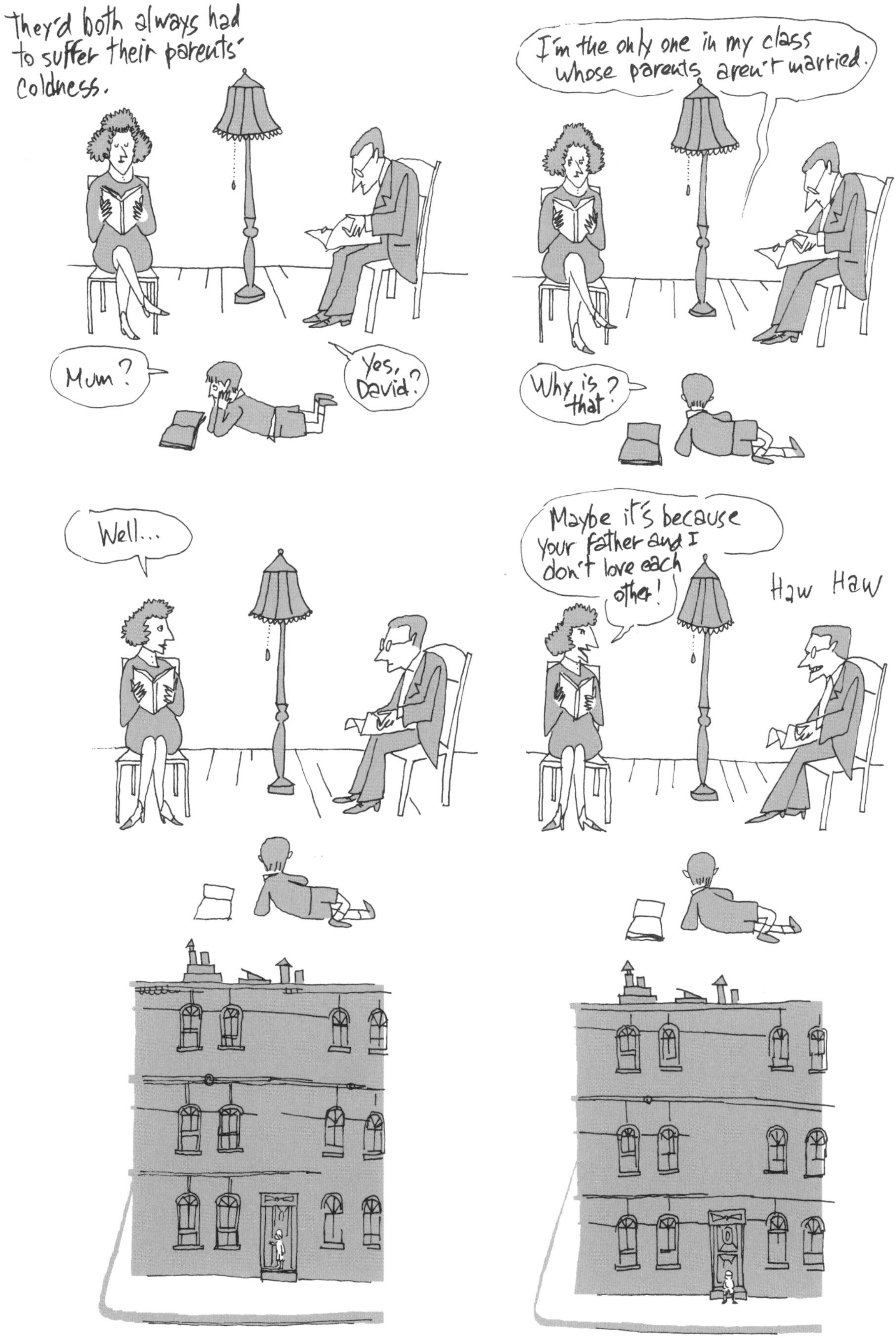
They'd both always had to suffer their parents' coldness.
Mum?
Yes, David?
I'm the only one in my class whose parents aren't married.
Why is that?
Well...
Maybe it's because your father and I don't love each other!
Haw Haw

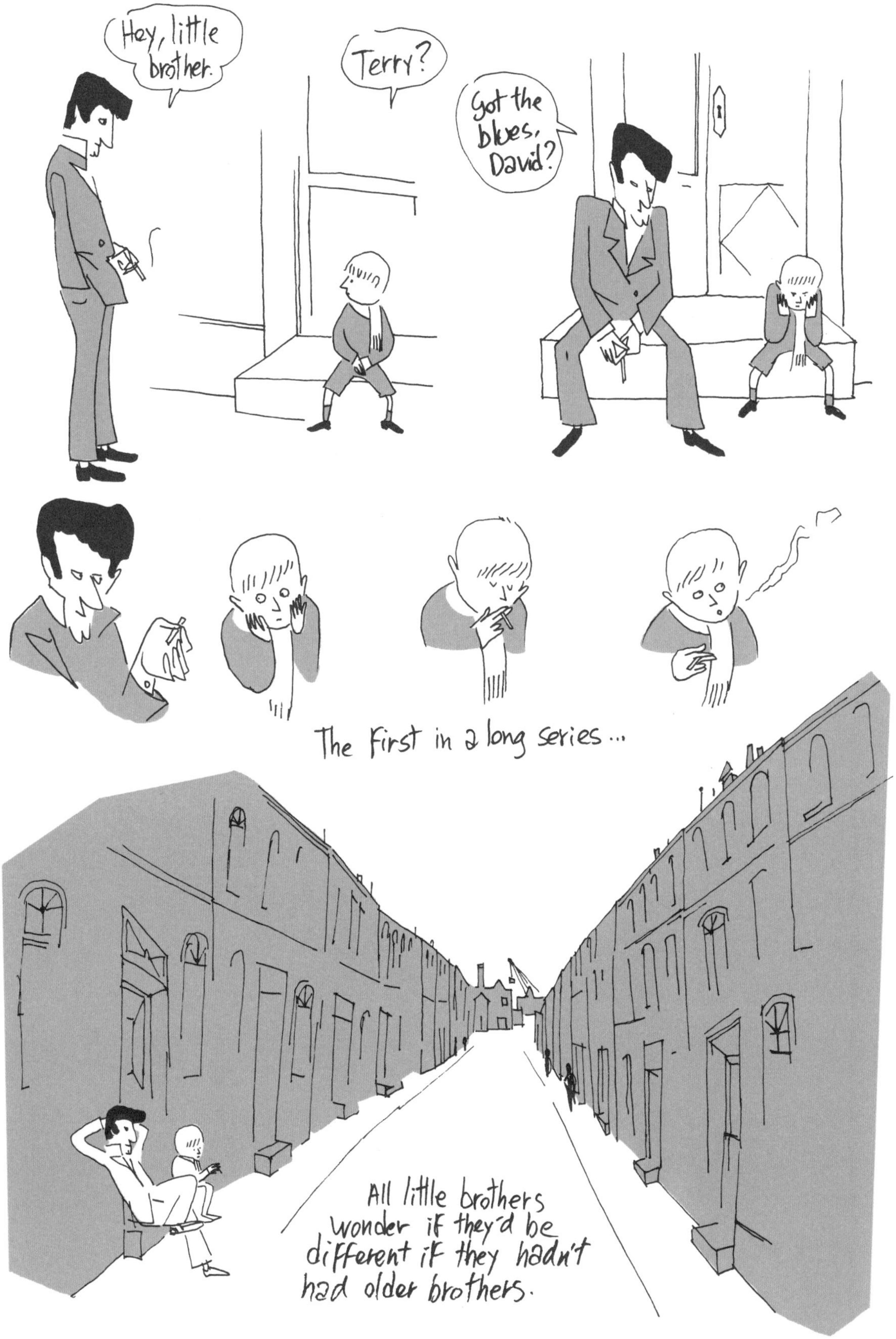
Hey, little brother.
Terry?
Got the blues, David?
The first in a long series...
All little brothers wonder if they'd be different if they hadn't had older brothers.

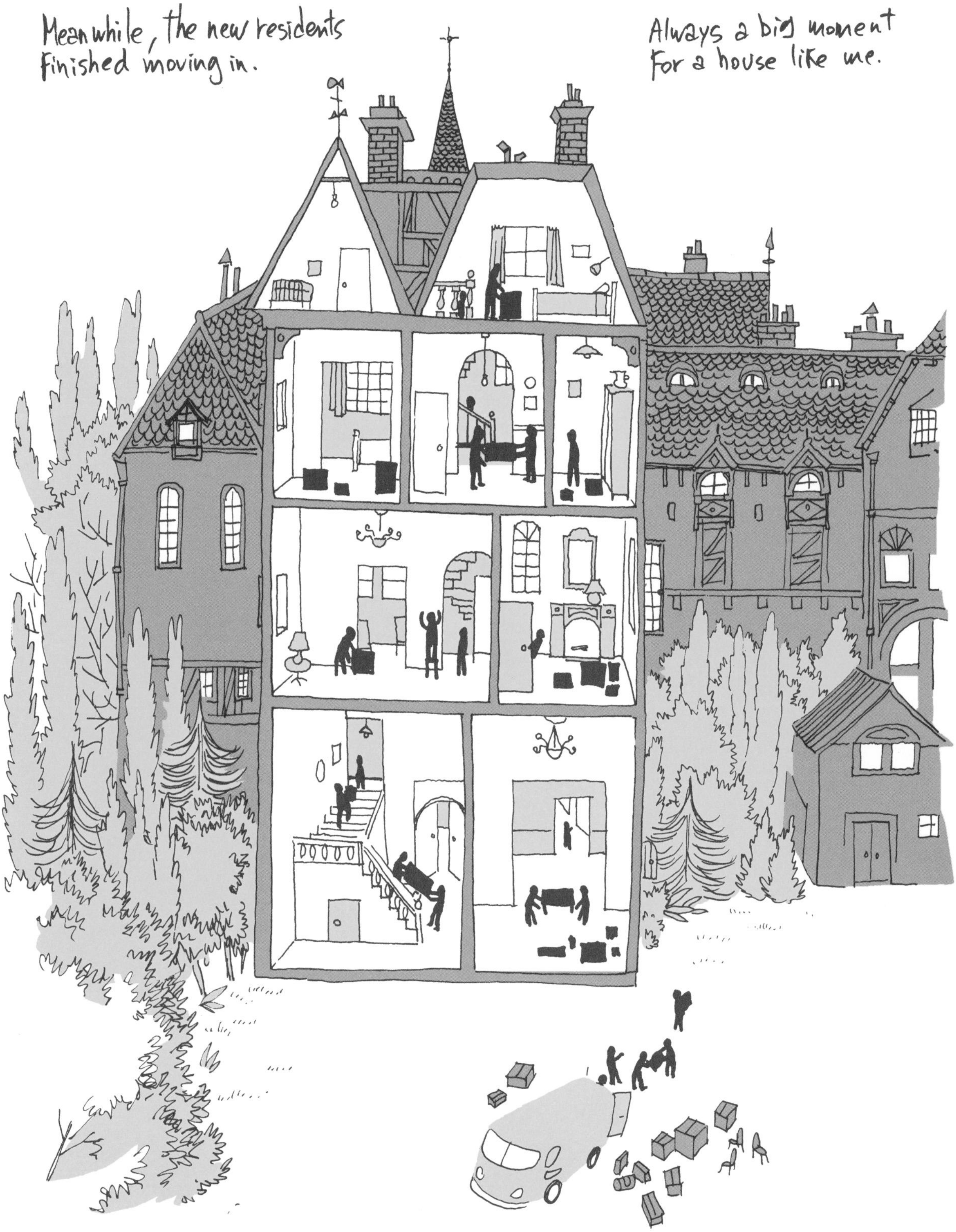
Meanwhile, the new residents finished moving in.
Always a big moment for a house like me.

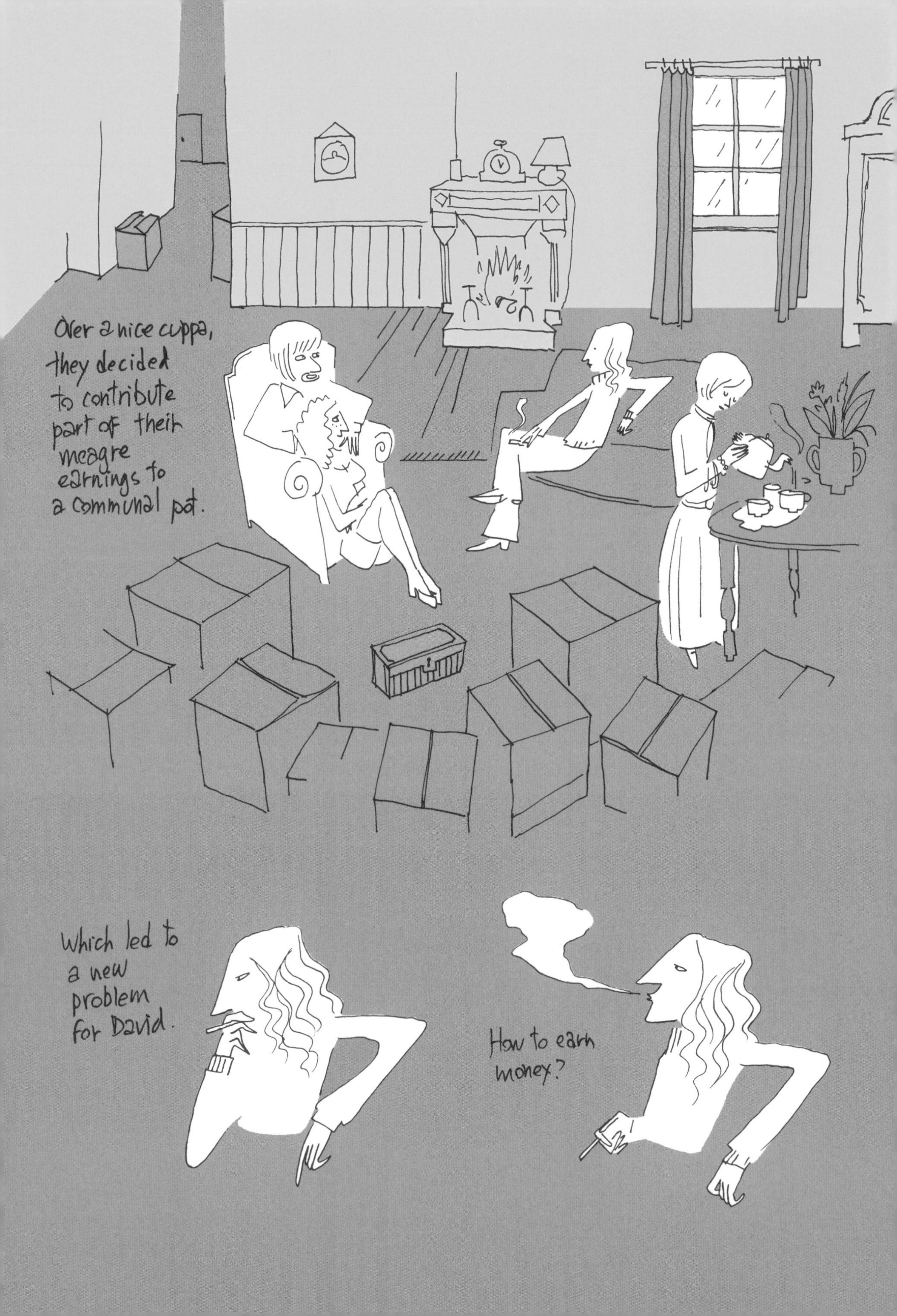
Over a nice cuppa, they decided to contribute part of their meagre earnings to a communal pot.
Which led to a new problem for David.
How to earn money?

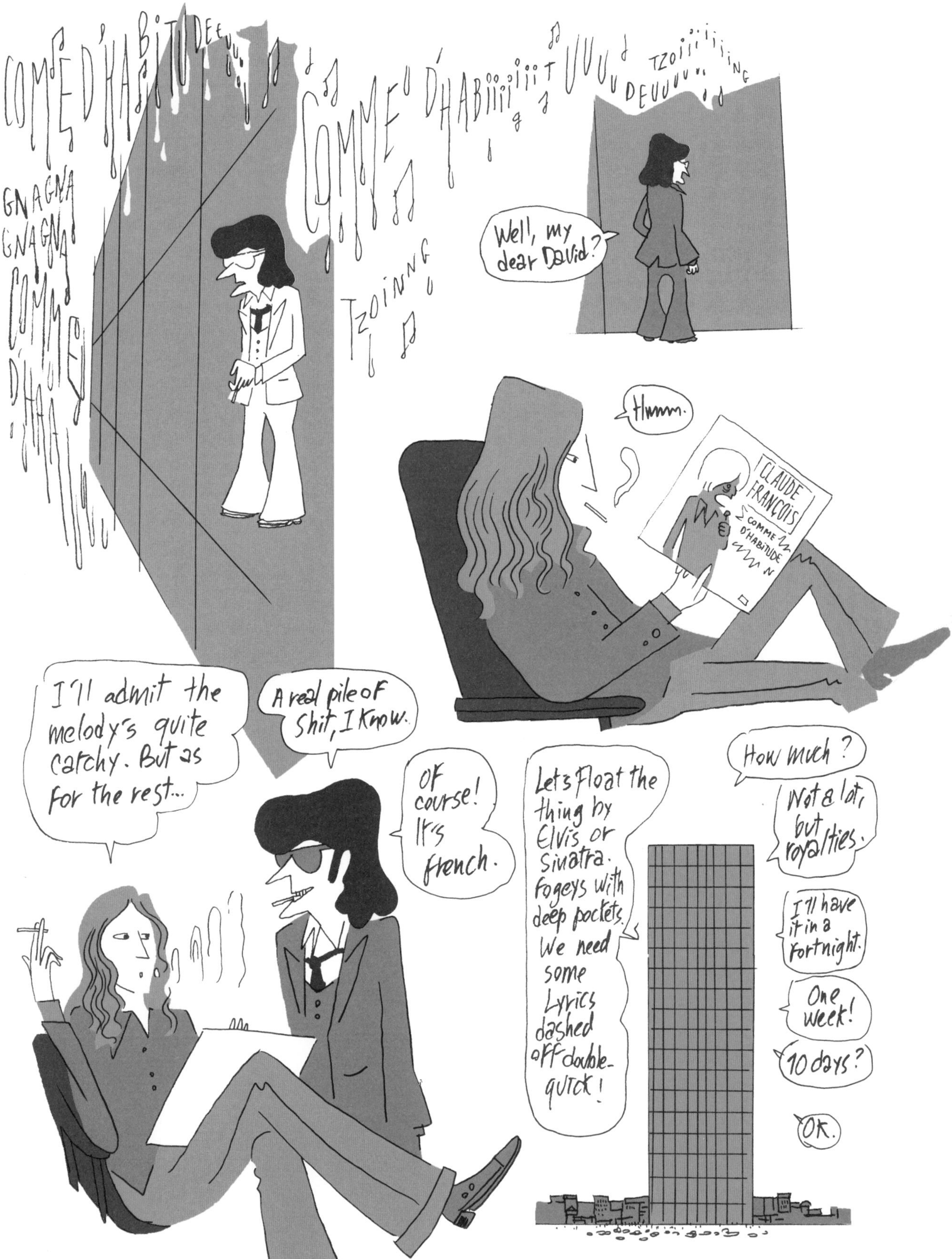
COMME D'HABITUDE
GNAGNA
GNAGNA
COMME D'HA
COMME D'HABIIIIIITUUUUDEUUUU
TZOIIIIING
TZOINNG
Well, my dear David?
Hmm.
CLAUDE FRANÇOIS
COMME D'HABITUDE
I'll admit the melody's quite catchy. But as for the rest...
A real pile of shit, I know.
Of course! It's French.
Let's float the thing by Elvis or Sinatra. Fogeys with deep pockets. We need some lyrics dashed off double-quick!
How much?
Not a lot, but royalties.
I'll have it in a fortnight.
One week!
10 days?
OK.

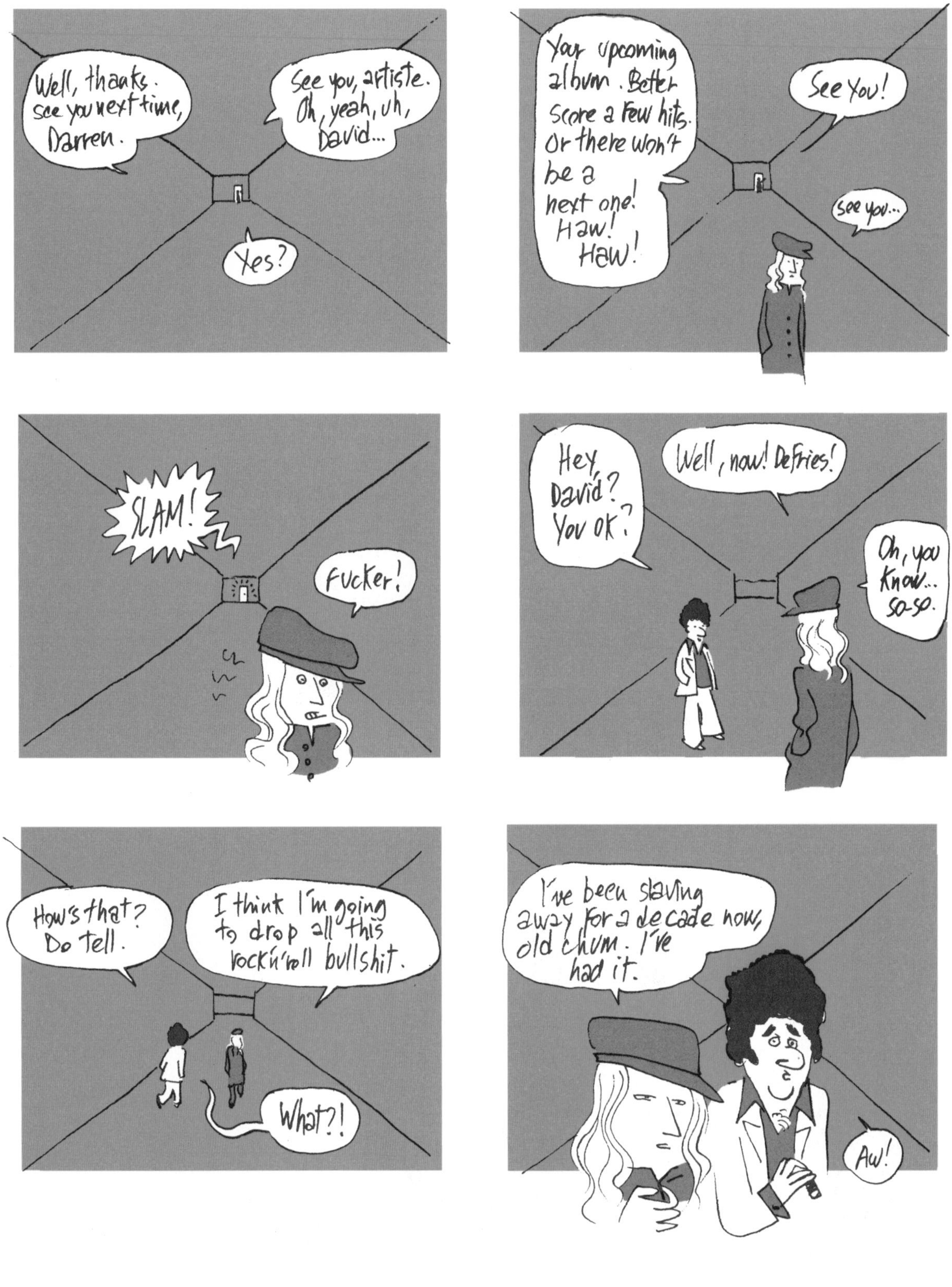

Well, thanks. see you next time, Darren.
See you, artiste. Oh, yeah, uh, David...
Yes?
Your upcoming album. Better score a few hits. Or there won't be a next one! Haw! Haw!
See You!
see you...
SLAM!
Fucker!
Hey, David? You ok?
Well, now! Defries!
Oh, you know... so-so.
How's that? Do tell.
I think I'm going to drop all this rock'n'roll bullshit.
What?!
I've been slaving away for a decade now, old chum. I've had it.
Aw!

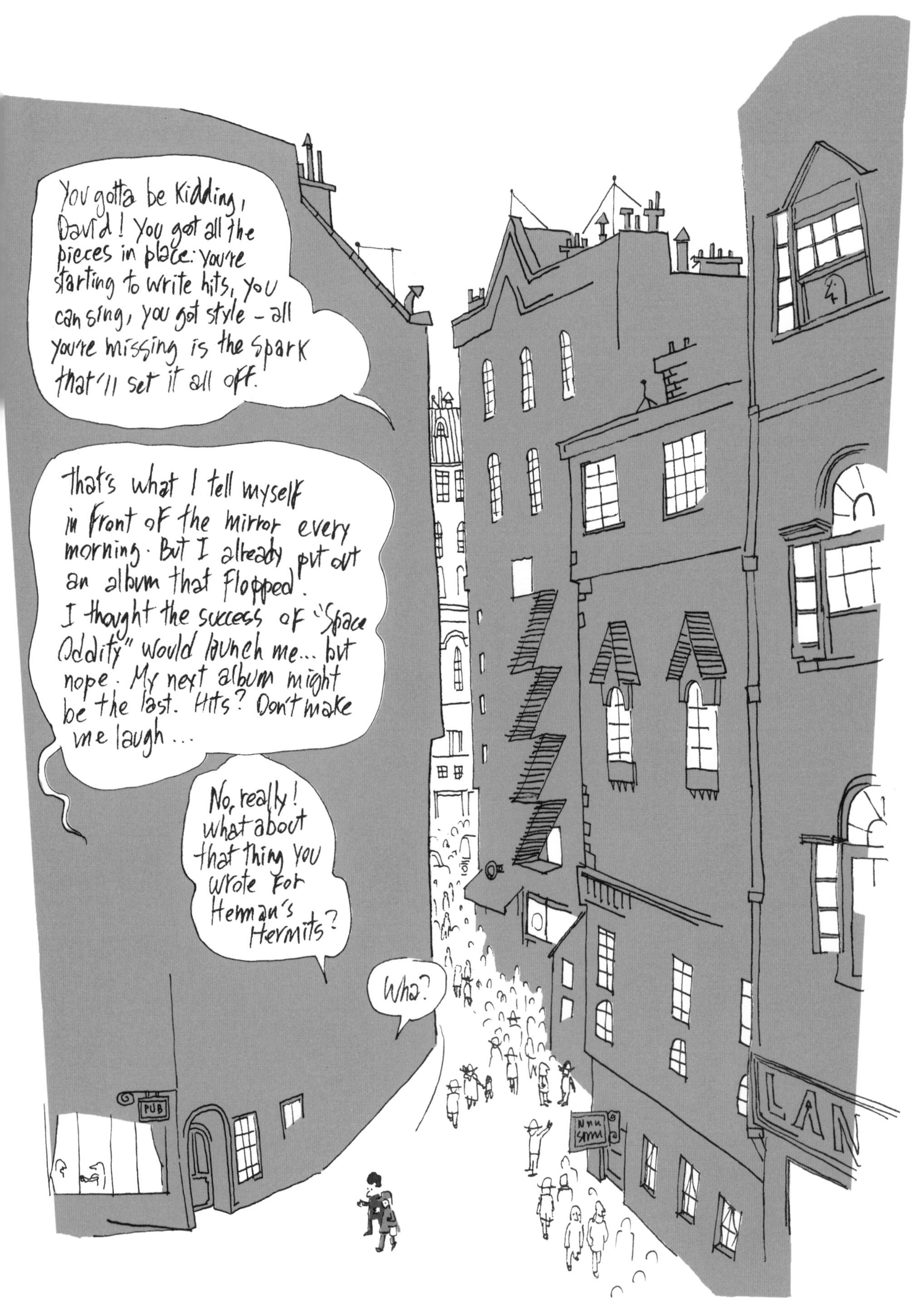
You gotta be kidding, David! You got all the pieces in place: you're starting to write hits, you can sing, you got style – all you're missing is the spark that'll set it all off.
That's what I tell myself in front of the mirror every morning. But I already put out an album that flopped. I thought the success of "Space Oddity" would launch me... but nope. My next album might be the last. Hits? Don't make me laugh...
No, really! What about that thing you wrote for Herman's Hermits?
Wha?
PUB

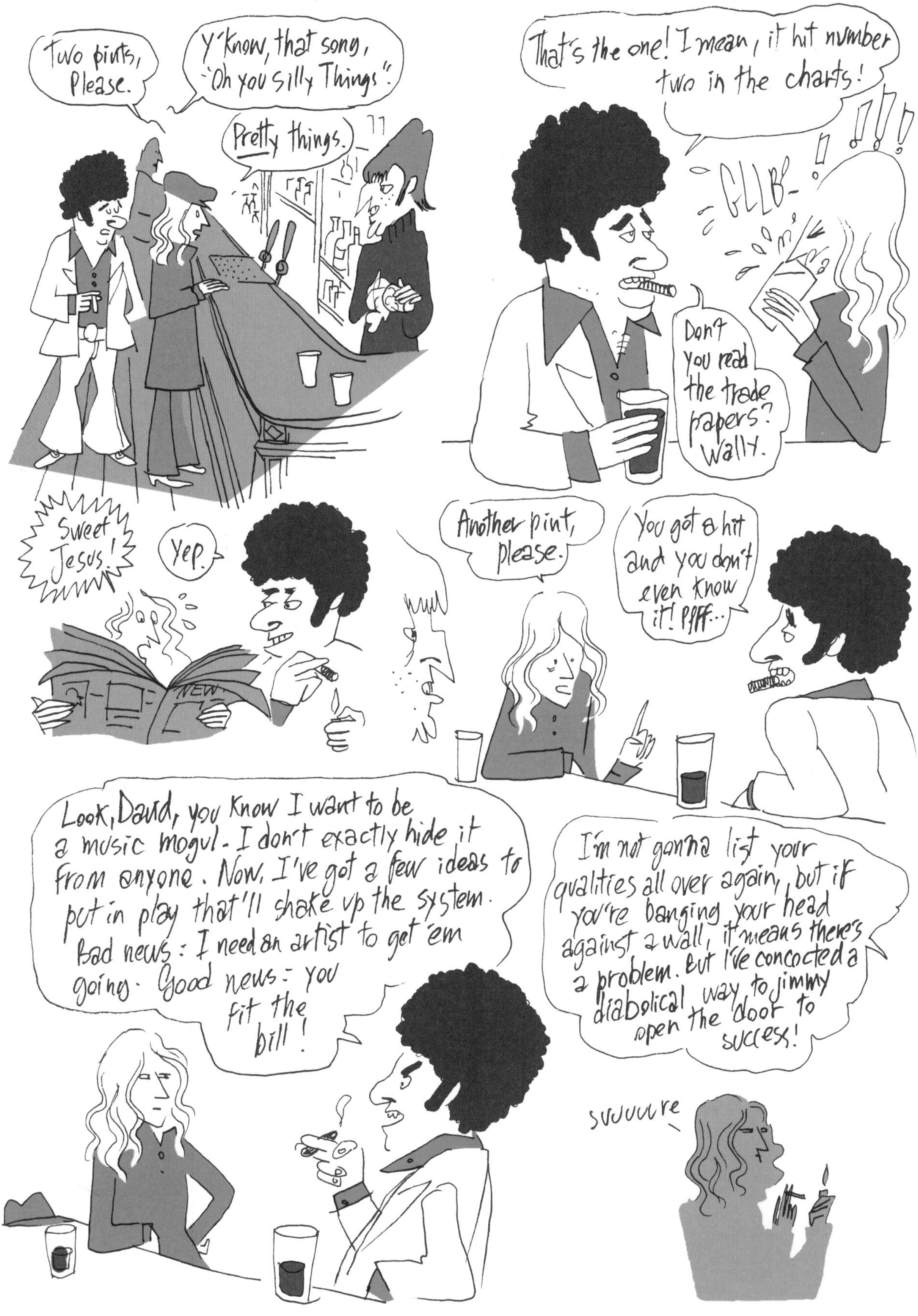
Two pints, Please.
Y'know, that song, "Oh you silly Things".
Pretty things.
That's the one! I mean, it hit number two in the charts!
GLLB-
Don't you read the trade papers? Wally.
Sweet Jesus!
Yep.
NEW
Another pint, please.
You got a hit and you don't even know it! Pfff...
Look, David, you know I want to be a music mogul. I don't exactly hide it from anyone. Now, I've got a few ideas to put in play that'll shake up the system. Bad news: I need an artist to get 'em going. Good news: you fit the bill!
I'm not gonna list your qualities all over again, but if you're banging your head against a wall, it means there's a problem. But I've concocted a diabolical way to jimmy open the door to success!
suuuure

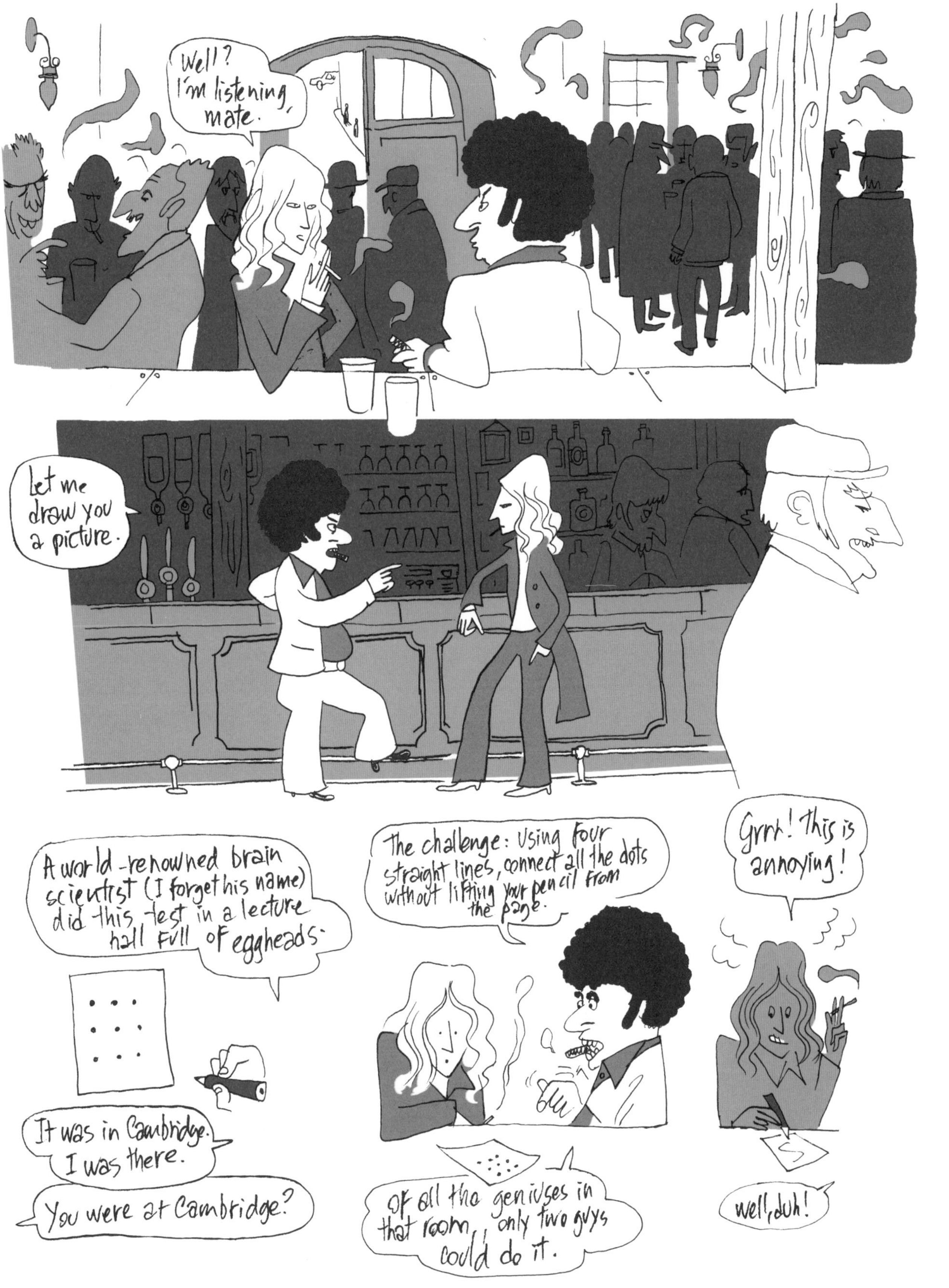
Well? I'm listening, mate.
Let me draw you a picture.
A world-renowned brain scientist (I forget his name) did this test in a lecture hall full of eggheads.
It was in Cambridge. I was there.
You were at Cambridge?
The challenge: Using four straight lines, connect all the dots without lifting your pencil from the page.
Of all the geniuses in that room, only two guys could do it.
Grrr! This is annoying!
Well, duh!

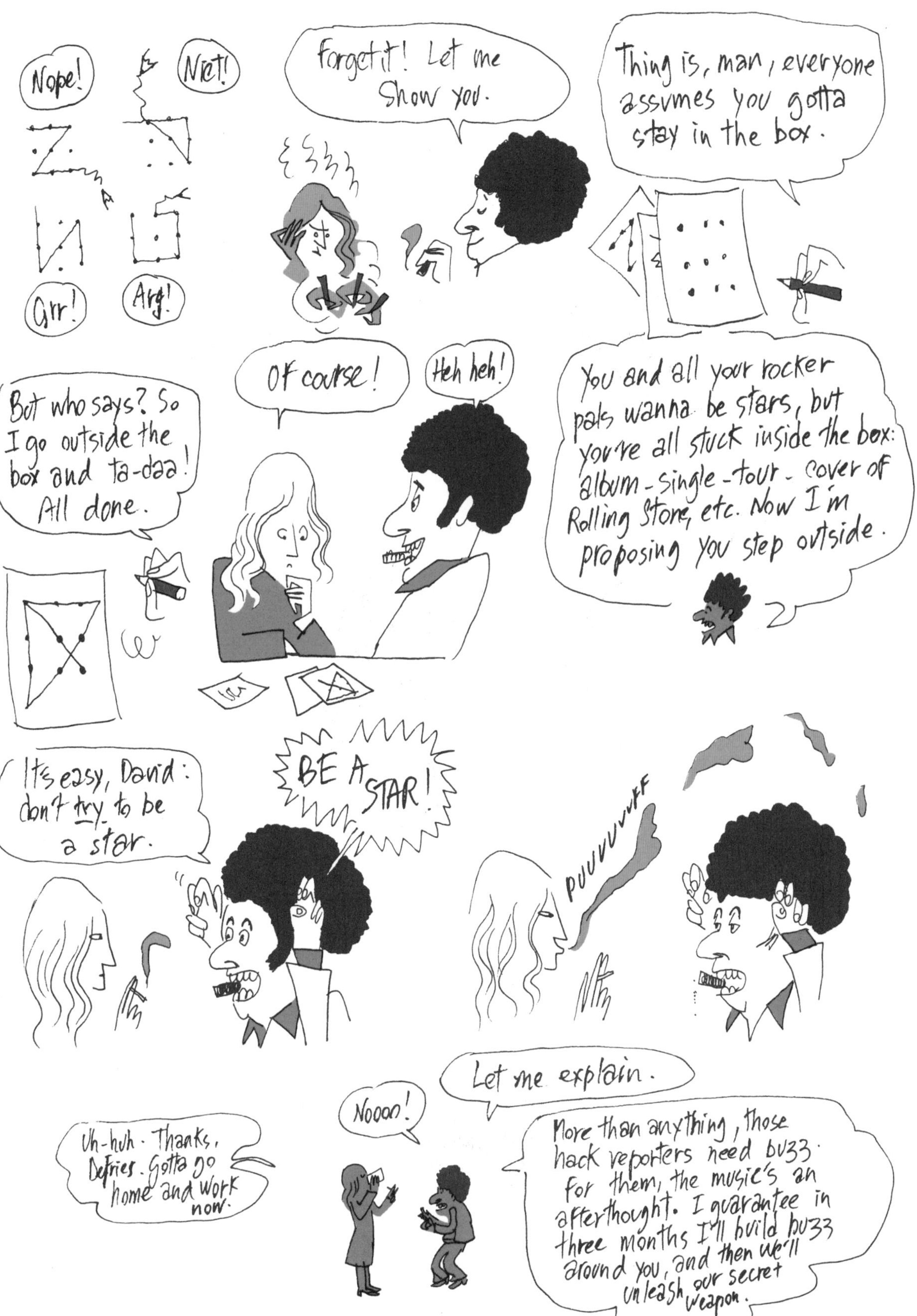
Nope!
Niet!
Grr!
Arg!
Forget it! Let me show you.
Thing is, man, everyone assumes you gotta stay in the box.
But who says? So I go outside the box and ta-daa! All done.
Of course!
Heh heh!
You and all your rocker pals wanna be stars, but you're all stuck inside the box: album - single - tour - cover of Rolling Stone, etc. Now I'm proposing you step outside.
It's easy, David: don't try to be a star.
BE A STAR!
PUUUUUUUF
Let me explain.
Nooon!
Uh-huh. Thanks, Defries. Gotta go home and work now.
More than anything, those hack reporters need buzz. For them, the music's an afterthought. I guarantee in three months I'll build buzz around you, and then we'll unleash our secret weapon.

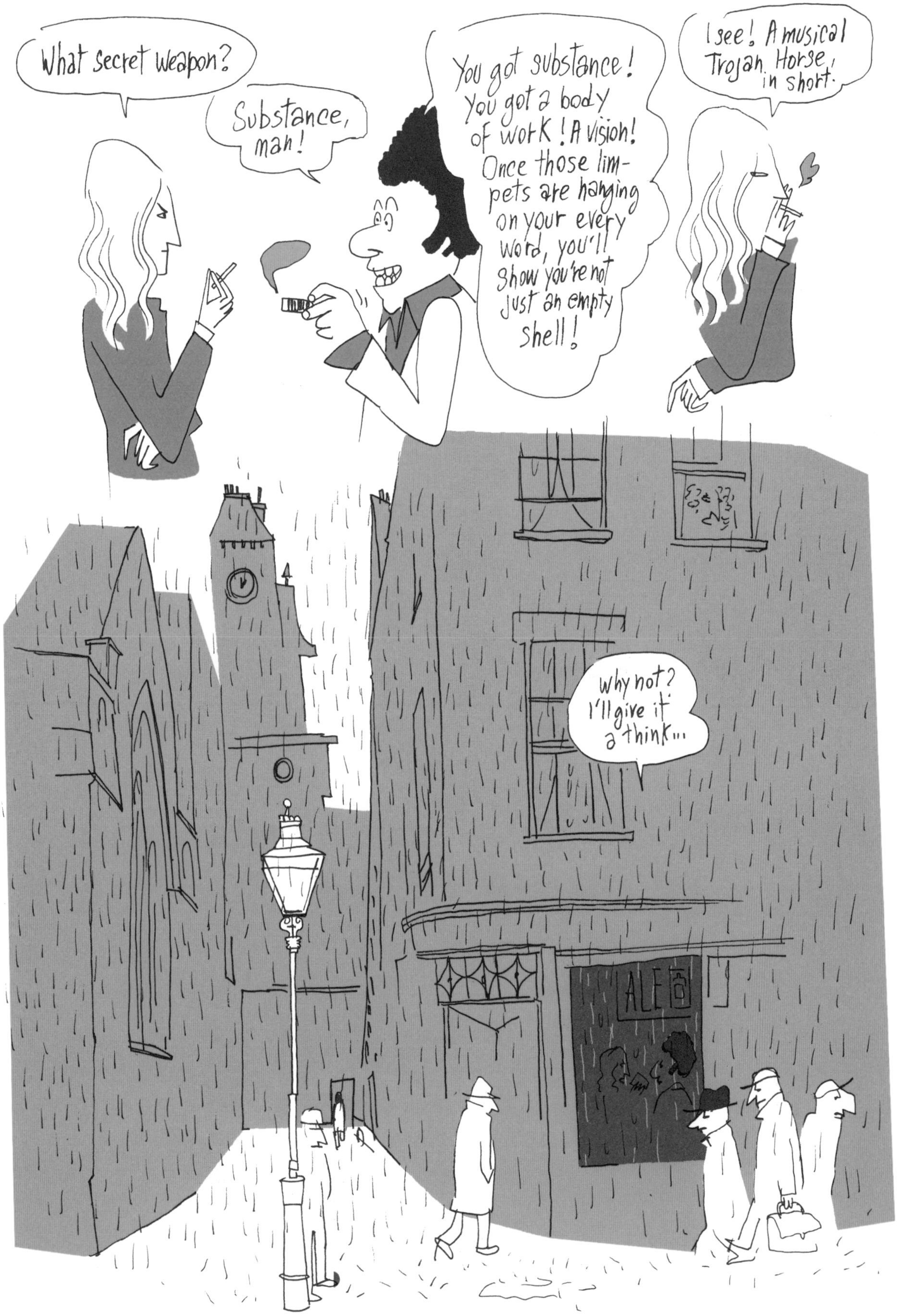
What secret weapon?
Substance, man!
You got substance! You got a body of work! A vision! Once those limpets are hanging on your every word, you'll show you're not just an empty shell!
I see! A musical Trojan Horse, in short.
Why not? I'll give it a think...
ALE

Meanwhile ... the competition.

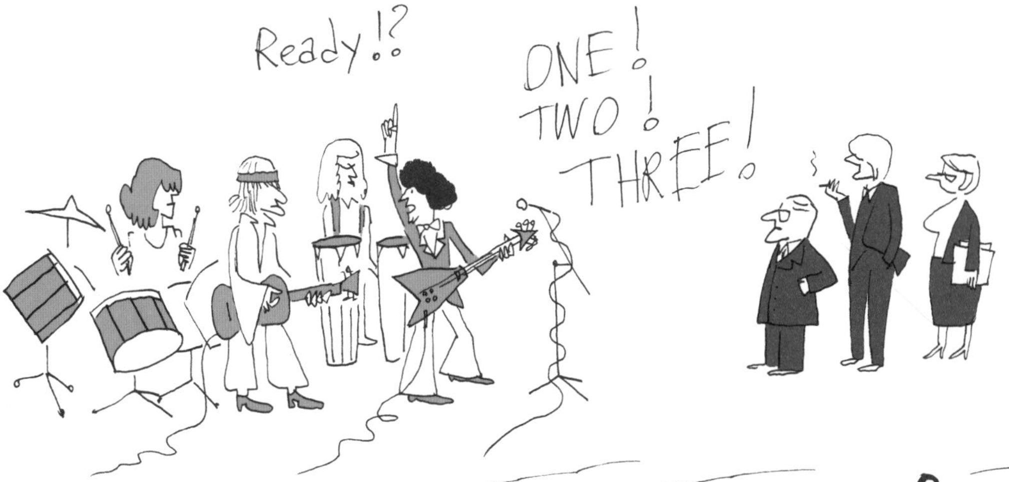
Ready!?
ONE! TWO! THREE!

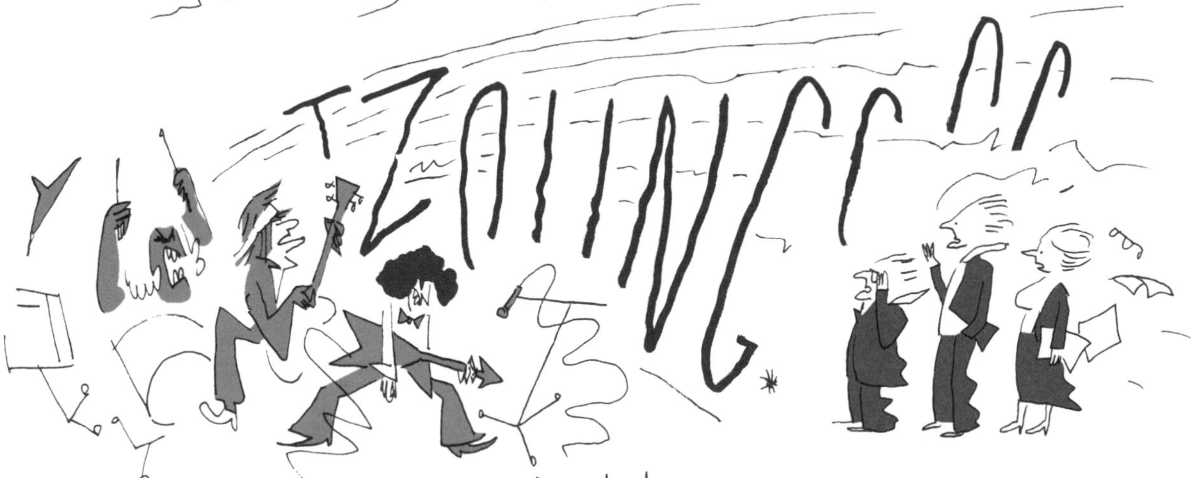
TZOIINGGGG*
* overpowering minor chord

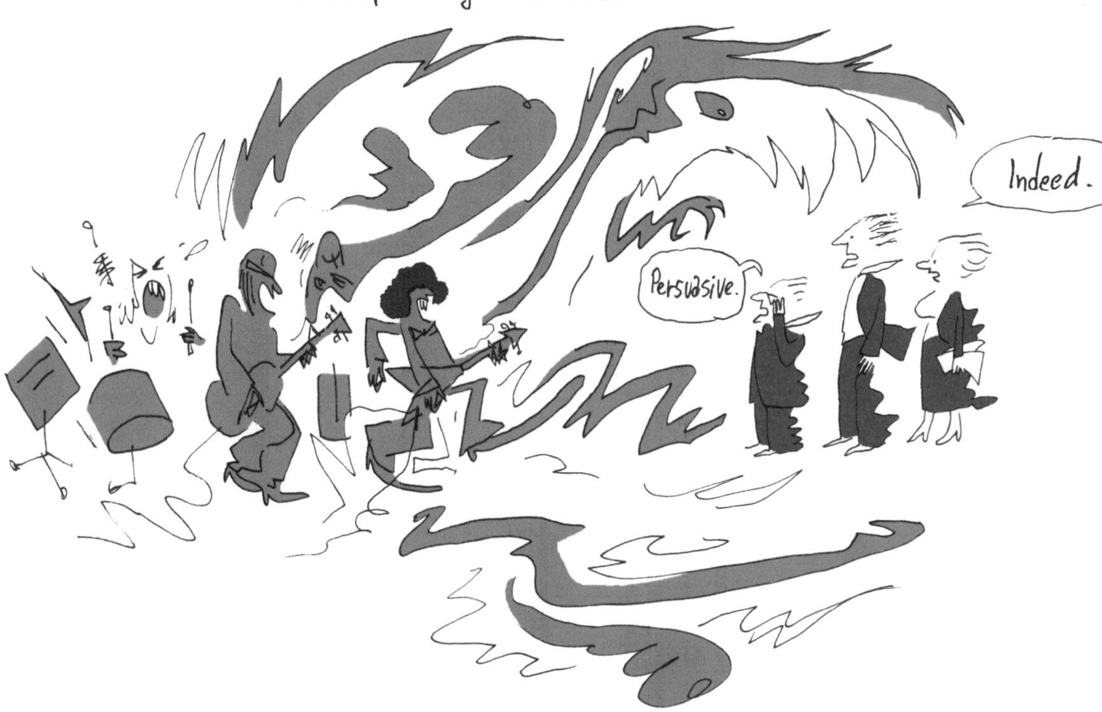
Persuasive.
Indeed.

And Marc was signed for three records.

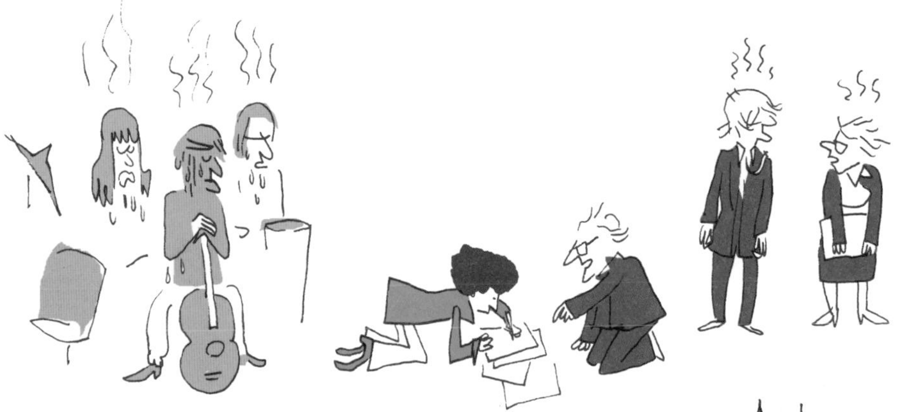

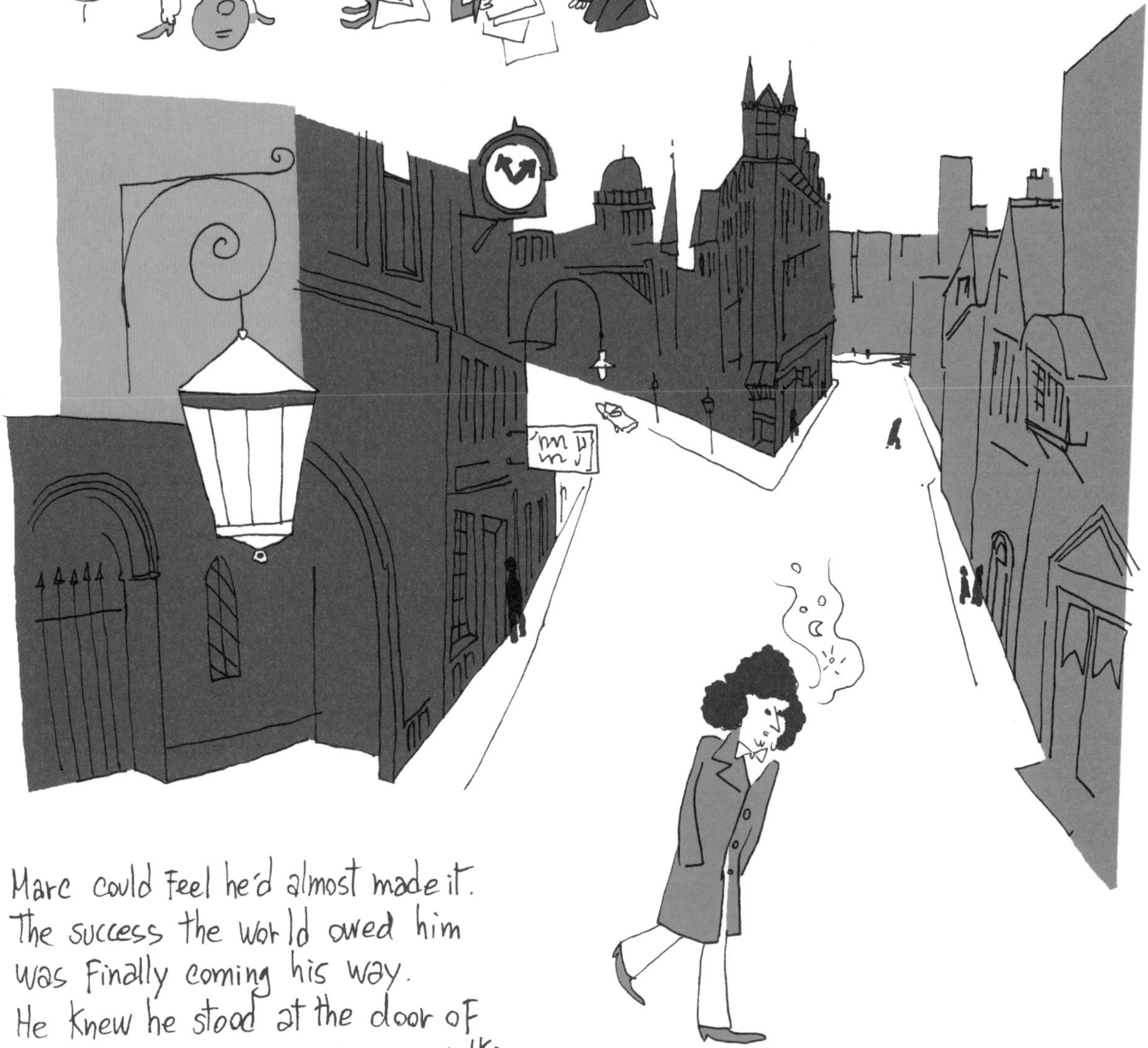

Marc could feel he'd almost made it. The success the world owed him was finally coming his way. He knew he stood at the door of everlasting fame, and was walking through the streets as a mere mortal for the last time.

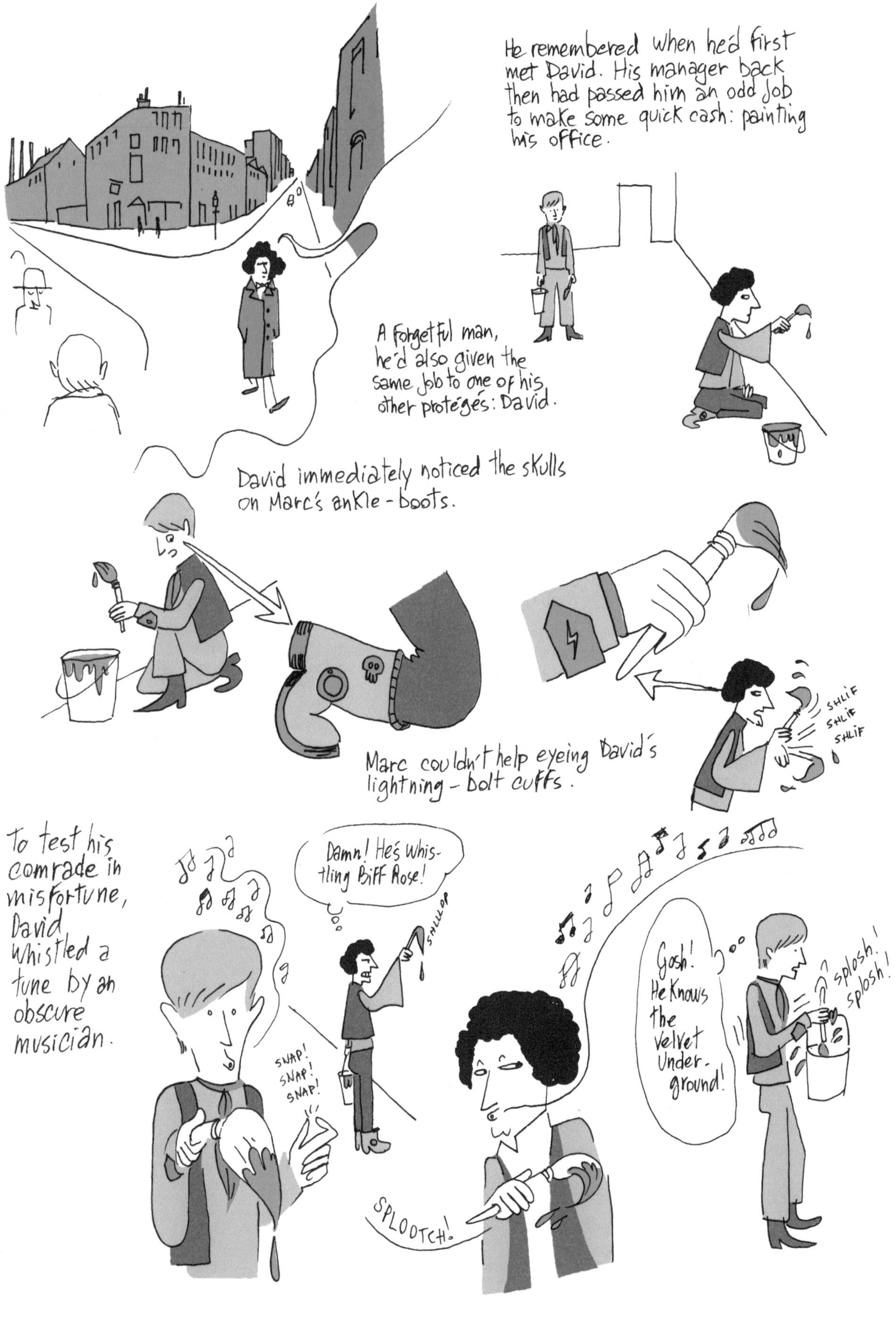
He remembered when he'd first met David. His manager back then had passed him an odd job to make some quick cash: painting his office.
A forgetful man, he'd also given the same job to one of his other protégés: David.
David immediately noticed the skulls on Marc's ankle-boots.
Marc couldn't help eyeing David's lightning-bolt cuffs.
SHLIF
SHLIF
SHLIF
To test his comrade in misfortune, David whistled a tune by an obscure musician.
Damn! He's whistling Biff Rose!
SHLLLOP
SNAP! SNAP! SNAP!
Gosh! He knows the Velvet Underground!
splosh! splosh!
SPLOOTCH!

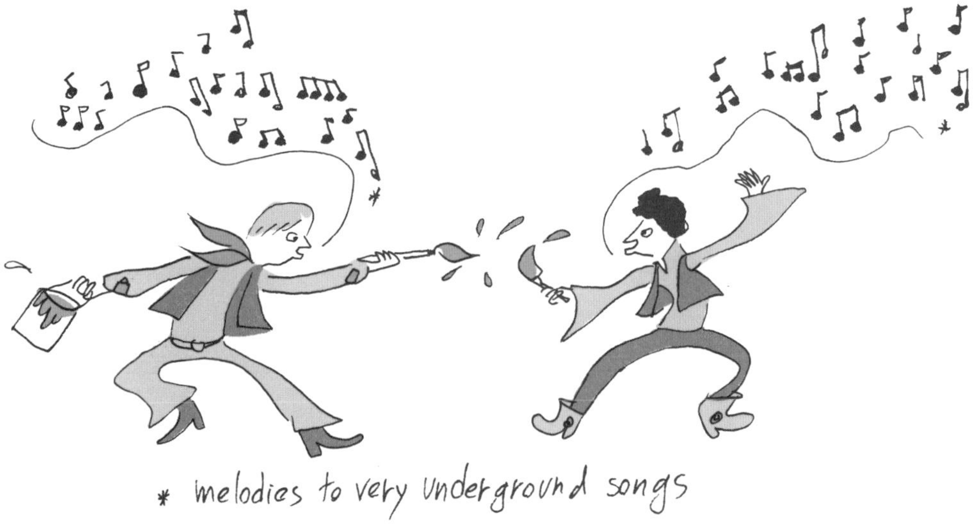
* melodies to very underground songs

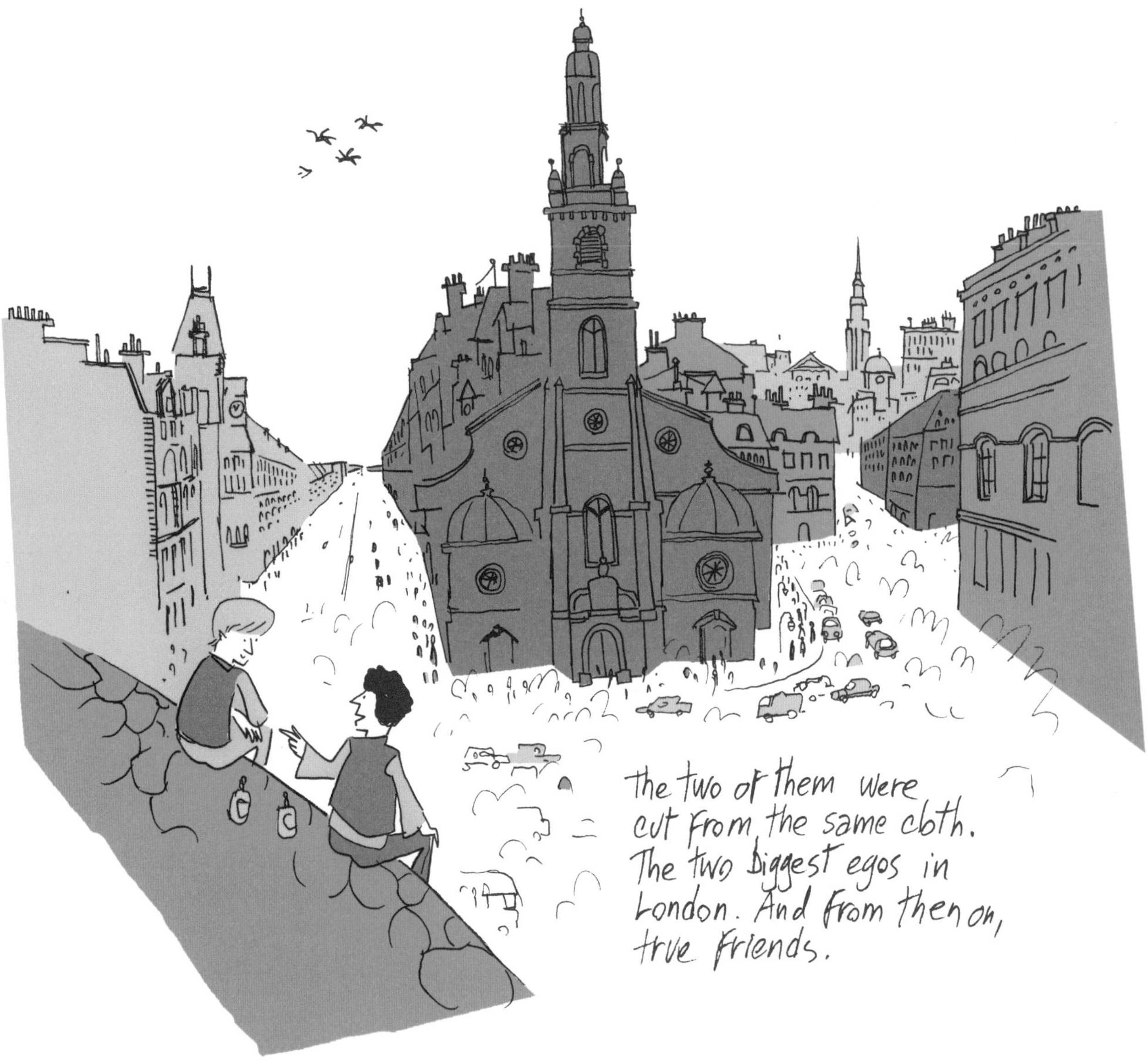
The two of them were cut from the same cloth. The two biggest egos in London. And from then on, true friends.

INTERMEZZO

de cappellibus evolutionatis

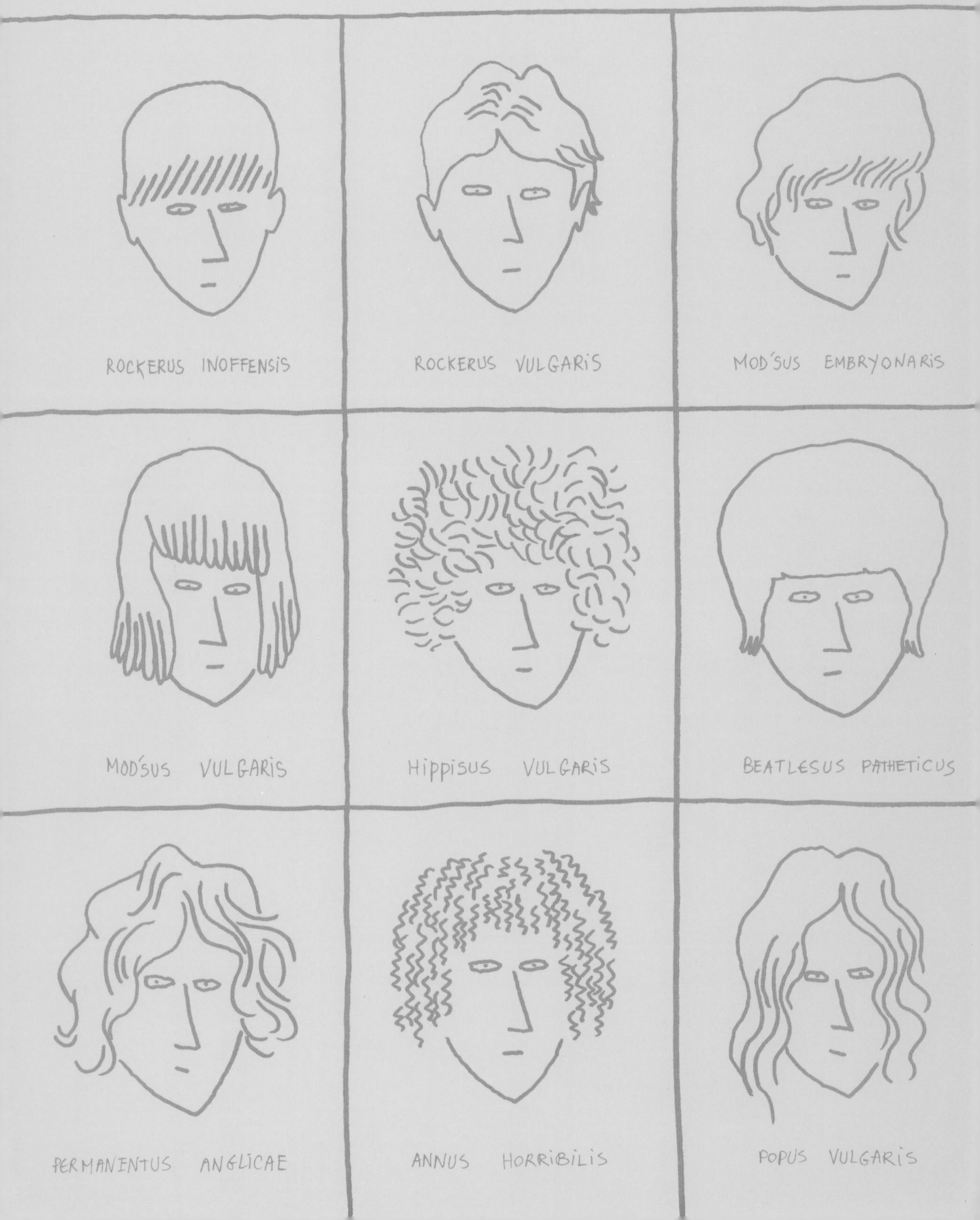
ROCKERUS INOFFENSIS
ROCKERUS VULGARIS
MOD'SUS EMBRYONARIS
MOD'SUS VULGARIS
Hippisus VULGARIS
BEATLESUS PATHETICUS
PERMANENTUS ANGLICAE
ANNUS HORRIBILIS
POPUS VULGARIS

At the time, music festivals were popping up all over like mushrooms. David never missed a chance to give a concert.

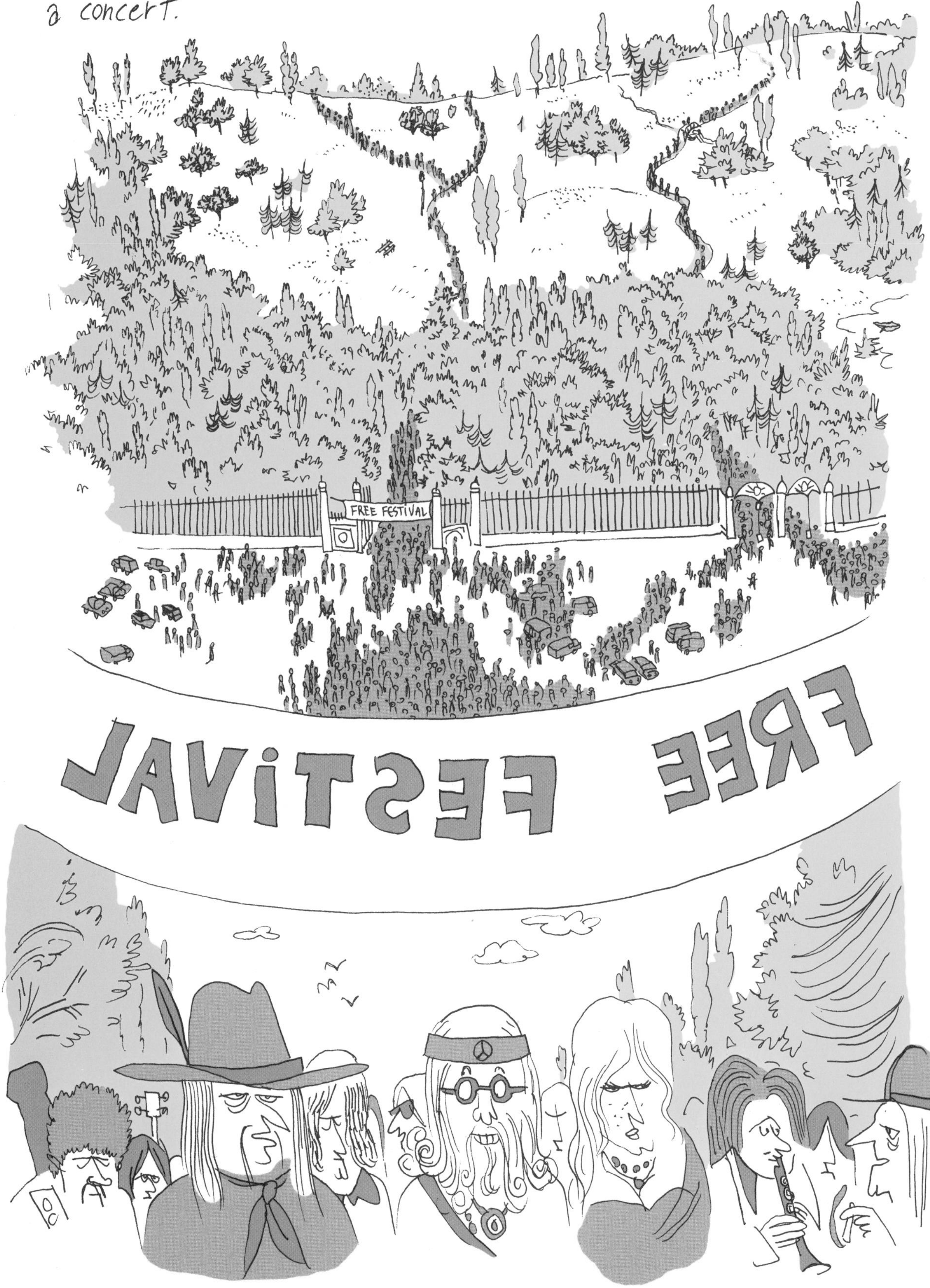
FREE FESTIVAL

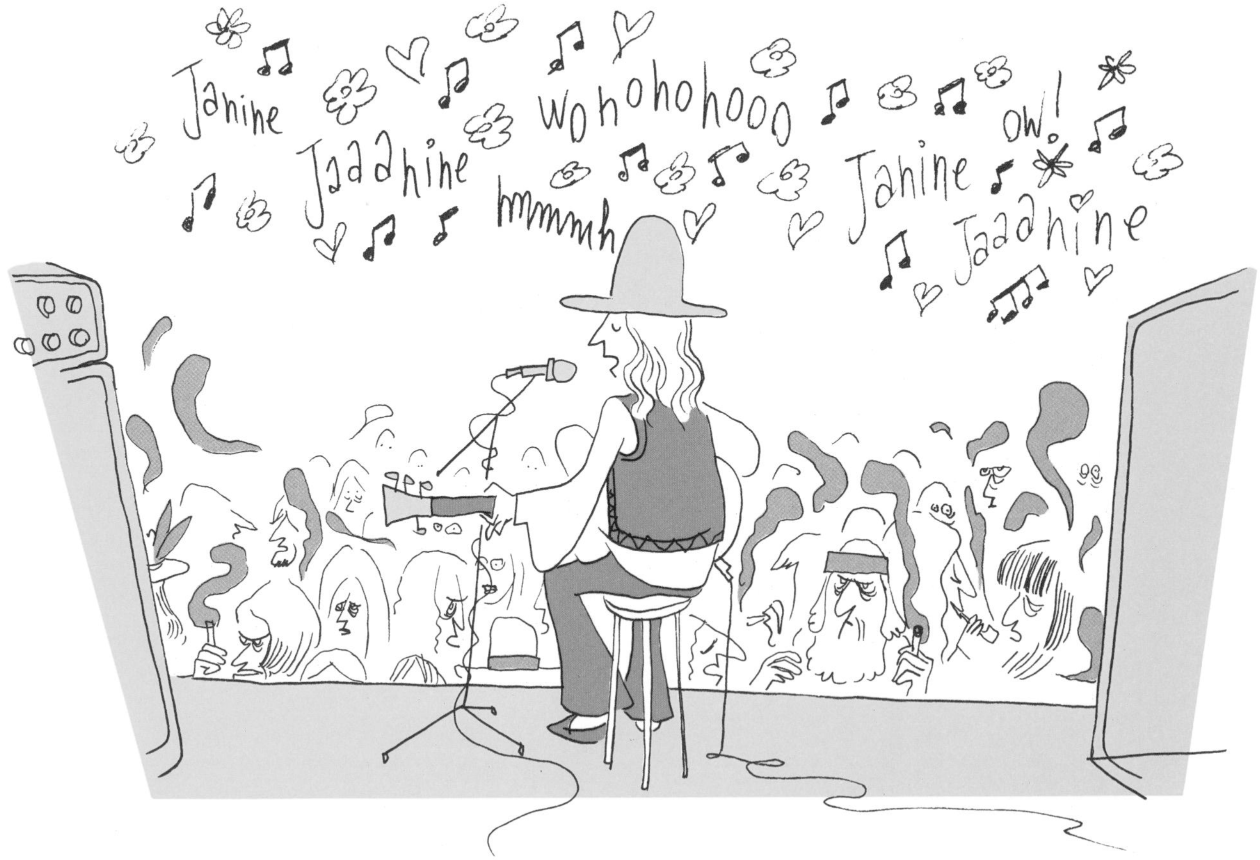
Janine
Jaaahine
wohohohooo
hmmmh
Janine ow!
Jaaahine

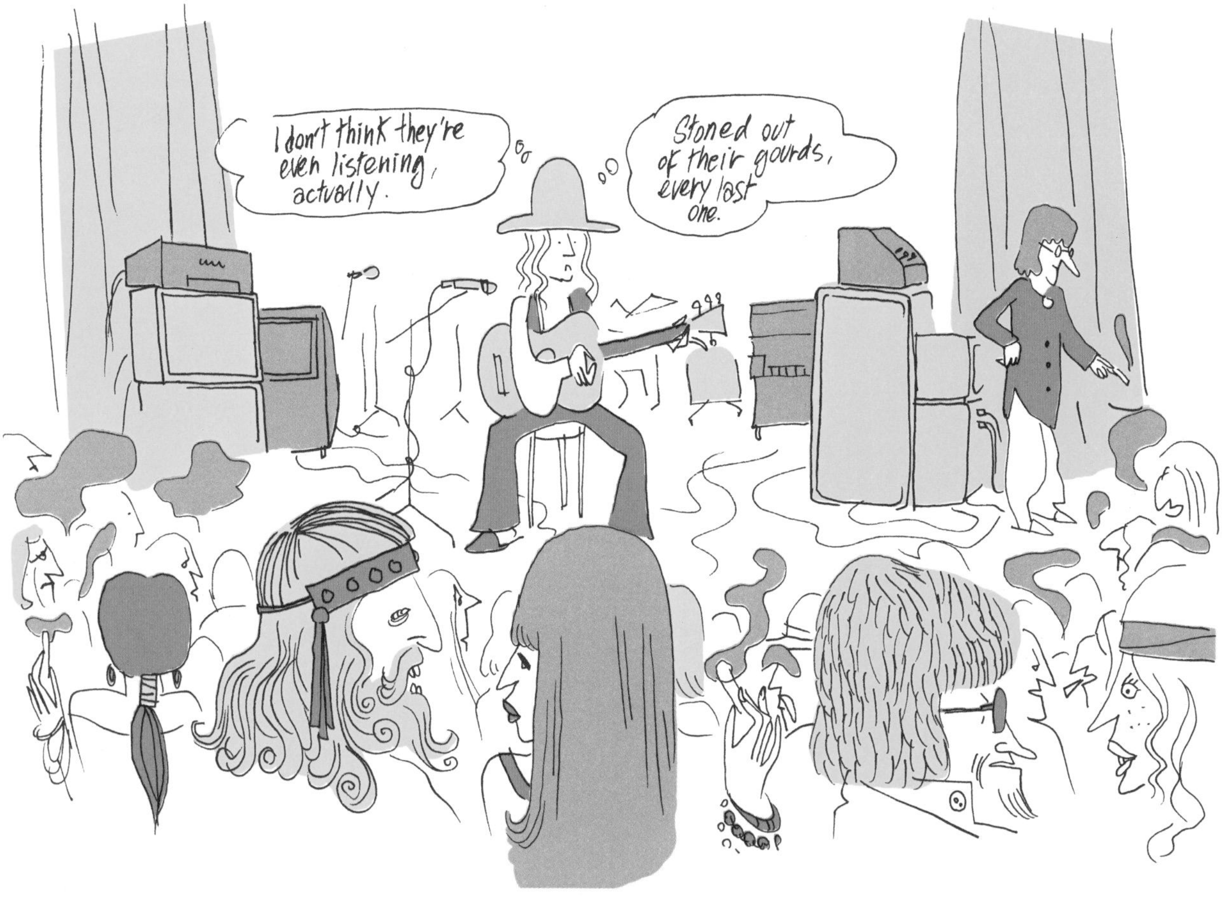
I don't think they're even listening, actually.
Stoned out of their gourds, every last one.

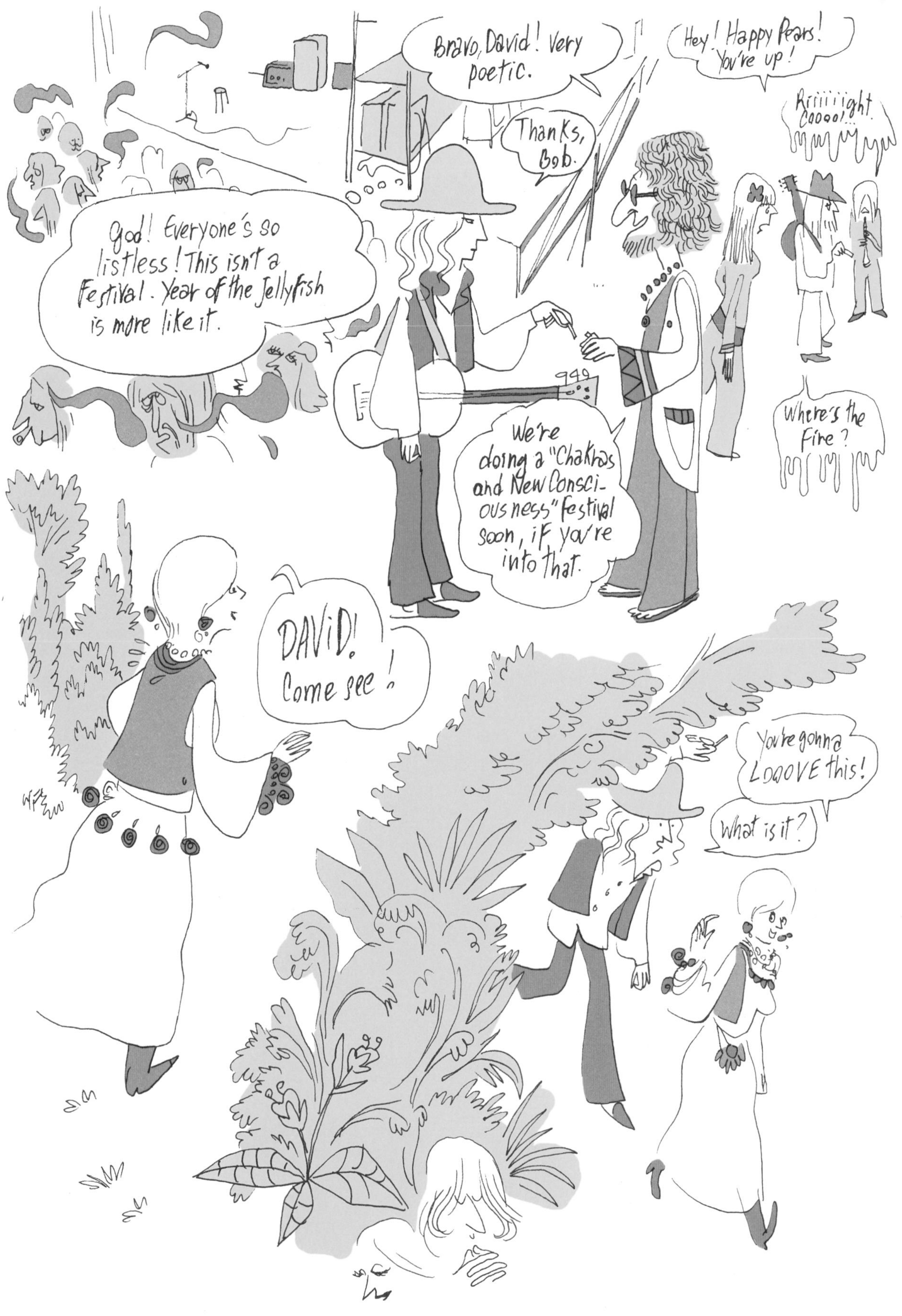
Bravo, David! Very poetic.
Hey! Happy Pears! You're up!
Thanks, Bob.
Riiiiiight. Cooool...
God! Everyone's so listless! This isn't a Festival. Year of the Jellyfish is more like it.
We're doing a "Chakras and New Consciousness" festival soon, if you're into that.
Where's the Fire?
DAVID! Come see!
You're gonna LOOOVE this!
What is it?

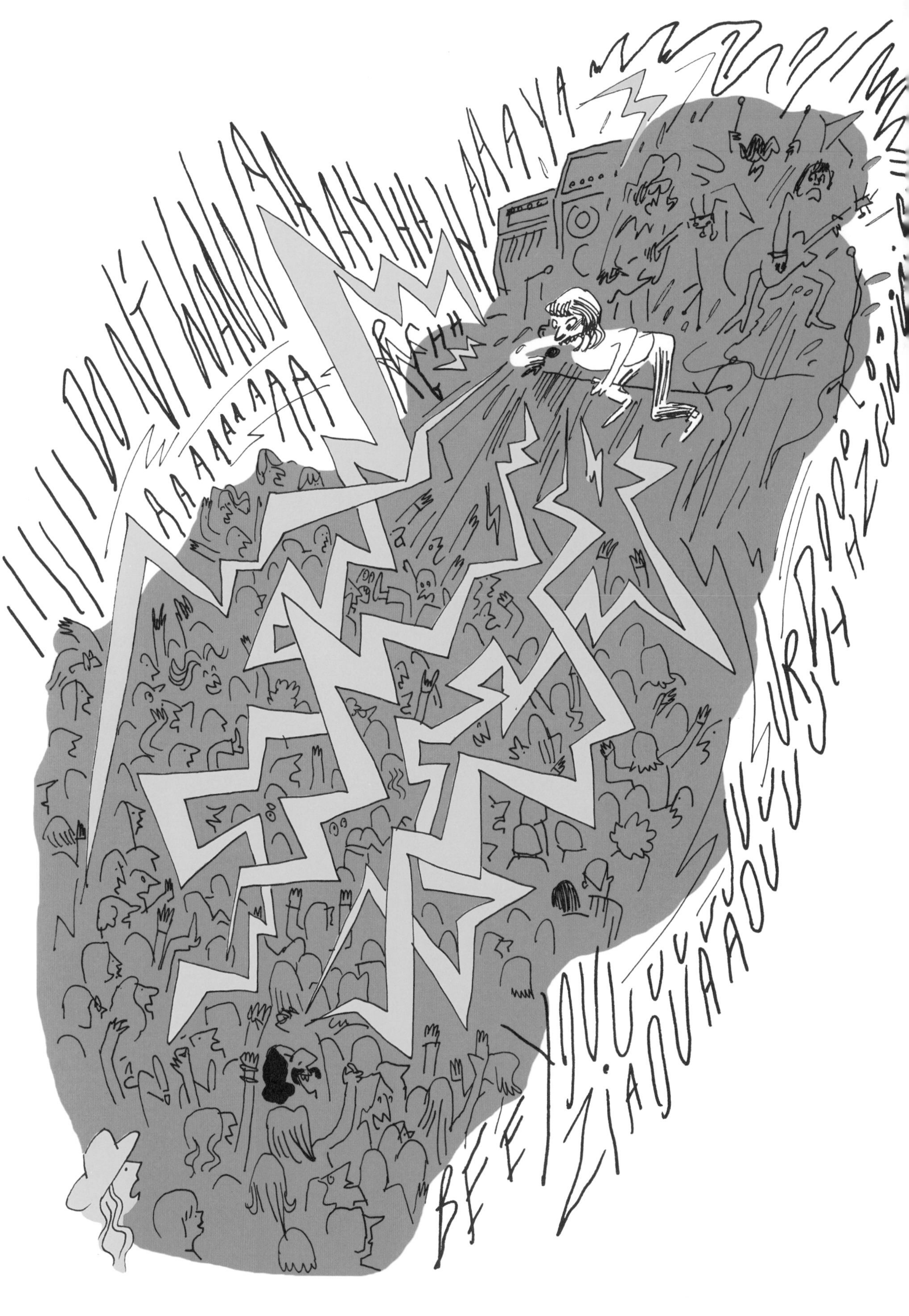

IIIII DO N'T WANT
AAAAAAAAAAA
BEE YOU
ZIAOUAAOU

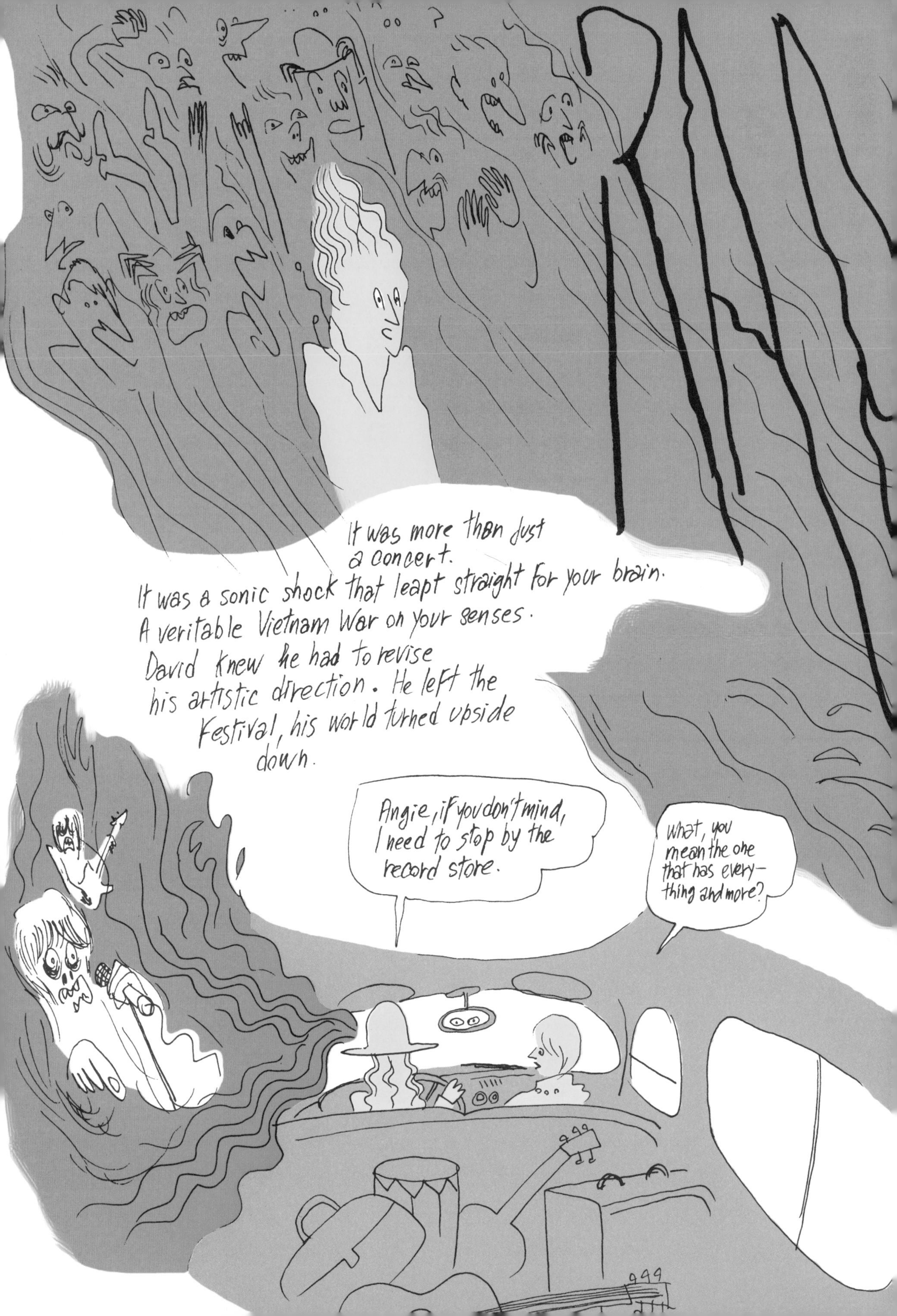

It was more than just a concert.
It was a sonic shock that leapt straight for your brain.
A veritable Vietnam War on your senses.
David knew he had to revise his artistic direction. He left the Festival, his world turned upside down.
Angie, if you don't mind, I need to stop by the record store.
What, you mean the one that has every-thing and more?

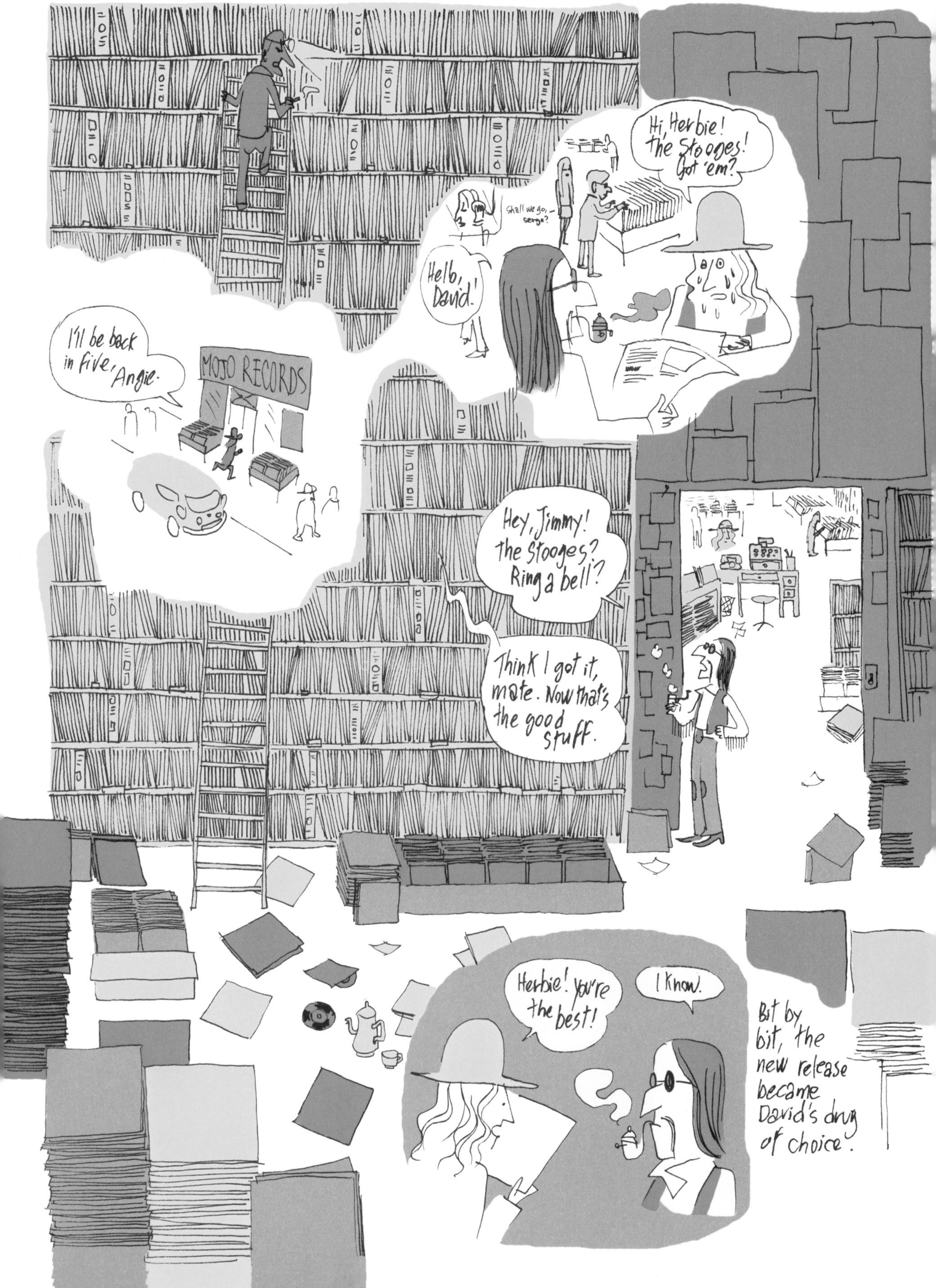
Hi, Herbie! the Stooges! Got 'em?
Shall we go, Serge?
Hello, David!
I'll be back in five, Angie.
MOJO RECORDS
Hey, Jimmy! the Stooges? Ring a bell?
Think I got it, mate. Now that's the good stuff.
Herbie! you're the best!
I know.
Bit by bit, the new release became David's drug of choice.

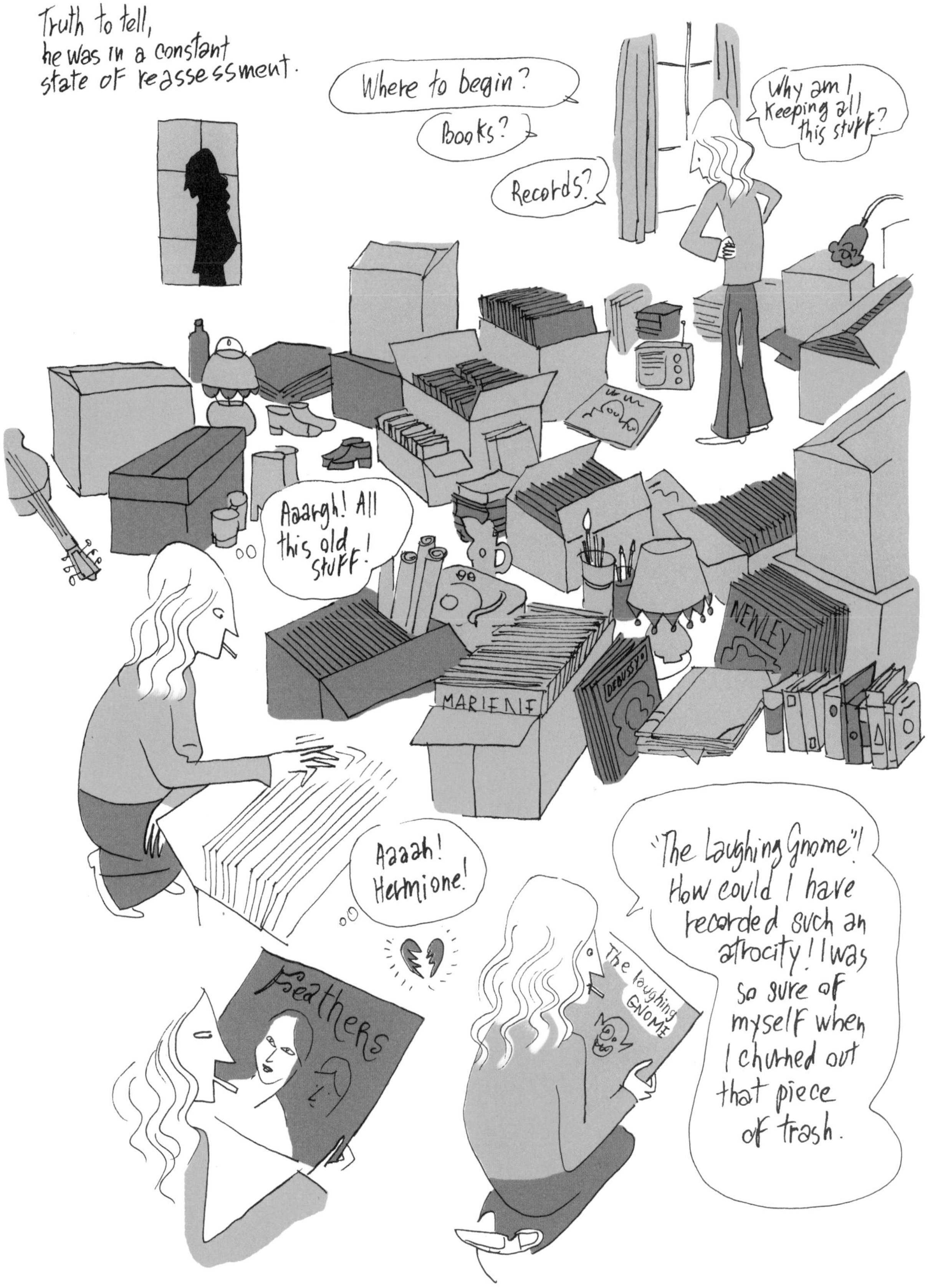

Truth to tell, he was in a constant state of reassessment.
Where to begin?
Books?
Records?
Why am I keeping all this stuff?
Aaargh! All this old stuff!
MARLENE
DEBUSSY
NEWLEY
Aaaah! Hermione!
Feathers
"The Laughing Gnome"! How could I have recorded such an atrocity! I was so sure of myself when I churned out that piece of trash.
The laughing GNOME

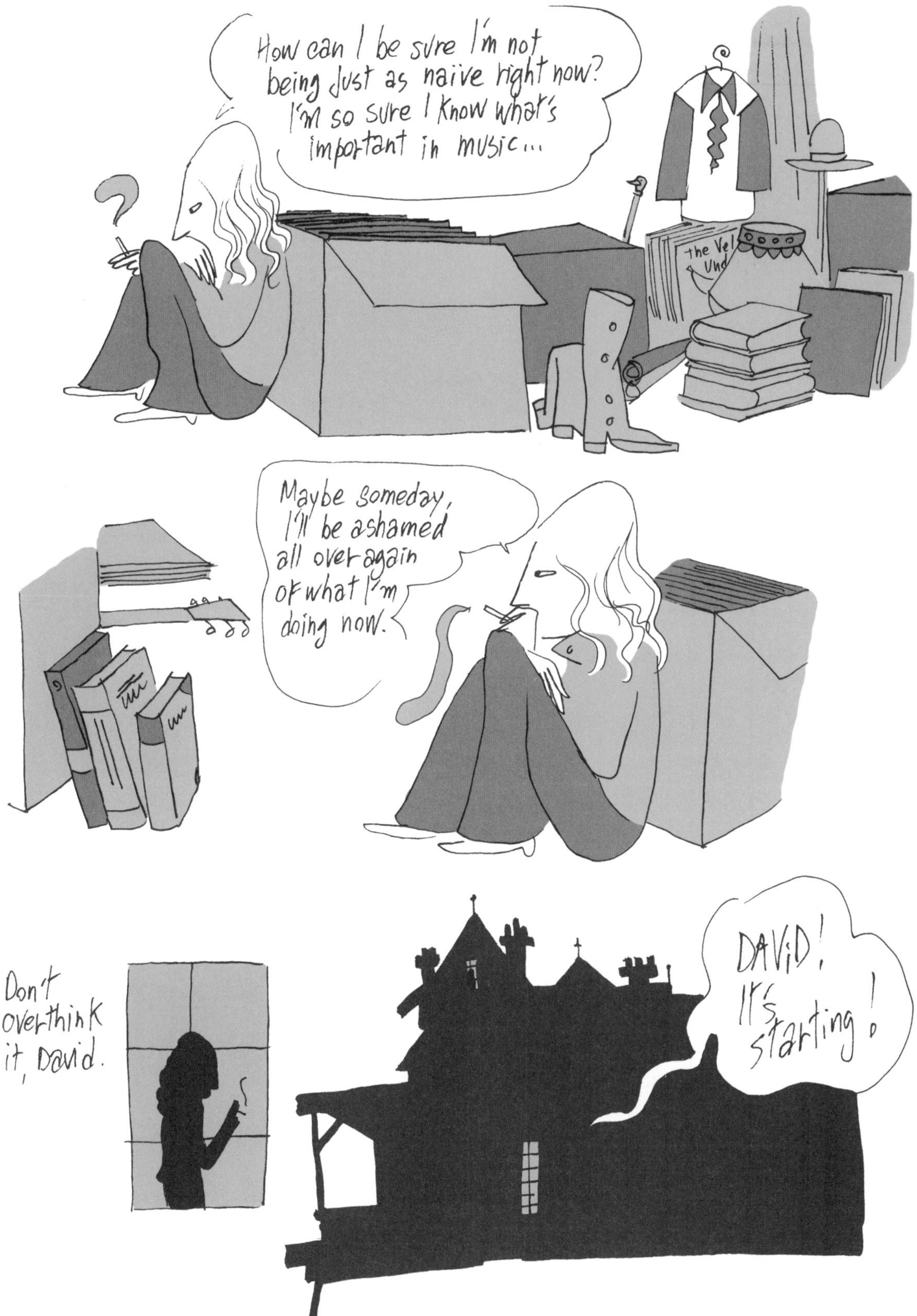
How can I be sure I'm not being just as naive right now? I'm so sure I know what's important in music...
the Vel Und
Maybe someday, I'll be ashamed all over again of what I'm doing now.
Don't overthink it, David.
DAVID! It's starting!

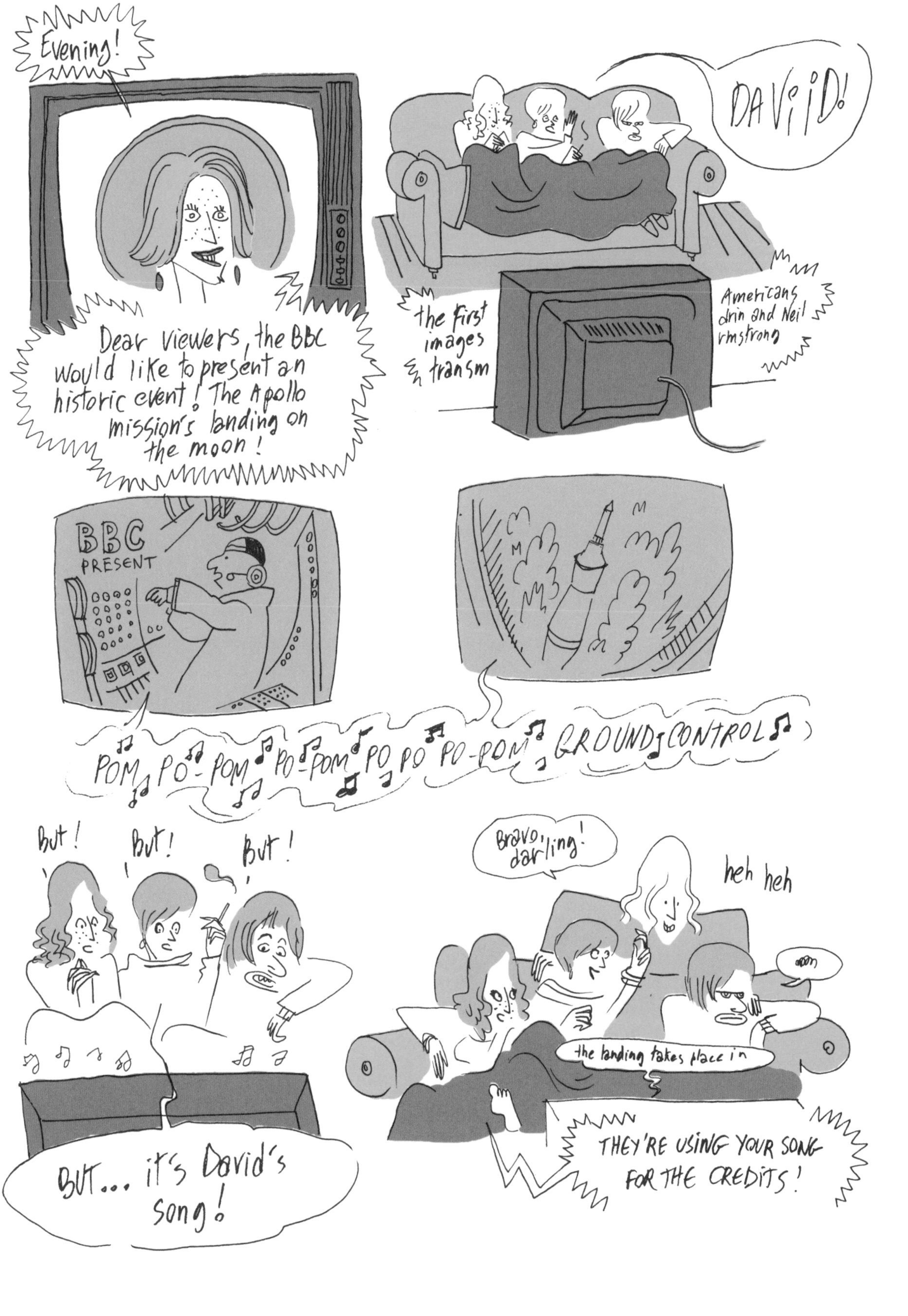
Evening!
Dear viewers, the BBC would like to present an historic event! The Apollo mission's landing on the moon!
DAVIiD!
the first images transm
Americans drin and Neil rmstrong
BBC PRESENT
POM PO-POM PO-POM PO PO PO-POM GROUND CONTROL
But!
But!
But!
BUT... it's David's song!
Bravo, darling!
heh heh
the landing takes place in
THEY'RE USING YOUR SONG FOR THE CREDITS!

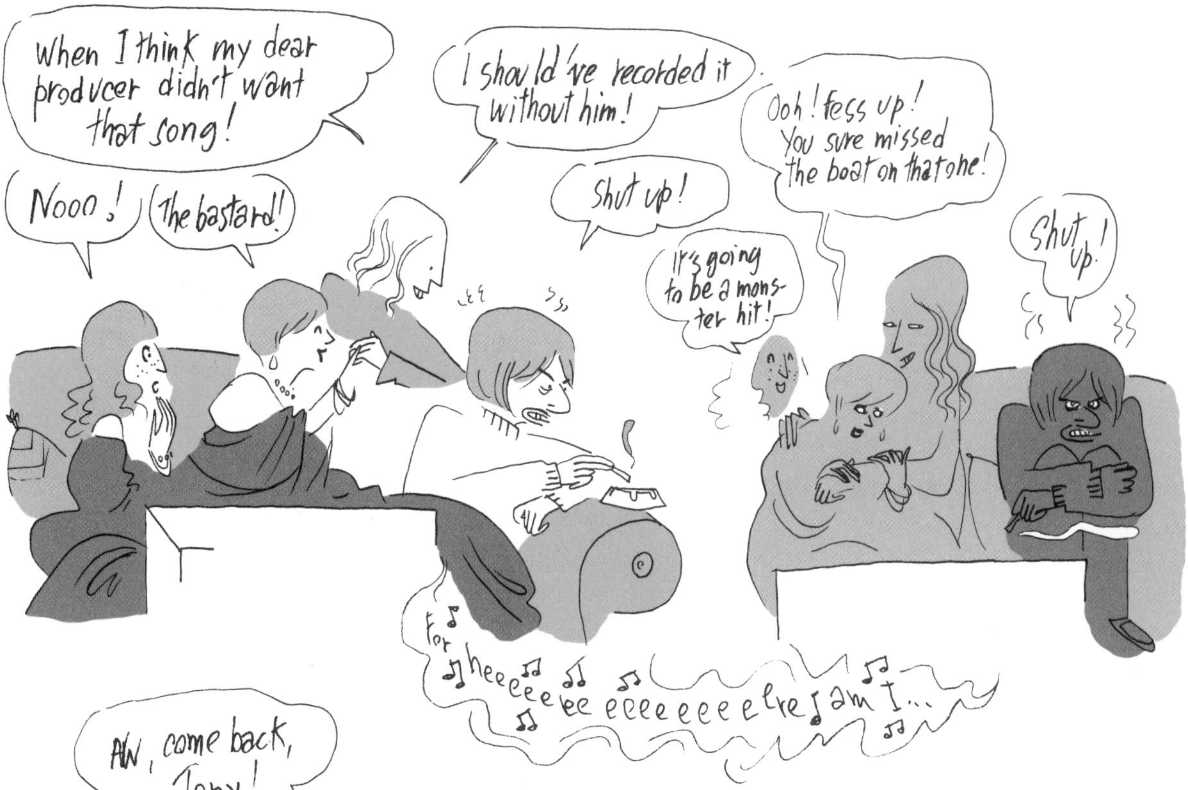

When I think my dear producer didn't want that song!
Nooo!
The bastard!
I should've recorded it without him!
Shut up!
It's going to be a monster hit!
Ooh! Fess up! You sure missed the boat on that one!
Shut up!
For heeeeeeee eeeeeeeeere I am I...

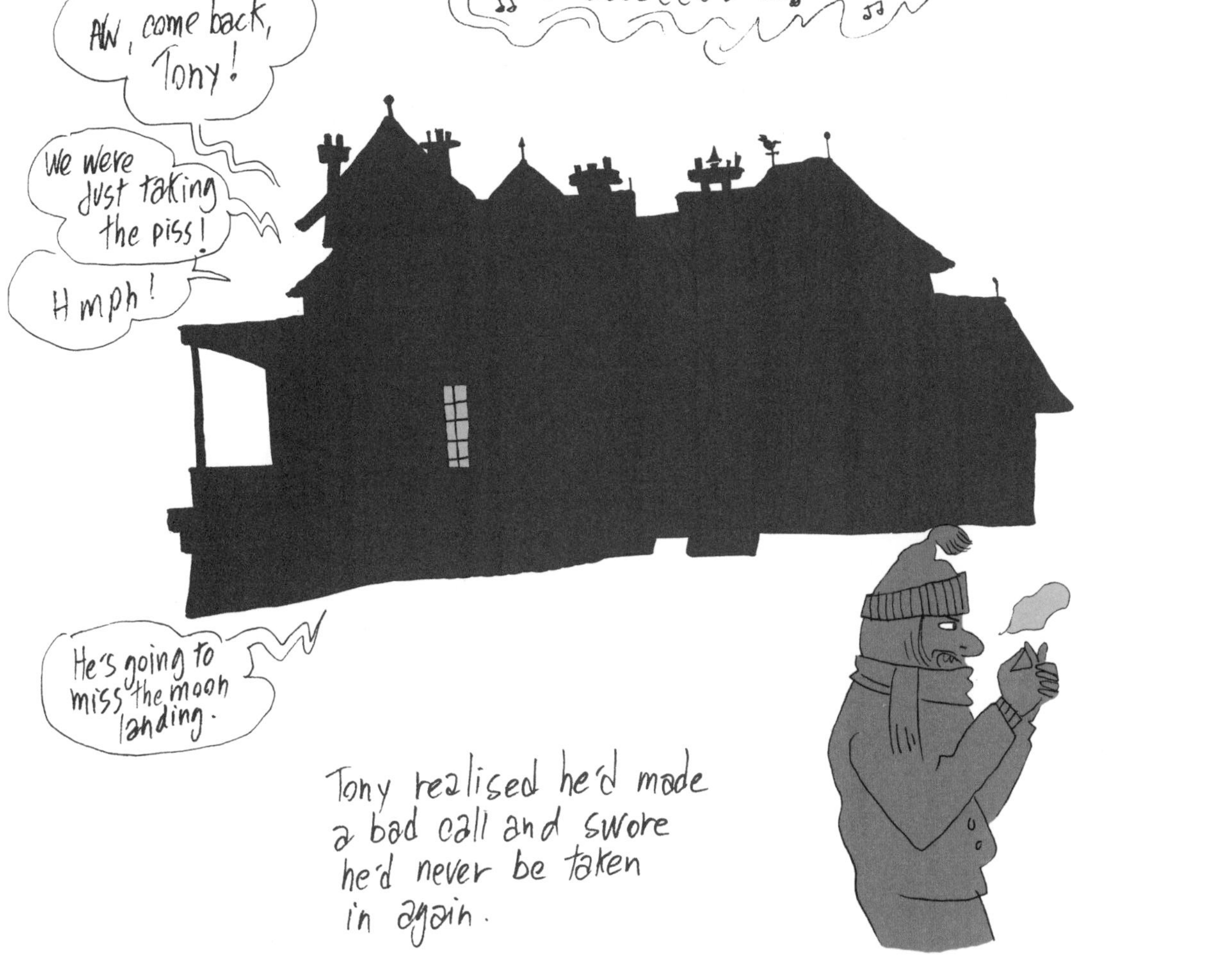

Aw, come back, Tony!
We were just taking the piss!
Hmph!
He's going to miss the moon landing.
Tony realised he'd made a bad call and swore he'd never be taken in again.

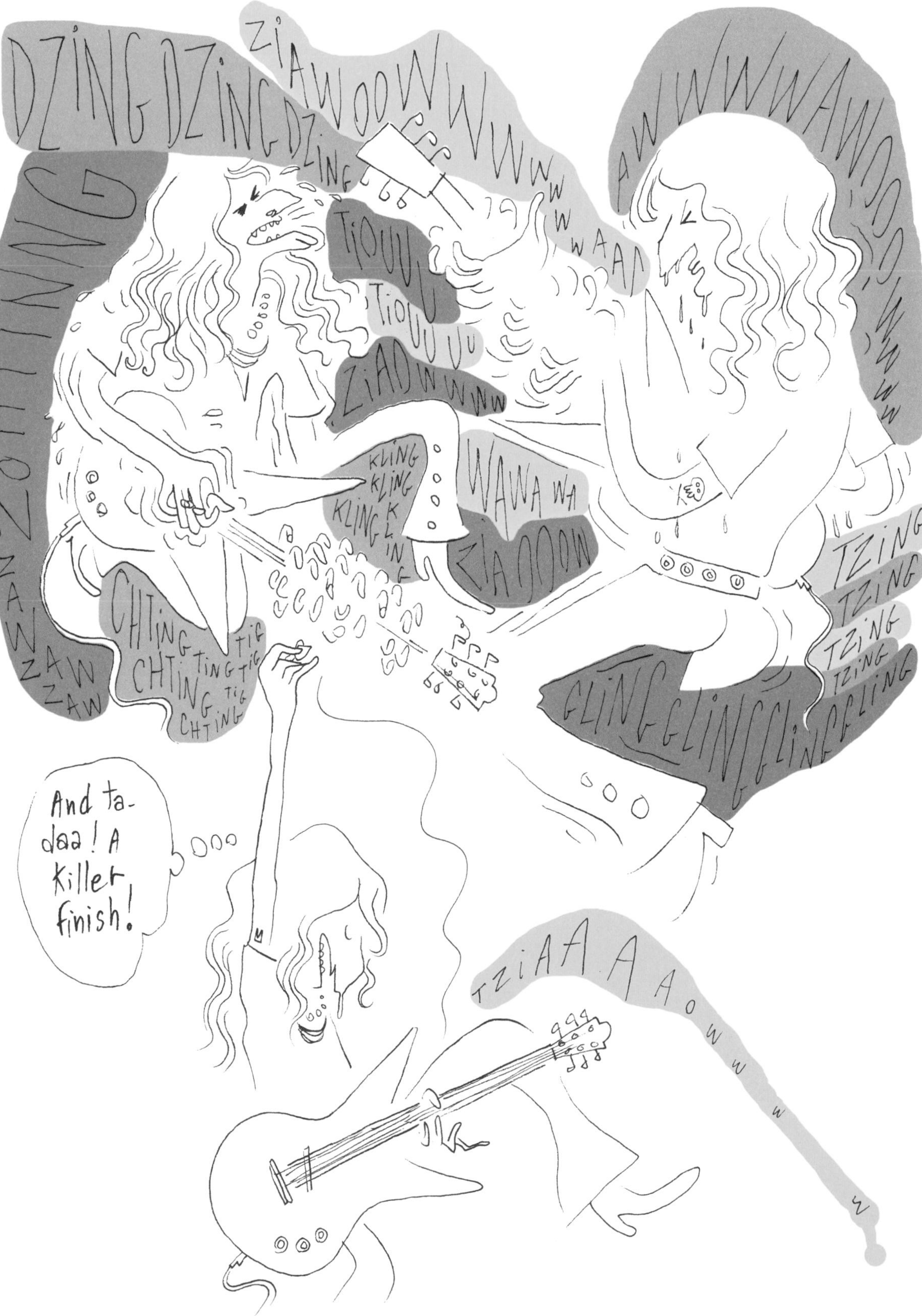
DZING DZING DZING DZING
ZIAWOOWWWWWW WAAA
AWWWWAWOOOWWWW
GNIIIIIOOIIIOONZAWZAWZAW
TIOUUU
TIOUUUUU
ZIAOWWWW
KLING KLING KLING KLING
WAWAWA WA
ZIAOOOW
CHTING TING TIG CHTING TIG CHTING
TZING TZING TZING TZING TZING
GLING GLING GLING GLING
And ta-daa! A killer finish!
TZIAAA A A O W W W W W

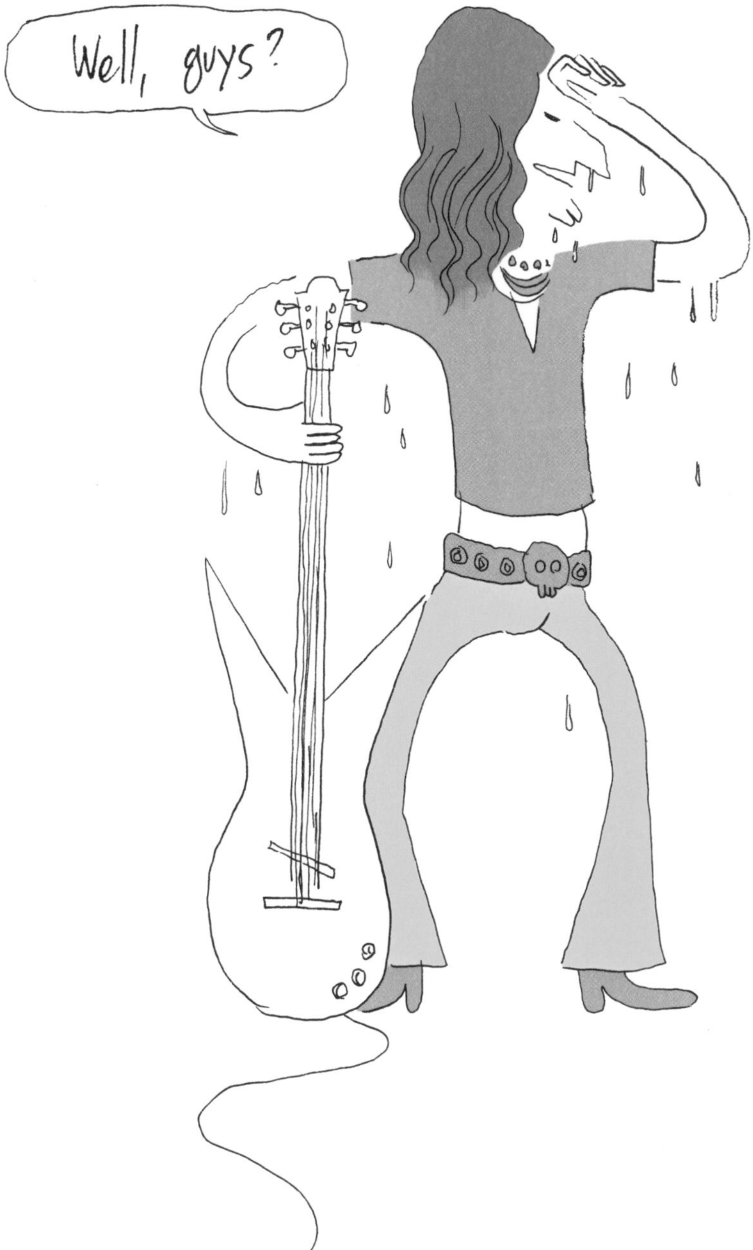
Well, guys?

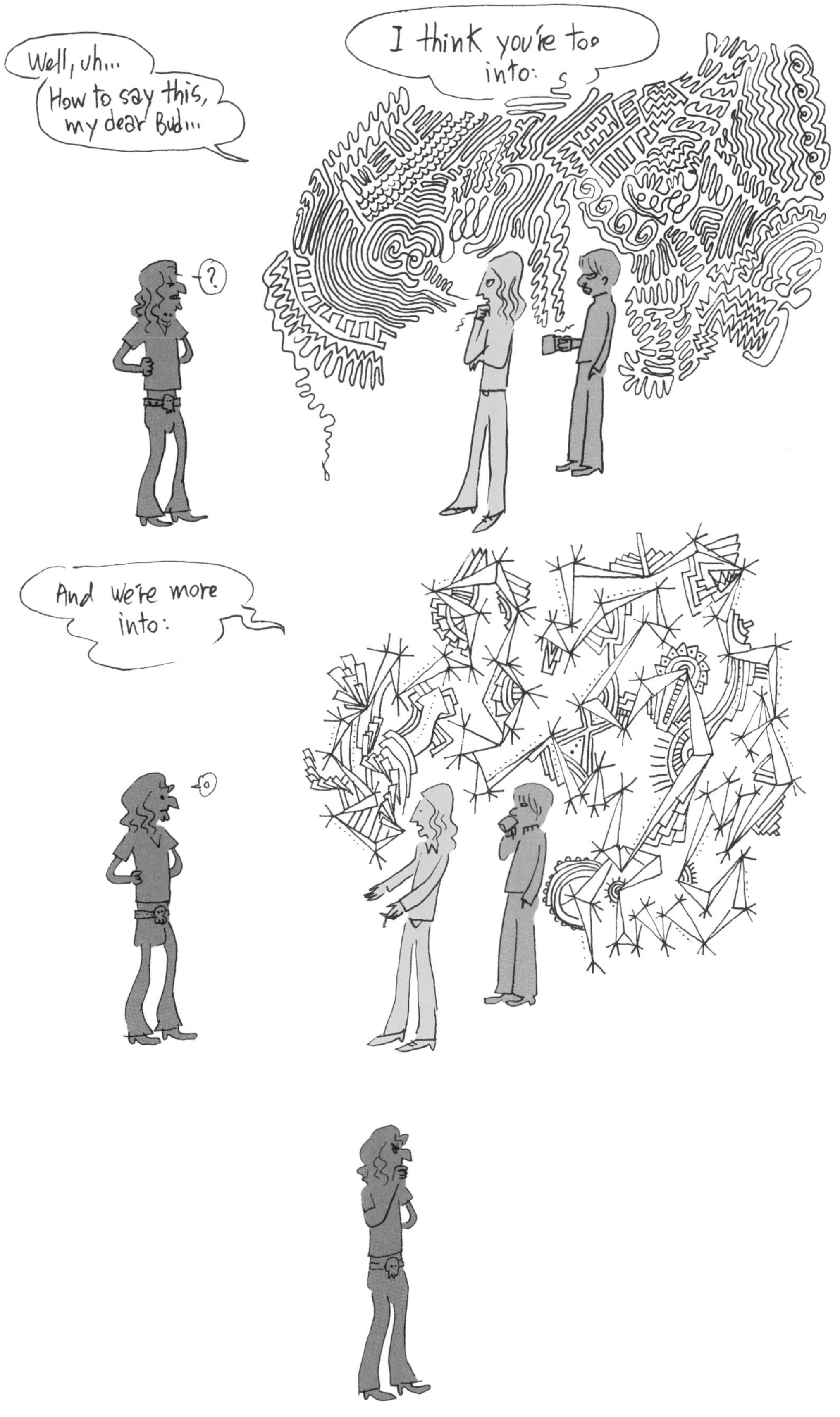
Well, uh...
How to say this, my dear Bud...
I think you're too into:
?
And we're more into:

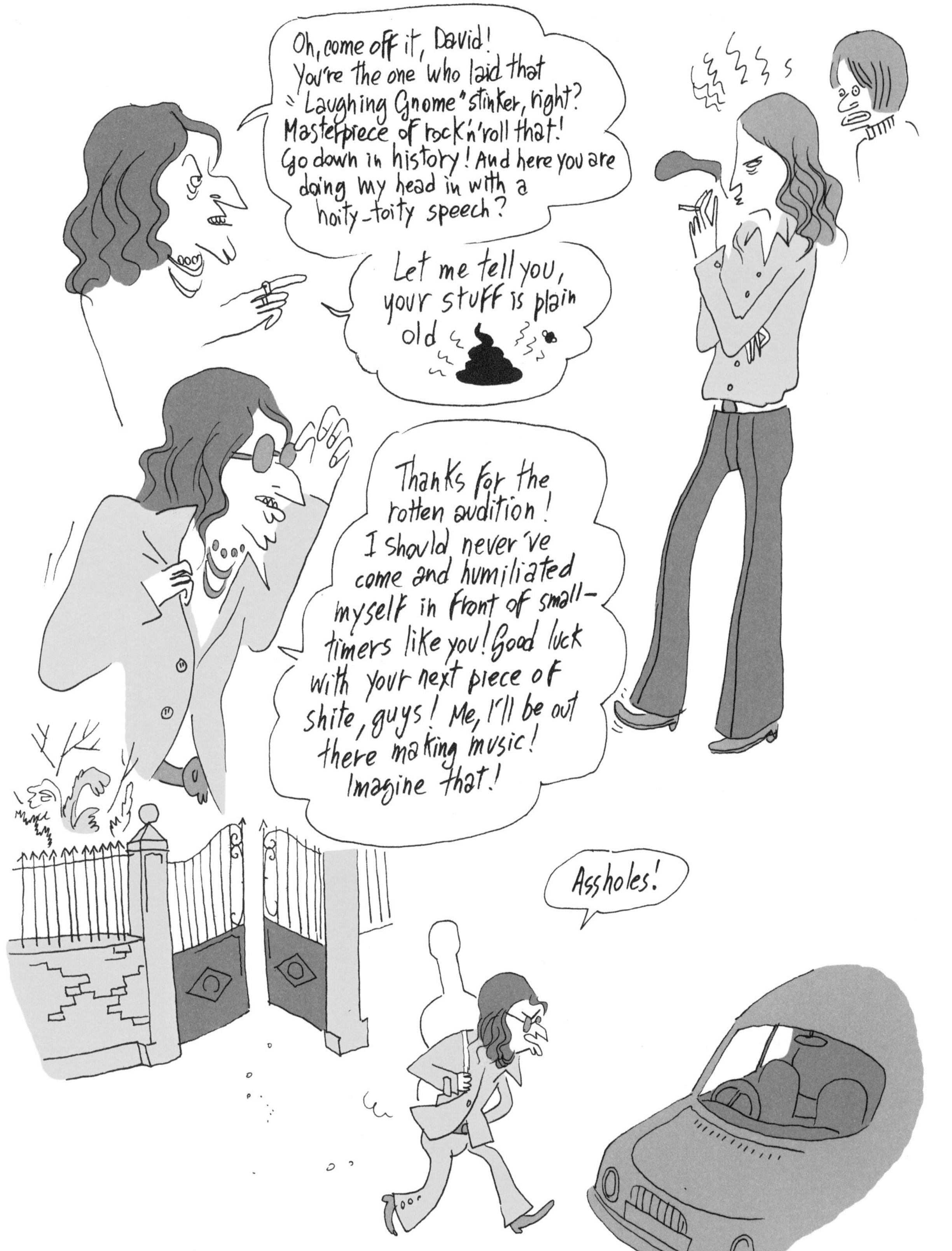
Oh, come off it, David! You're the one who laid that "Laughing Gnome" stinker, right? Masterpiece of rock'n'roll that! Go down in history! And here you are doing my head in with a hoity-toity speech?
Let me tell you, your stuff is plain old
Thanks for the rotten audition! I should never've come and humiliated myself in front of small-timers like you! Good luck with your next piece of shite, guys! Me, I'll be out there making music! Imagine that!
Assholes!

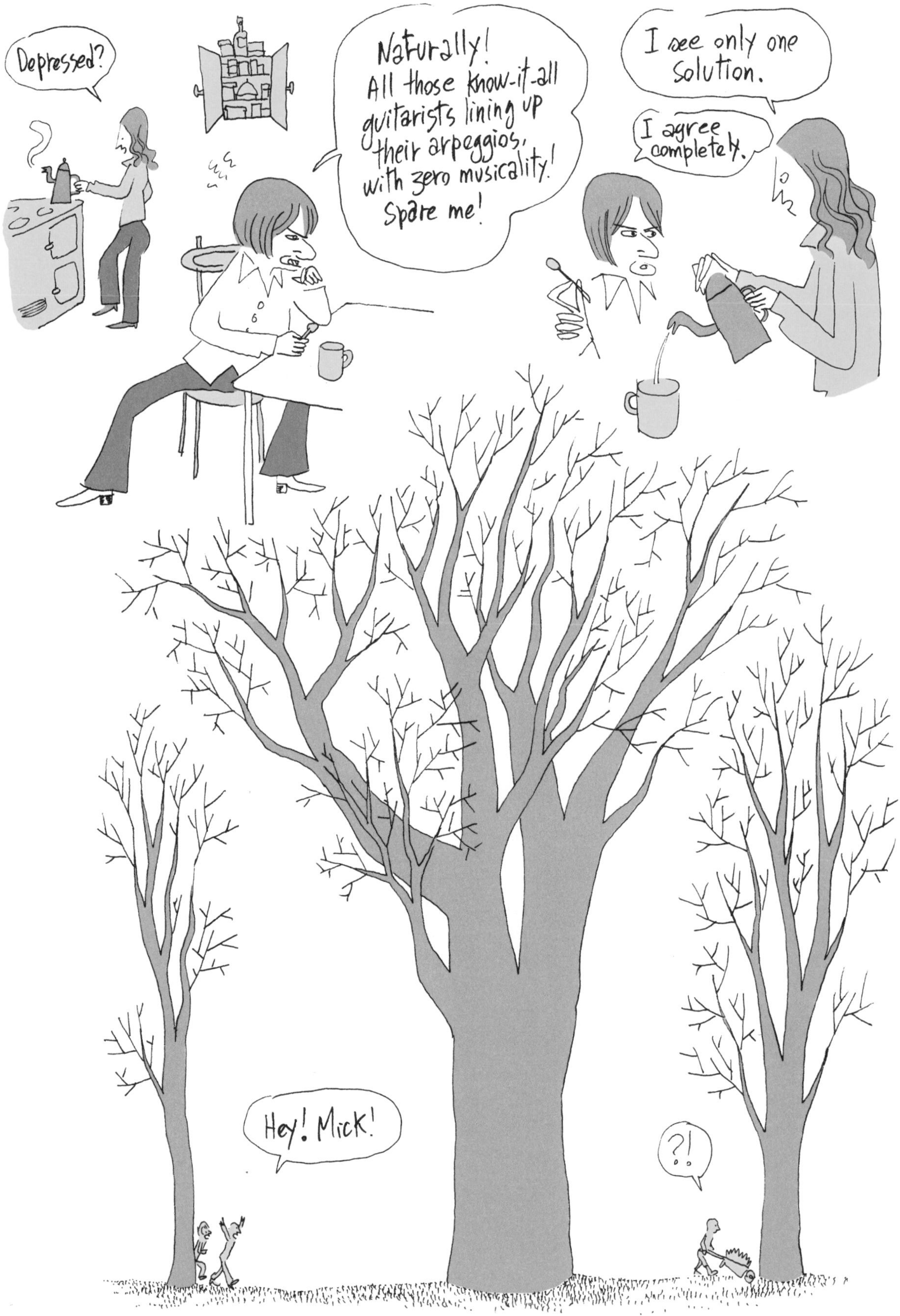
Depressed?
Naturally! All those know-it-all guitarists lining up their arpeggios, with zero musicality! Spare me!
I see only one solution.
I agree completely.
Hey! Mick!
?!

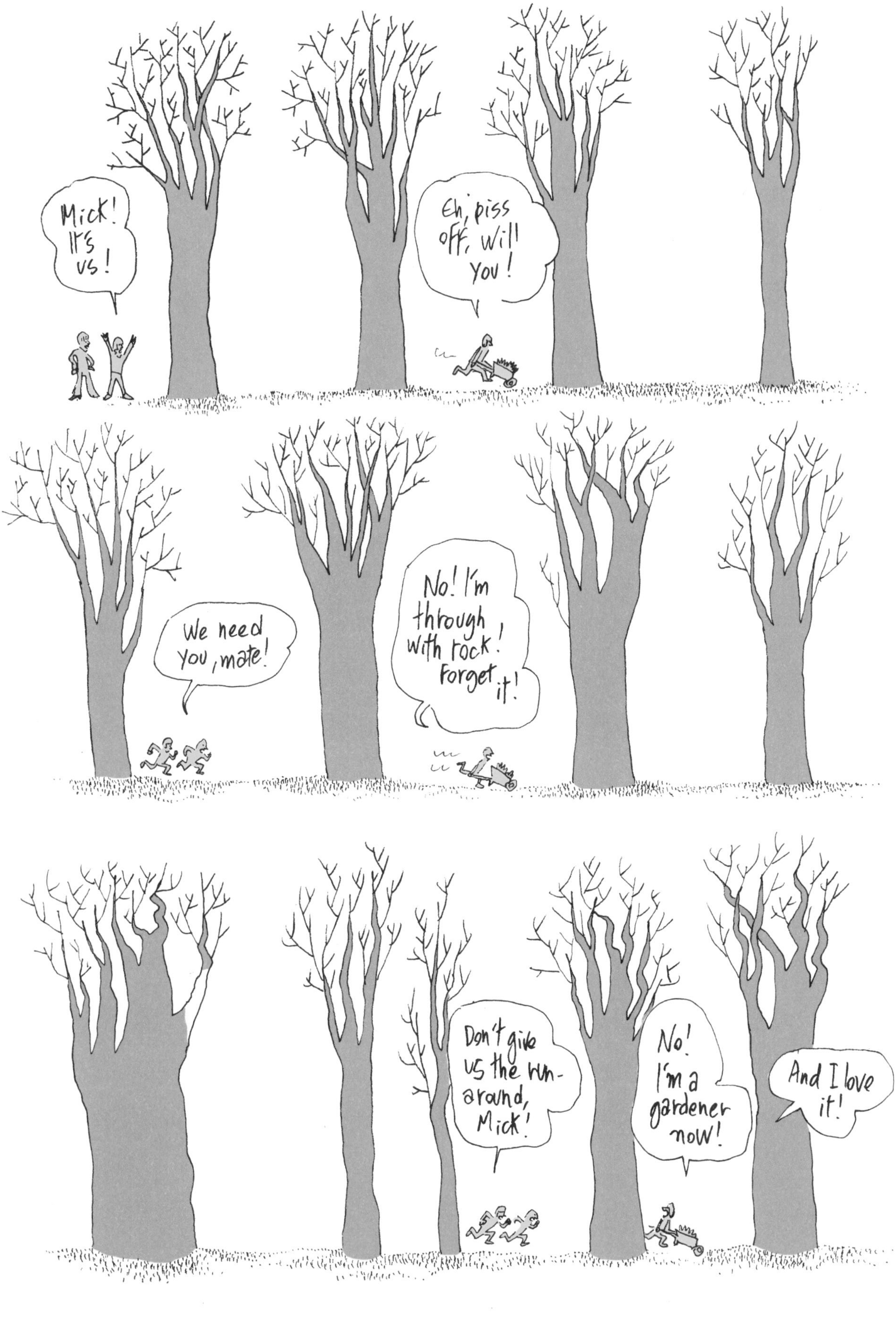
Mick! It's us!
Eh, piss off, will you!
We need you, mate!
No! I'm through with rock! Forget it!
Don't give us the run-around, Mick!
No! I'm a gardener now!
And I love it!

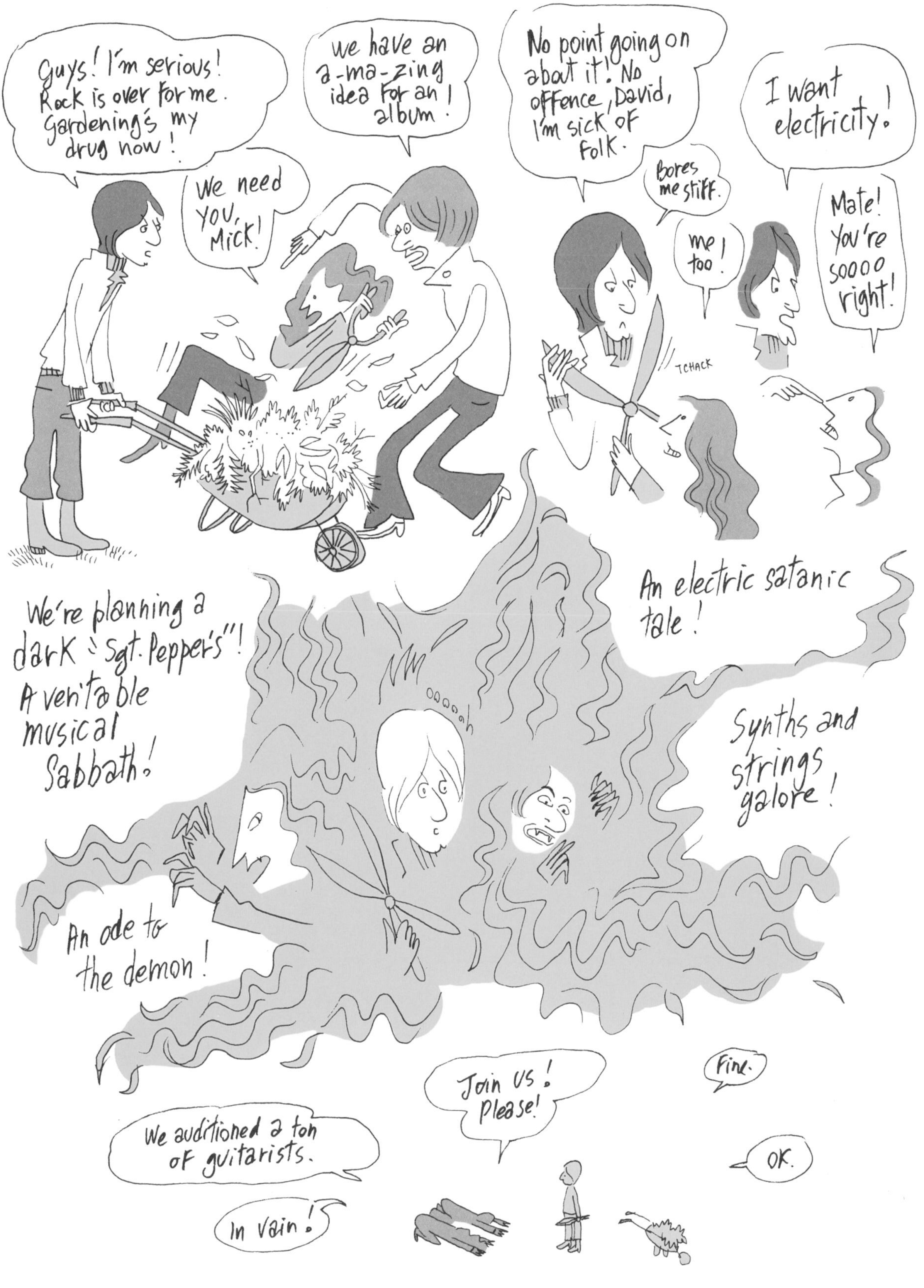
Guys! I'm serious! Rock is over for me. Gardening's my drug now!
We have an a-ma-zing idea for an album!
We need you, Mick!
No point going on about it! No offence, David, I'm sick of folk.
Bores me stiff.
Me too!
I want electricity!
Mate! You're soooo right!
TCHACK
We're planning a dark "Sgt. Pepper's"! A veritable musical Sabbath!
An electric satanic tale!
Ooooh
Synths and strings galore!
An ode to the demon!
We auditioned a ton of guitarists.
In vain!
Join us! Please!
Fine.
OK.

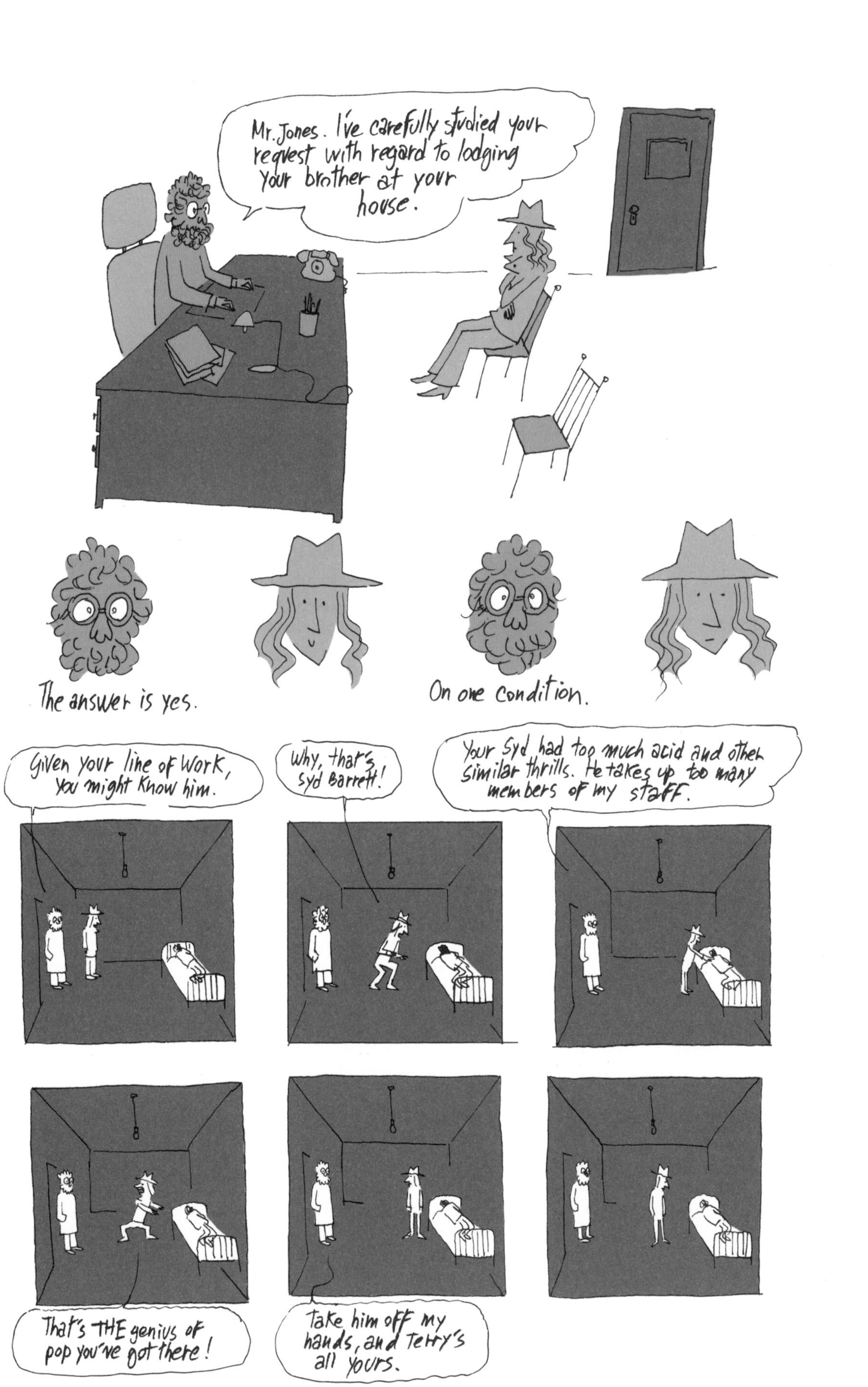
Mr. Jones. I've carefully studied your request with regard to lodging your brother at your house.
The answer is yes.
On one condition.
Given your line of work, you might know him.
Why, that's Syd Barrett!
Your Syd had too much acid and other similar thrills. He takes up too many members of my staff.
That's THE genius of pop you've got there!
Take him off my hands, and Terry's all yours.

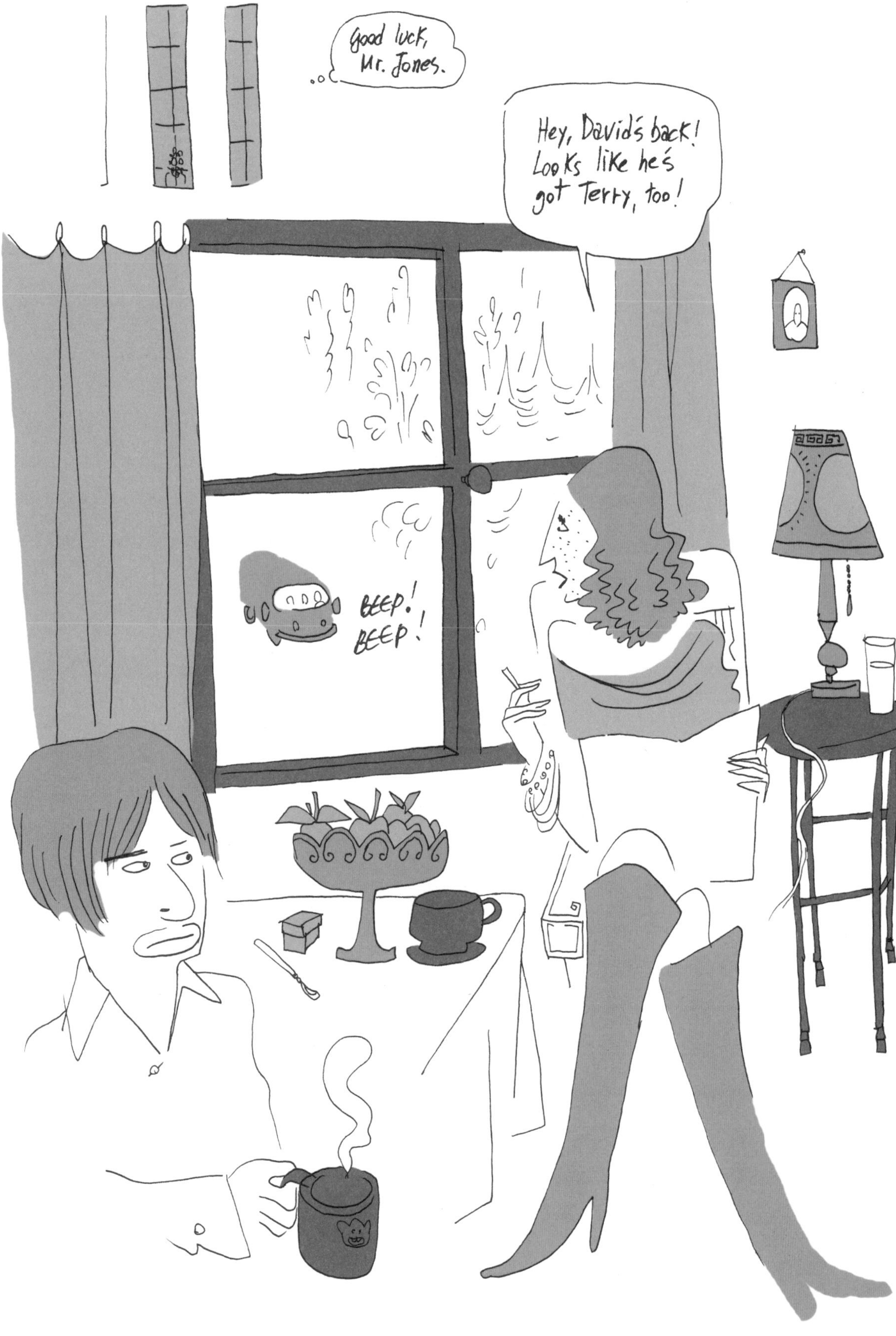
Good luck, Mr. Jones.
Hey, David's back! Looks like he's got Terry, too!
BEEP! BEEP!

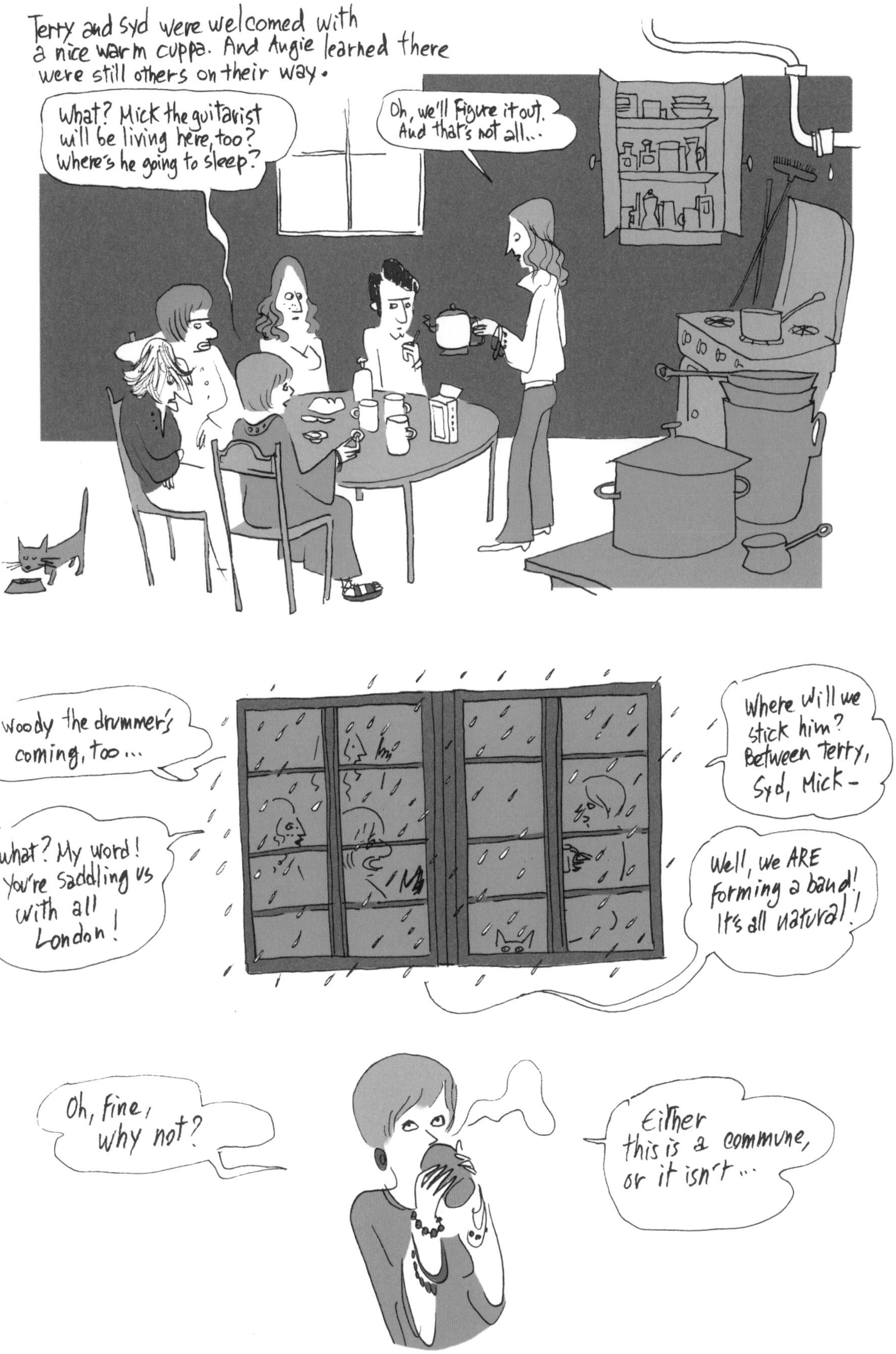
Terry and Syd were welcomed with a nice warm cuppa. And Angie learned there were still others on their way.
What? Mick the guitarist will be living here, too? Where's he going to sleep?
Oh, we'll figure it out. And that's not all...
Woody the drummer's coming, too...
Where will we stick him? Between Terry, Syd, Mick –
What? My word! You're saddling us with all London!
Well, we ARE forming a band! It's all natural!
Oh, fine, why not?
Either this is a commune, or it isn't...

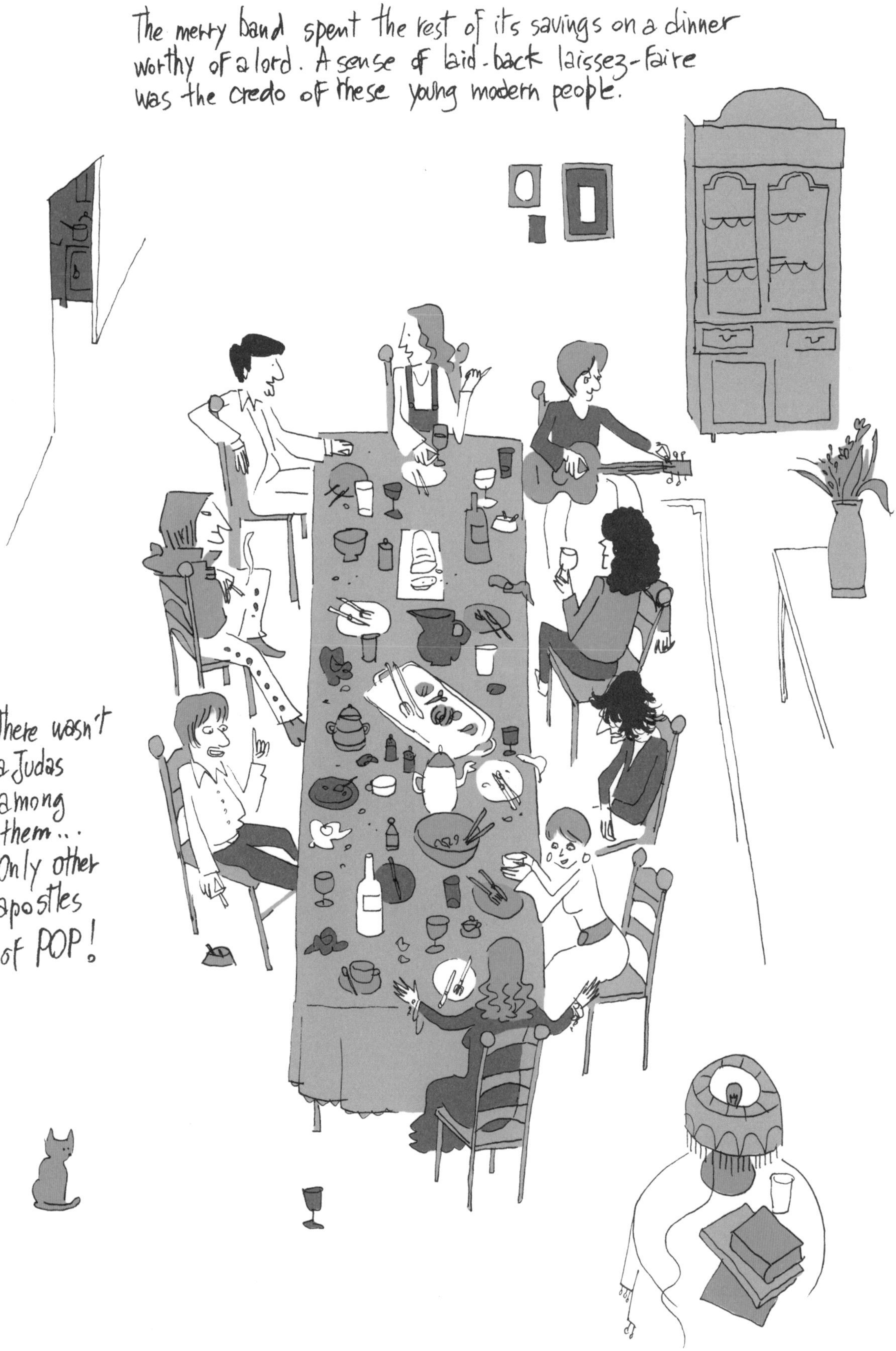
The merry band spent the rest of its savings on a dinner worthy of a lord. A sense of laid-back laissez-faire was the credo of these young modern people.
There wasn't a Judas among them... Only other apostles of POP!

INTERMEZZO

pop star insomnia

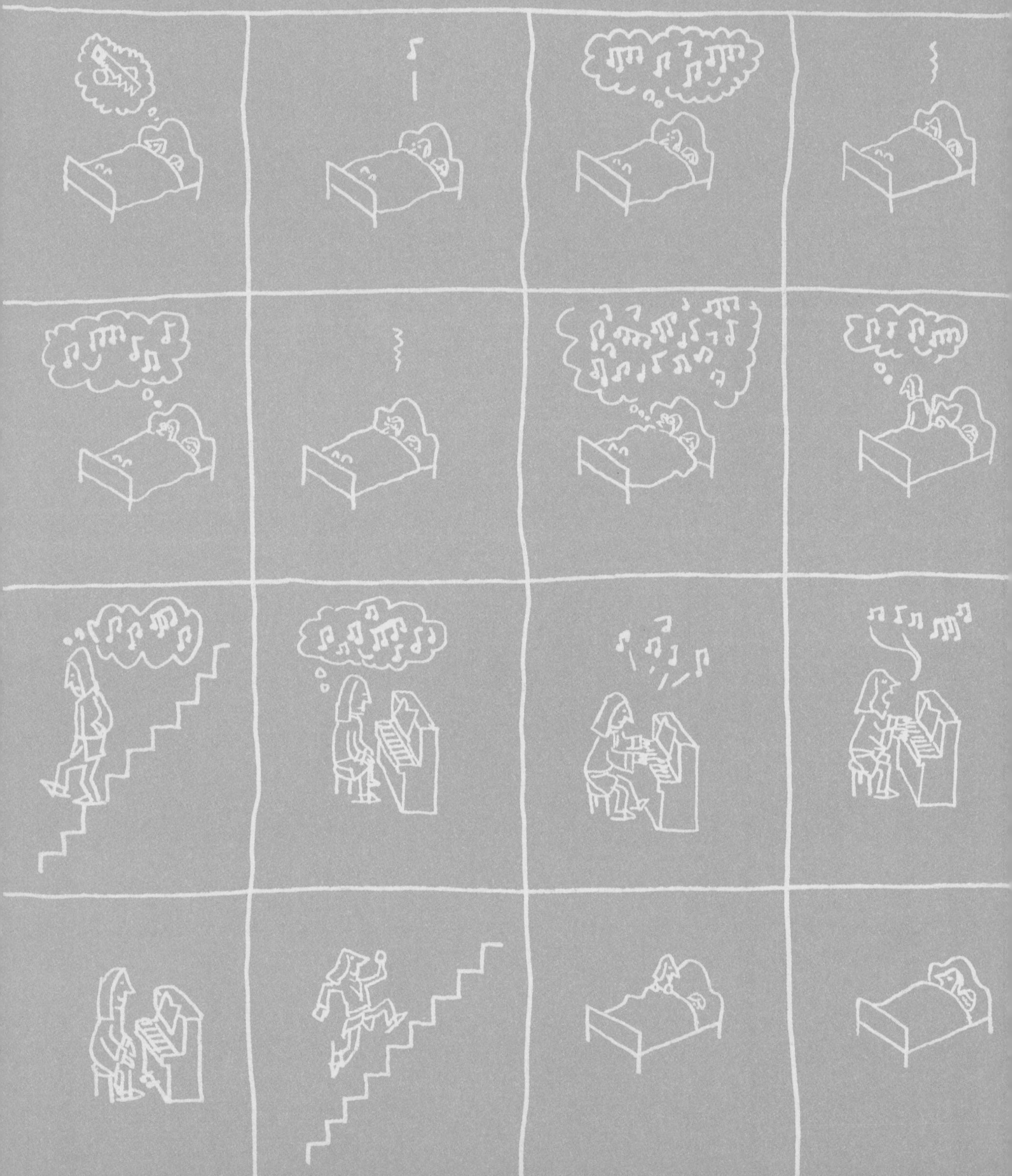

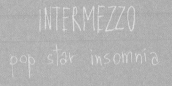

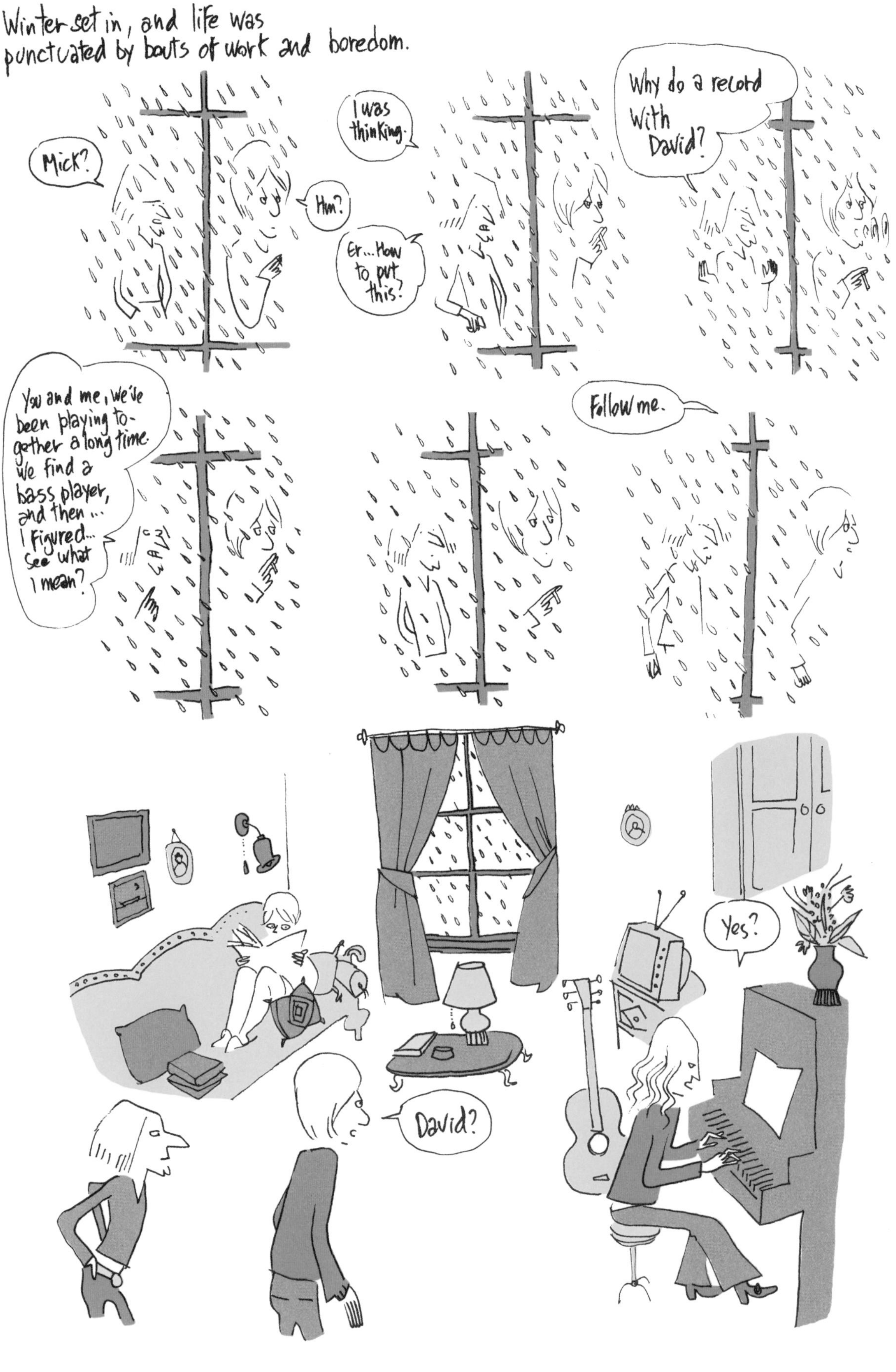
Winter set in, and life was punctuated by bouts of work and boredom.
Mick?
Hm?
I was thinking.
Er... How to put this?
Why do a record with David?
You and me, we've been playing together a long time. We find a bass player, and then... I figured... See what I mean?
Follow me.
Yes?
David?

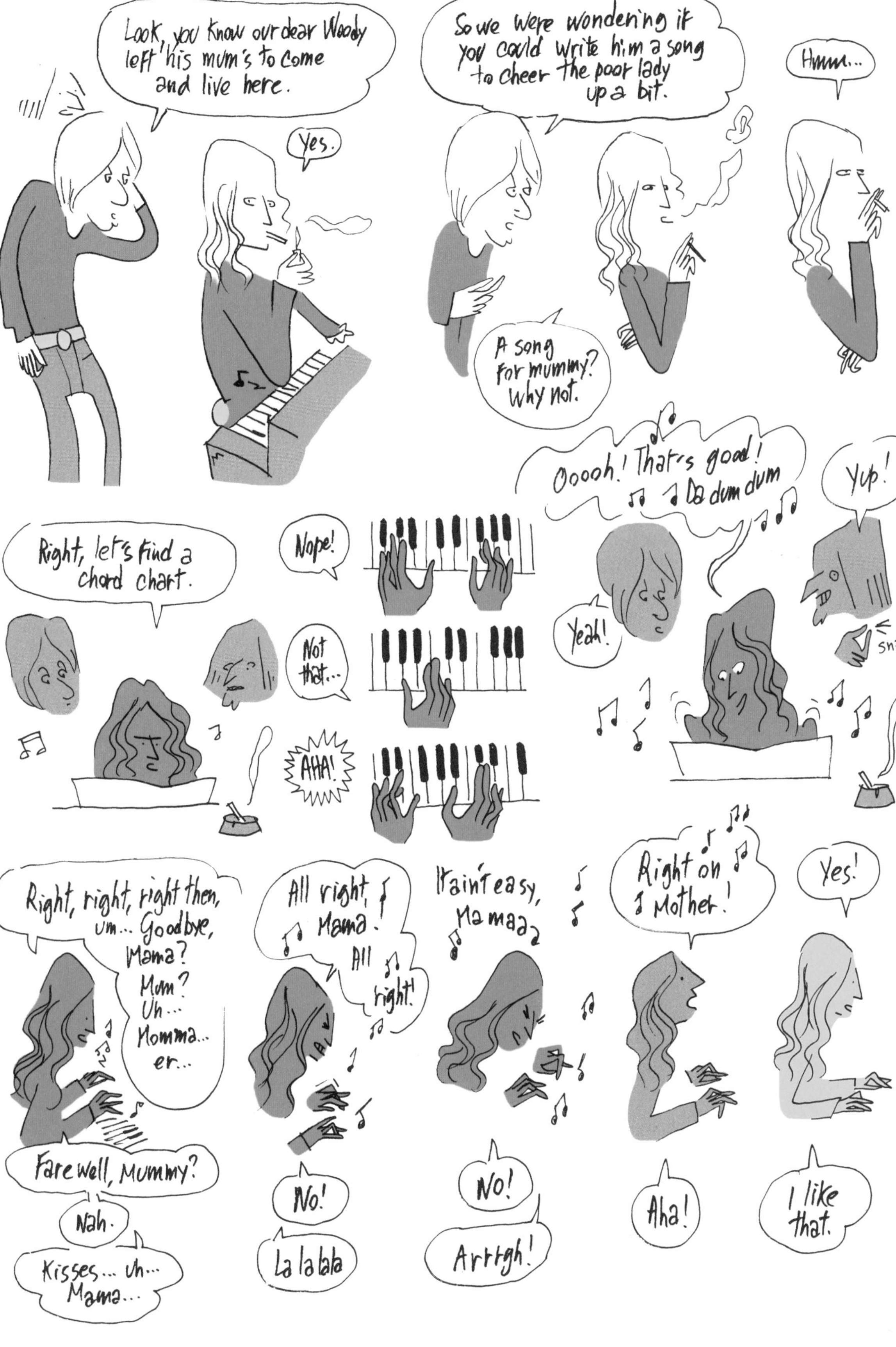
Look, you know our dear Woody left his mum's to come and live here.
Yes.
So we were wondering if you could write him a song to cheer the poor lady up a bit.
A song for mummy? Why not.
Hmm...
Right, let's find a chord chart.
Nope!
Not that...
AHA!
Ooooh! That's good! Da dum dum
Yeah!
Yup!
snap!
Right, right, right then, um... Goodbye, Mama? Mum? Uh... Momma... er...
Farewell, Mummy?
Nah.
Kisses... uh... Mama...
All right, Mama. All right!
No!
La la la la
It ain't easy, Mamaa
No!
Arrrgh!
Right on Mother!
Aha!
Yes!
I like that.

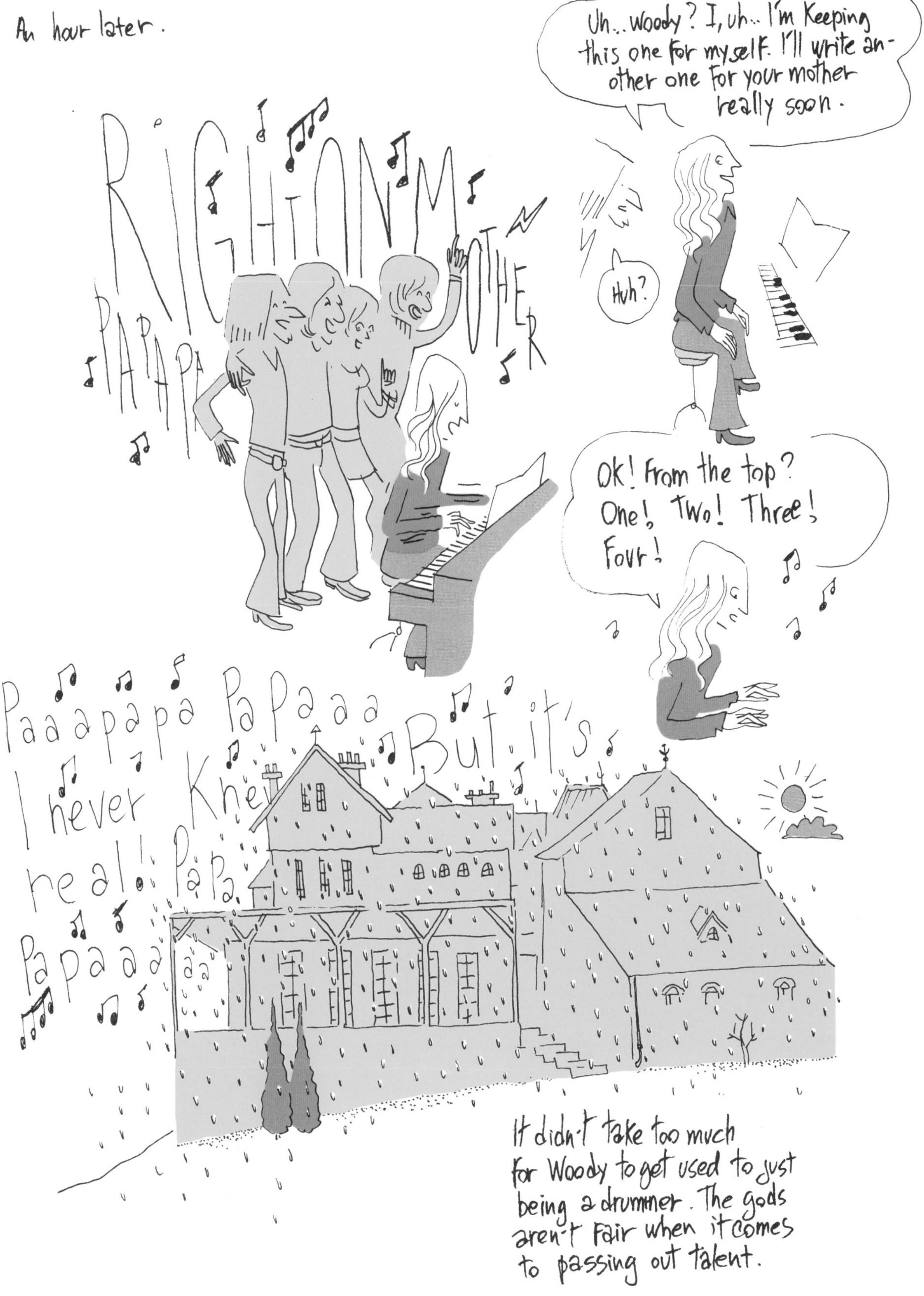
An hour later.
RIGHTON MOTHER
PAPAPA
Uh.. Woody? I, uh.. I'm Keeping this one for myself. I'll write another one for your mother really soon.
Huh?
Ok! From the top? One! Two! Three! Four!
Paaapapa Papaaa
I never Kne
But it's
real! PaPa
Papaaaaa
It didn't take too much for Woody to get used to just being a drummer. The gods aren't fair when it comes to passing out talent.

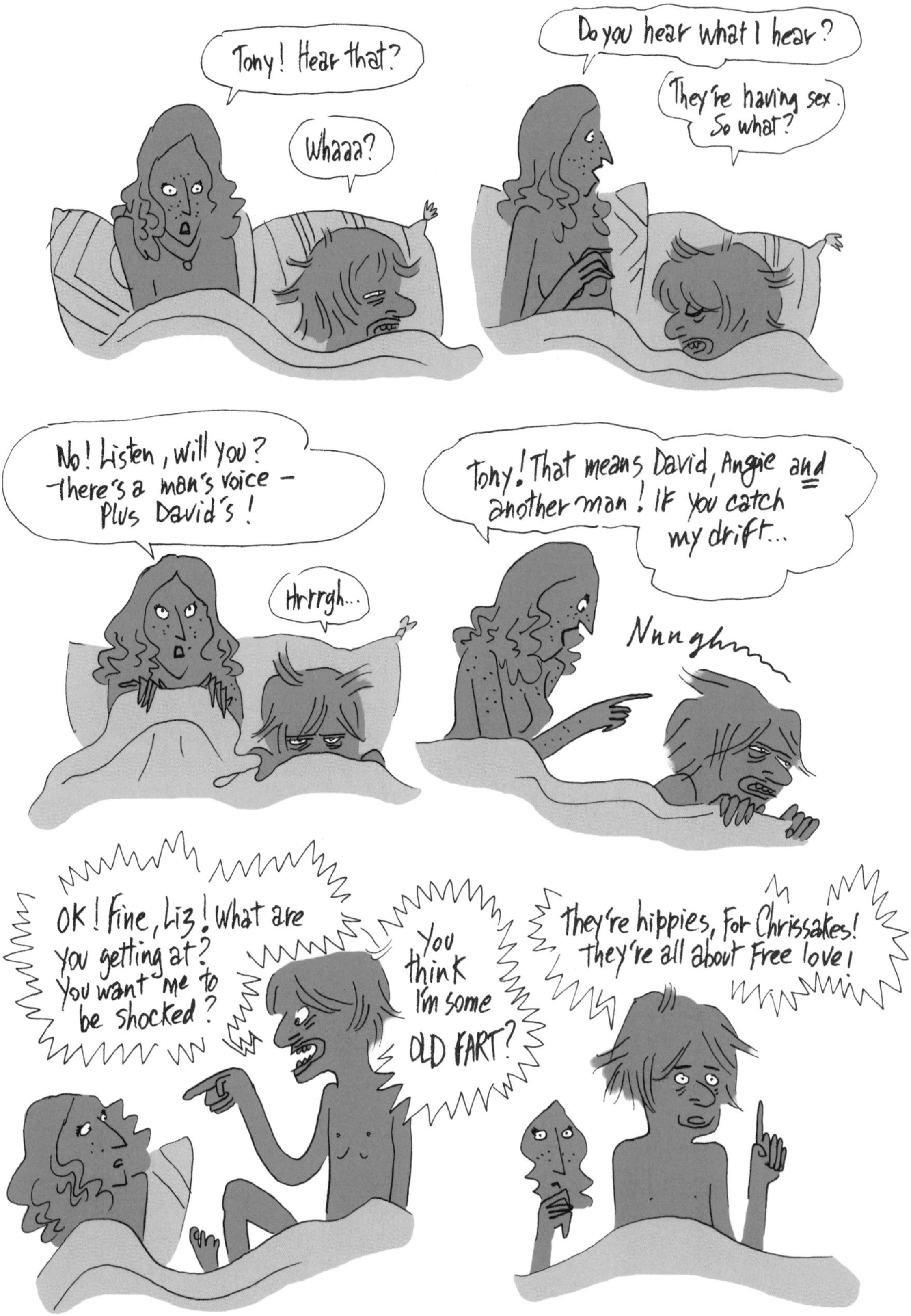
Tony! Hear that?
Whaaa?
Do you hear what I hear?
They're having sex. So what?
No! Listen, will you? There's a man's voice - Plus David's!
Hrrrgh...
Tony! That means David, Angie and another man! If you catch my drift...
Nunghhh
OK! Fine, Liz! What are you getting at? You want me to be shocked?
You think I'm some OLD FART?
They're hippies, for Chrissakes! They're all about free love!

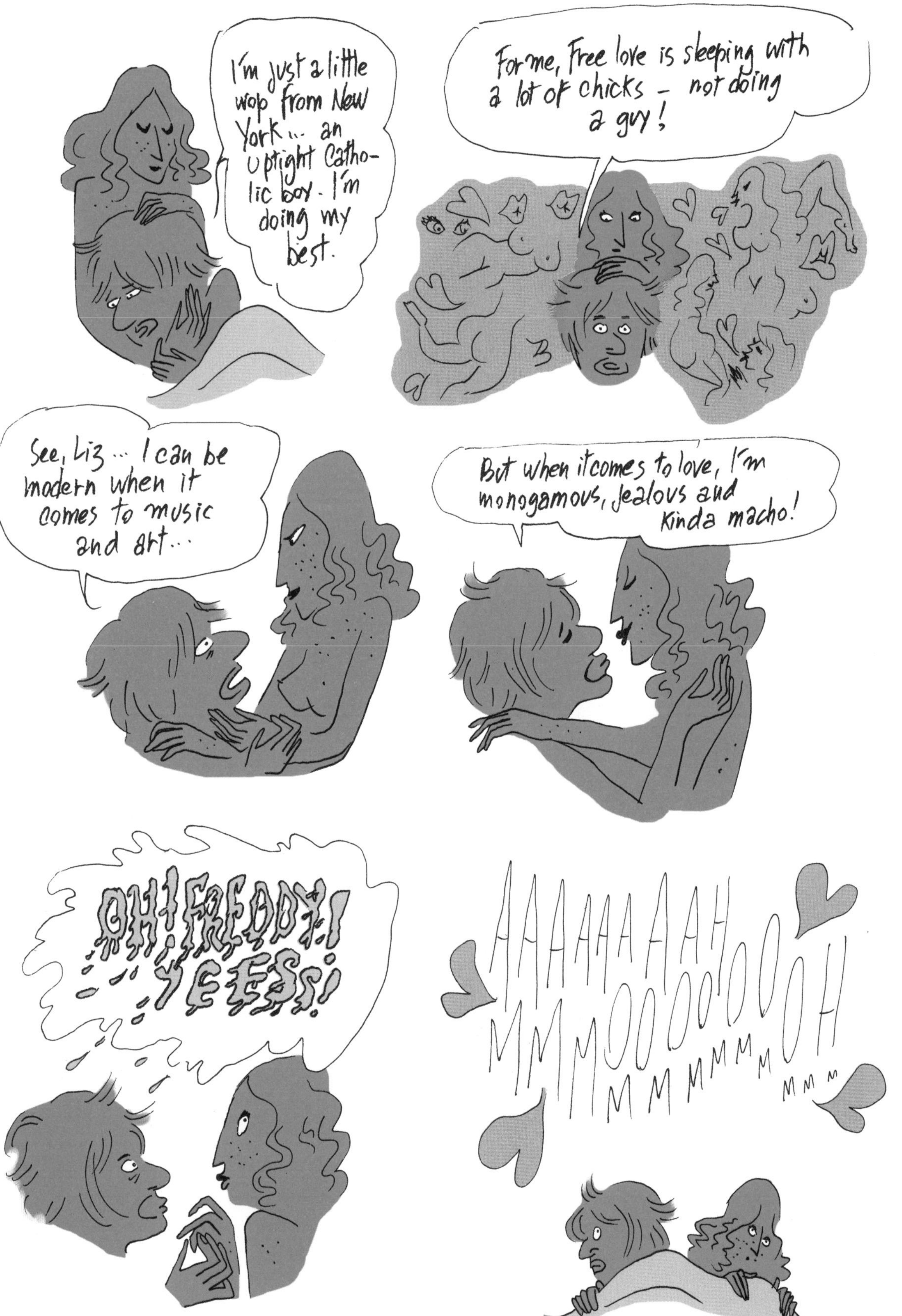
I'm just a little wop from New York... an uptight Catholic boy. I'm doing my best.
For me, Free love is sleeping with a lot of chicks – not doing a guy!
See, Liz... I can be modern when it comes to music and art...
But when it comes to love, I'm monogamous, jealous and kinda macho!
OH! FREDDY! YEESS!
AAAAAAAAH
MMOOOOOOOH
MMMMMMM
MMM

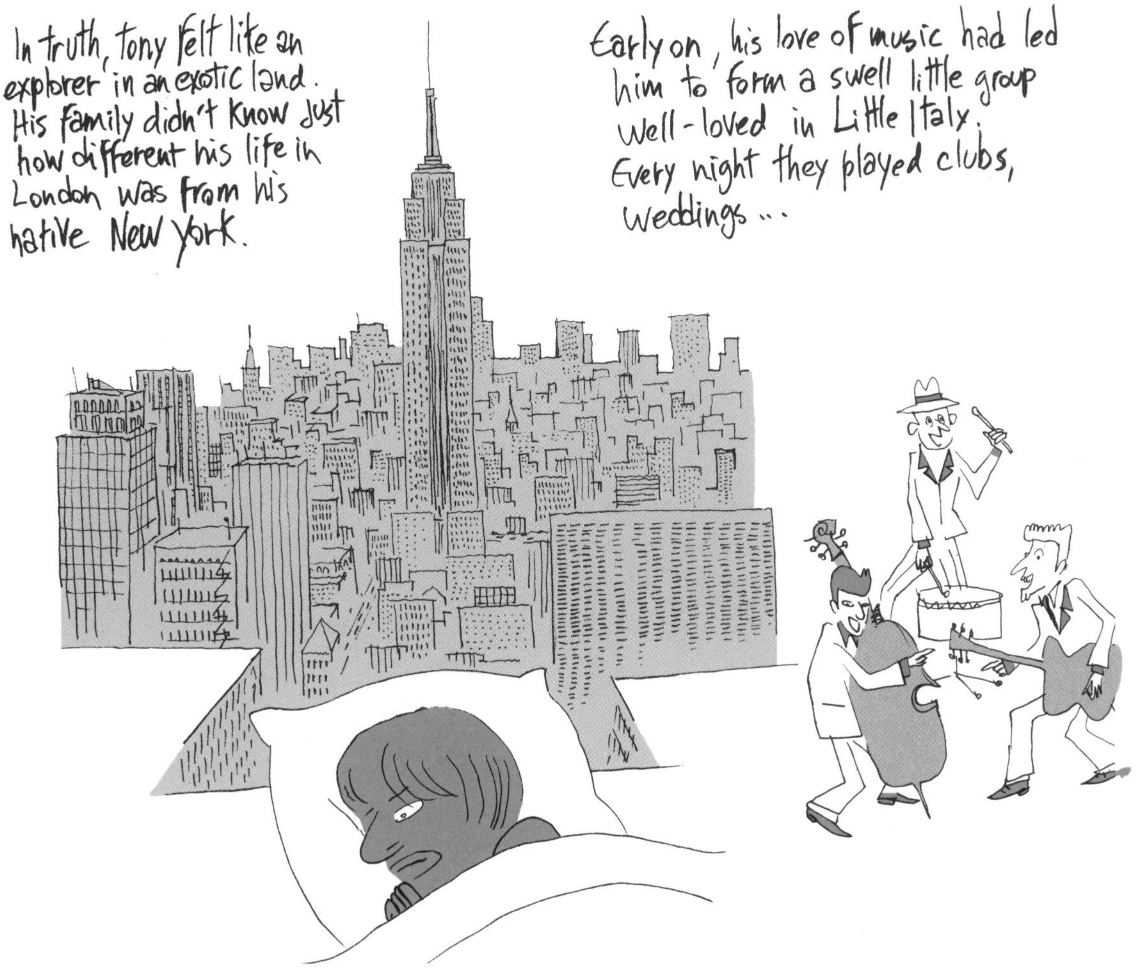
In truth, tony felt like an explorer in an exotic land. His family didn't know just how different his life in London was from his native New York.
Early on, his love of music had led him to form a swell little group well-loved in Little Italy. Every night they played clubs, weddings...

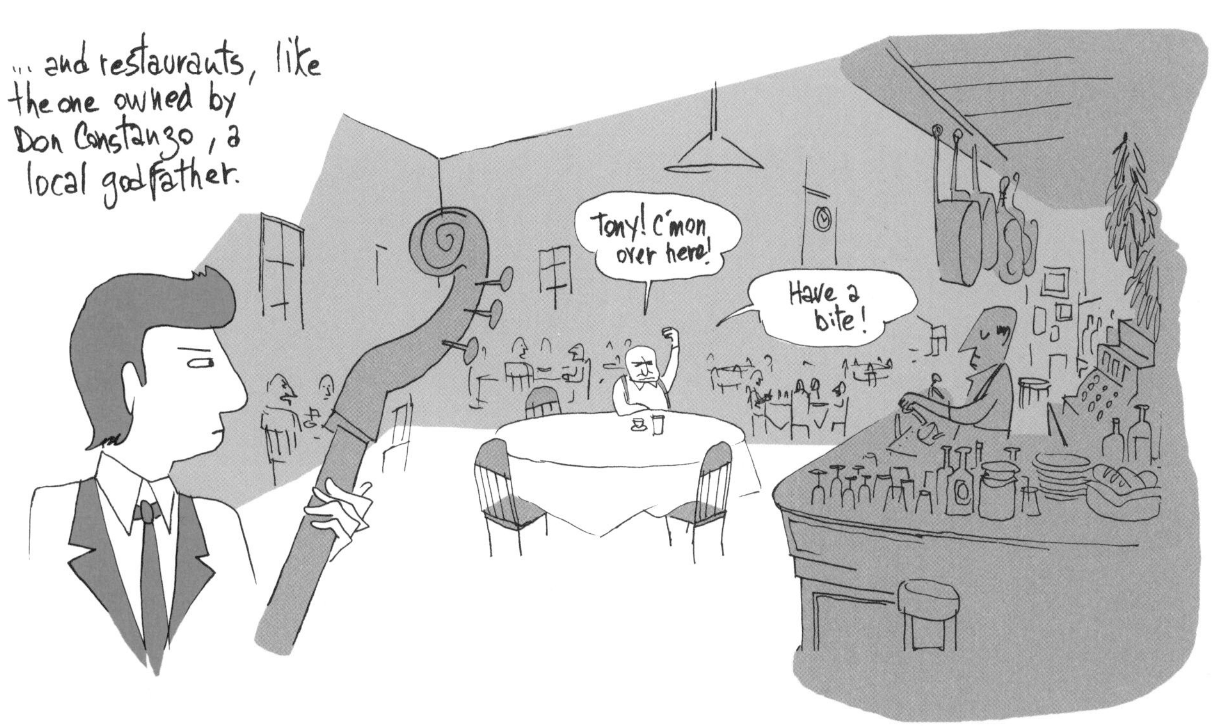
...and restaurants, like the one owned by Don Constanzo, a local godfather.
Tony! C'mon over here!
Have a bite!

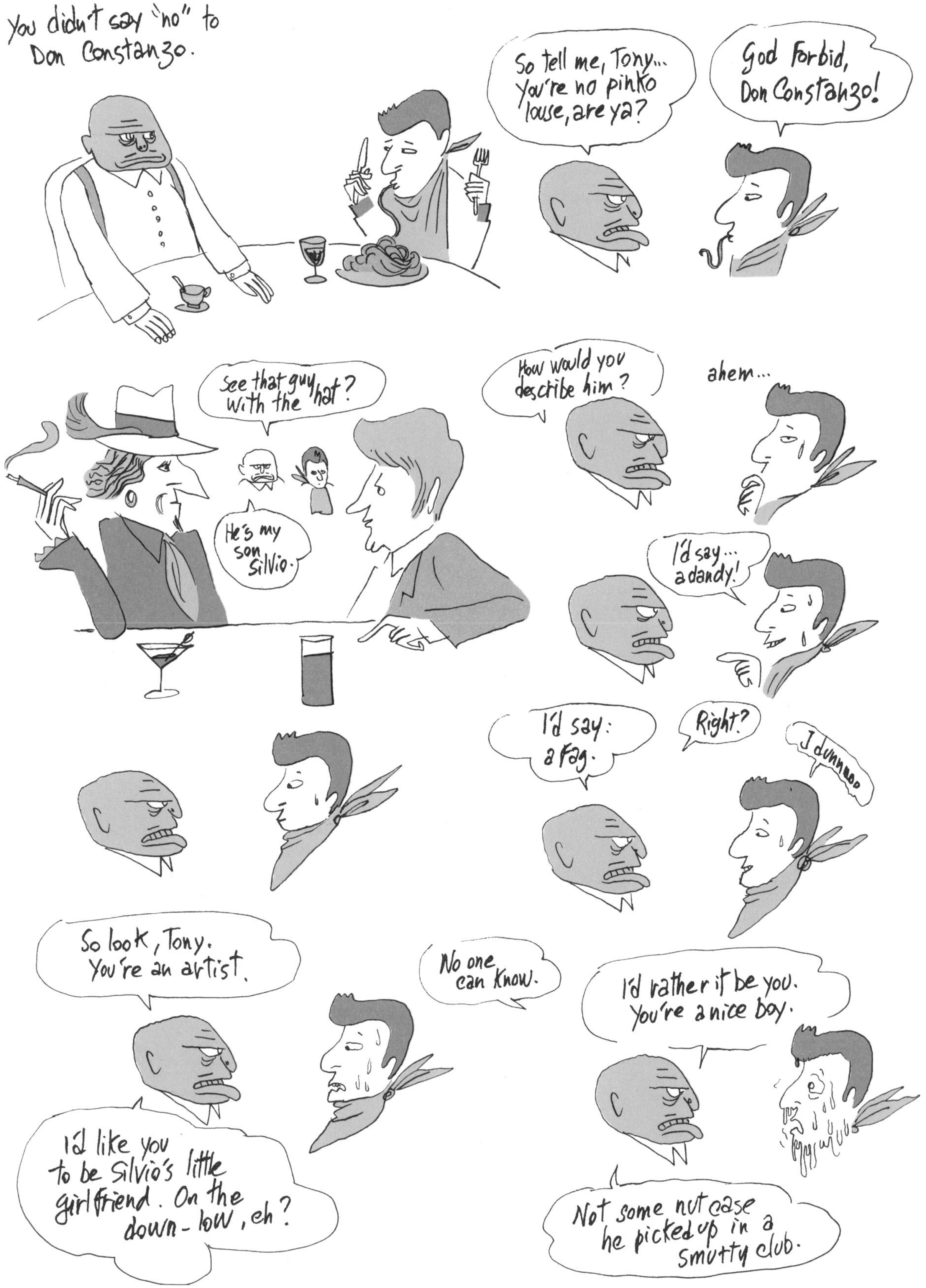
You didn't say "no" to Don Constanzo.
So tell me, Tony... You're no pinko louse, are ya?
God forbid, Don Constanzo!
See that guy with the hat?
He's my son Silvio.
How would you describe him?
ahem...
I'd say... a dandy!
I'd say: a fag.
Right?
I dunno...
So look, Tony. You're an artist.
I'd like you to be Silvio's little girlfriend. On the down-low, eh?
No one can know.
I'd rather it be you. You're a nice boy.
Not some nut case he picked up in a smutty club.

Like many musicians, Tony dreamed of going to work in London, where everything exciting in music was happening.

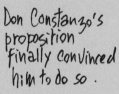

Don Constanzo's proposition finally convinced him to do so.

LONDON

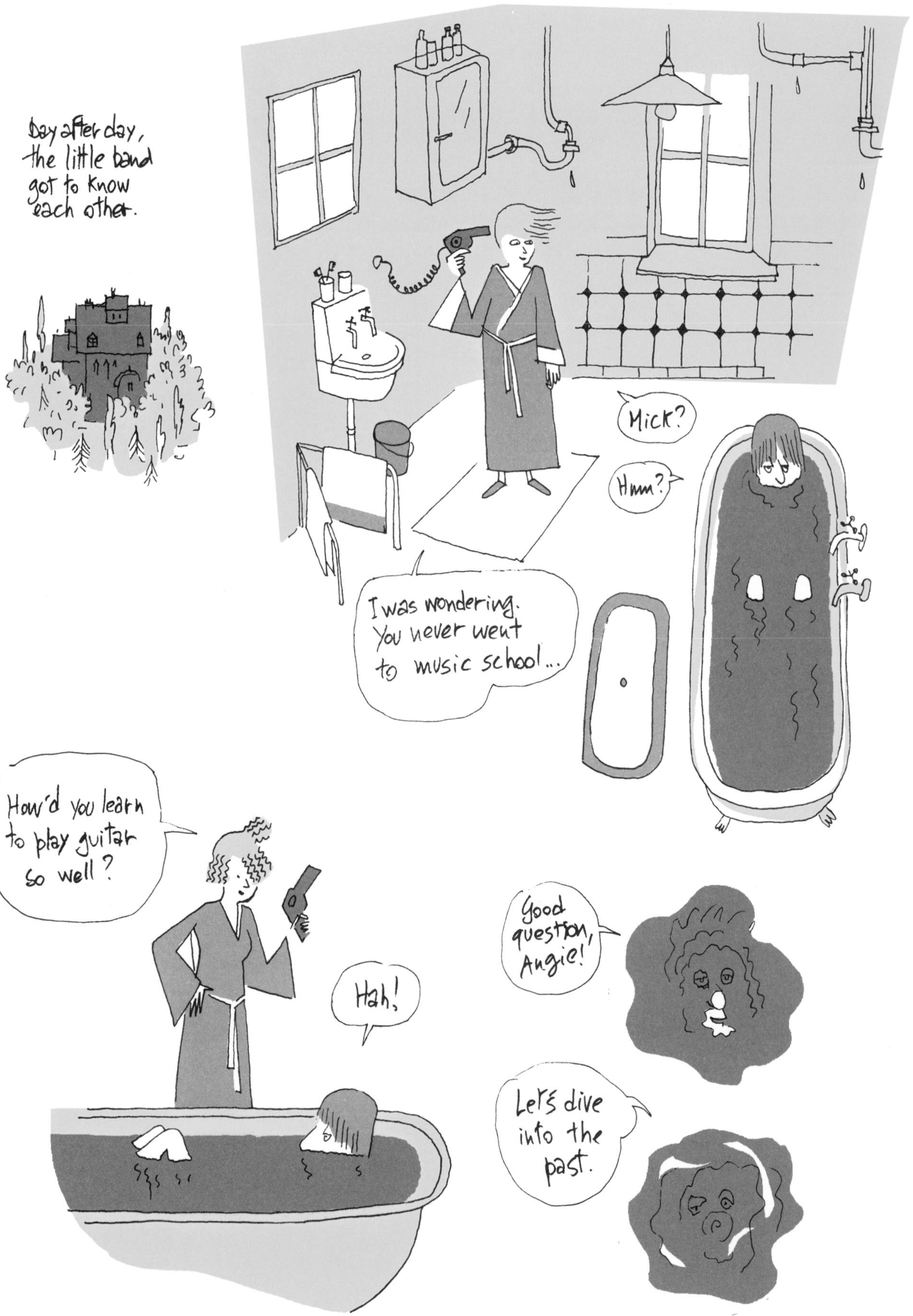
Day after day, the little band got to know each other.
Mick?
Hmm?
I was wondering. You never went to music school...
How'd you learn to play guitar so well?
Hah!
Good question, Angie!
Let's dive into the past.

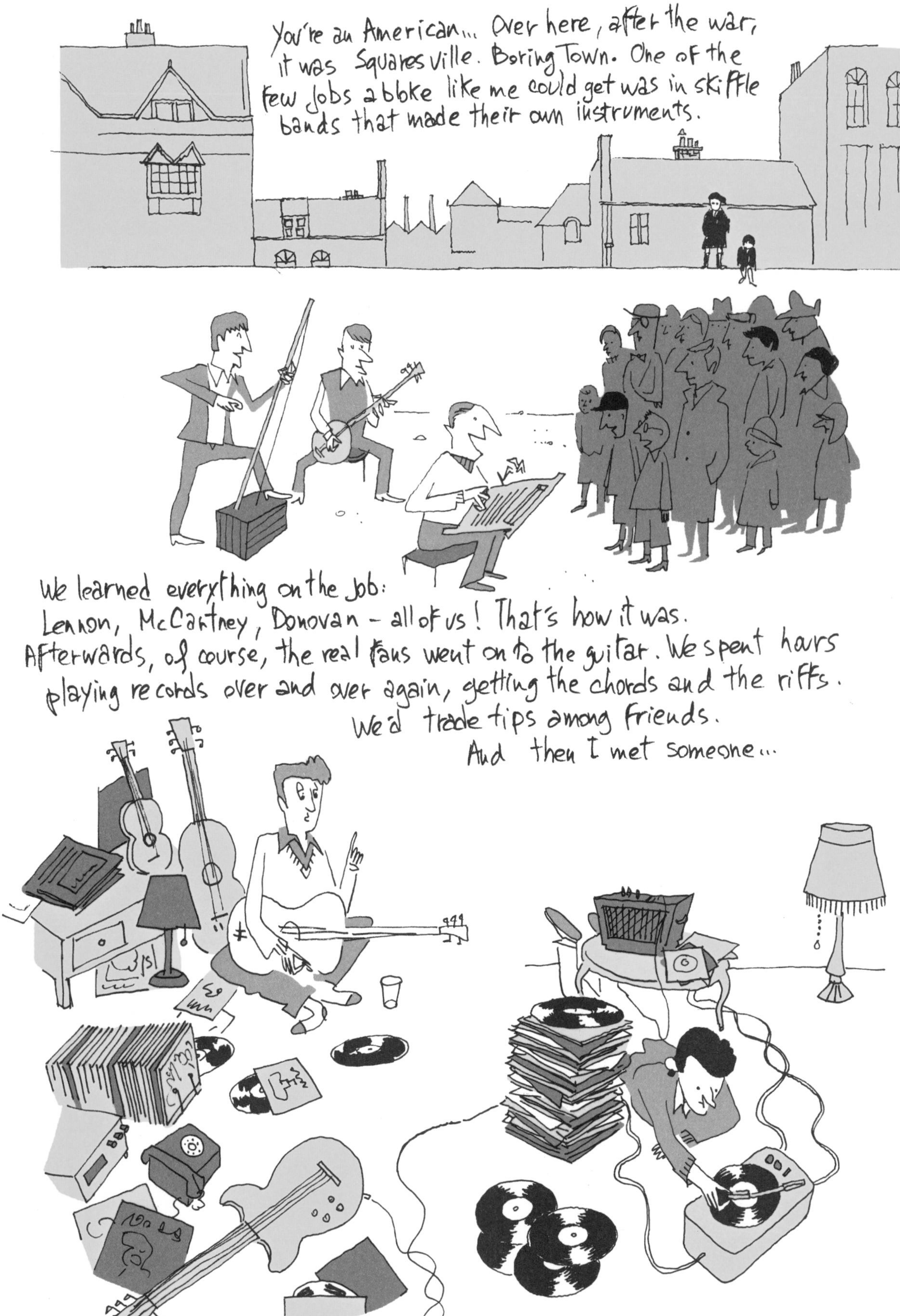

You're an American... Over here, after the war, it was Squaresville. Boring Town. One of the few jobs a bloke like me could get was in skiffle bands that made their own instruments.
We learned everything on the job: Lennon, McCartney, Donovan – all of us! That's how it was.
Afterwards, of course, the real fans went on to the guitar. We spent hours playing records over and over again, getting the chords and the riffs.
We'd trade tips among friends.
And then I met someone...

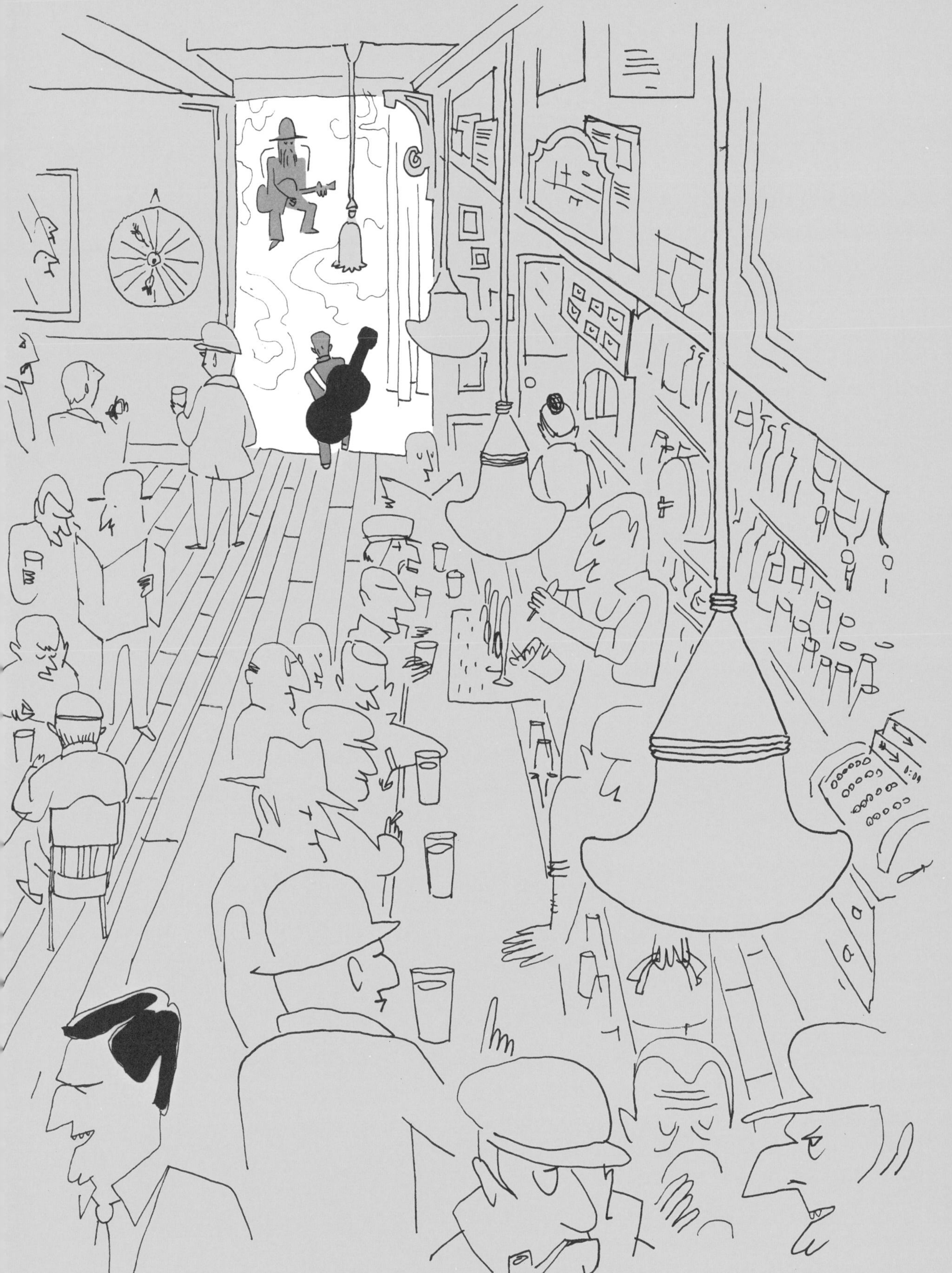

There was this odd beatnik who gave concerts on Thursday and Friday evenings. He was a wizard on the guitar. He knew everything there was to know about the instrument. I'd go watch him play religiously.

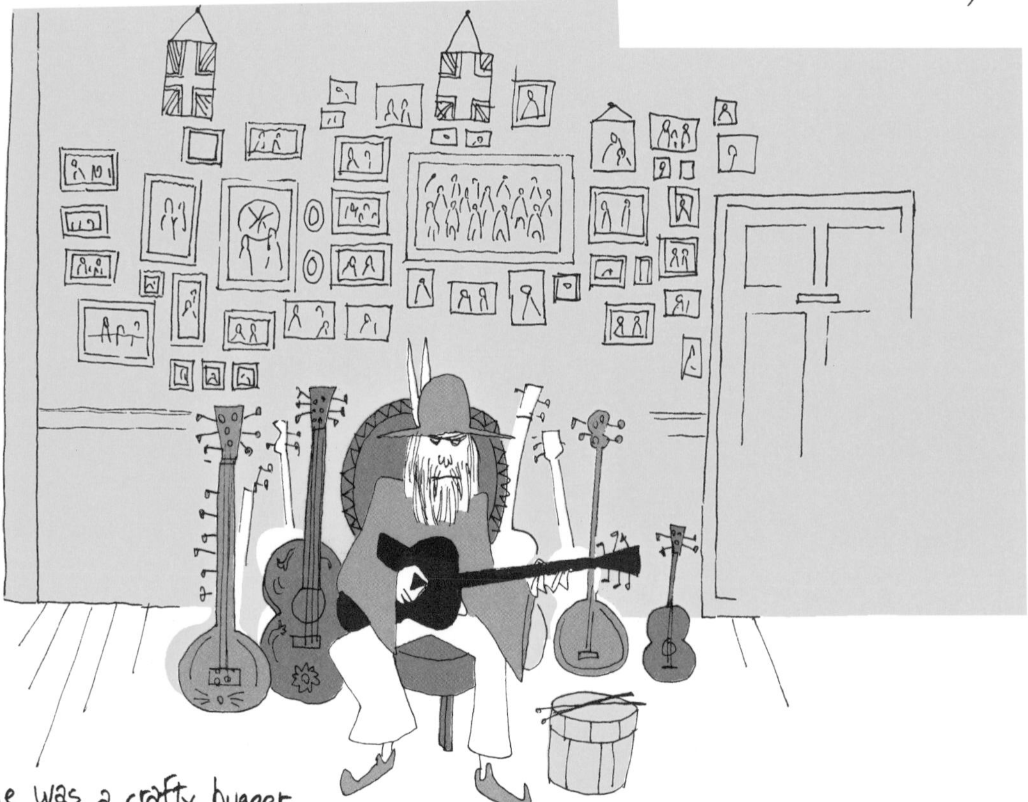

But he was a crafty bugger, and whenever he saw me, he'd twist his body around so I couldn't see his fingering. But it took more than that to discourage me. So we played cat and mouse like that for months.

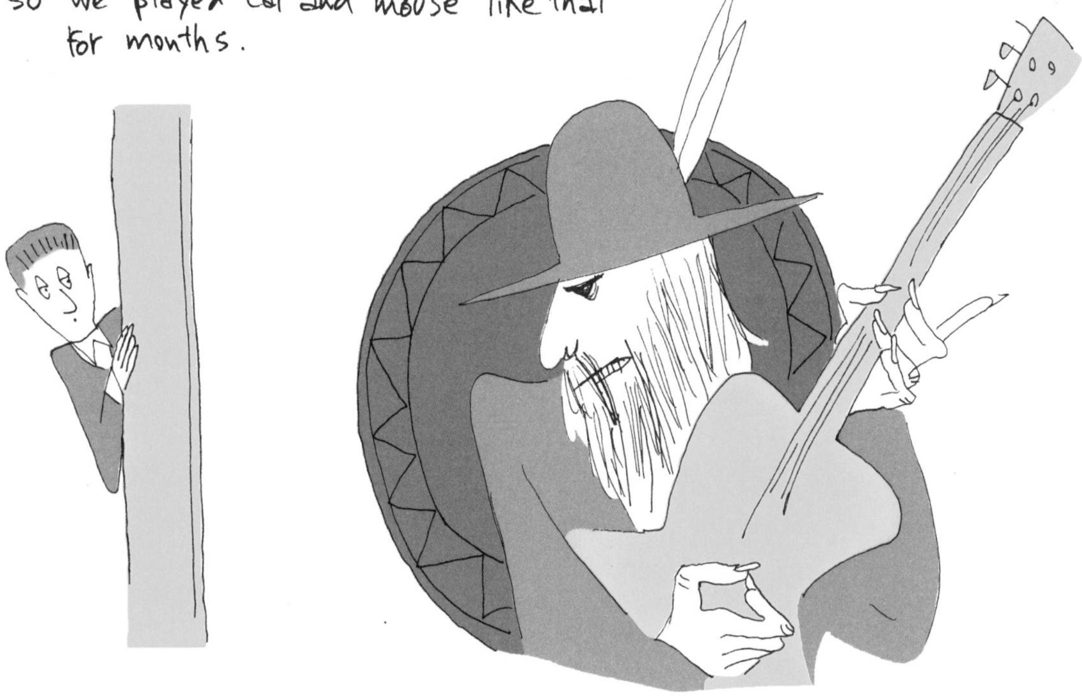

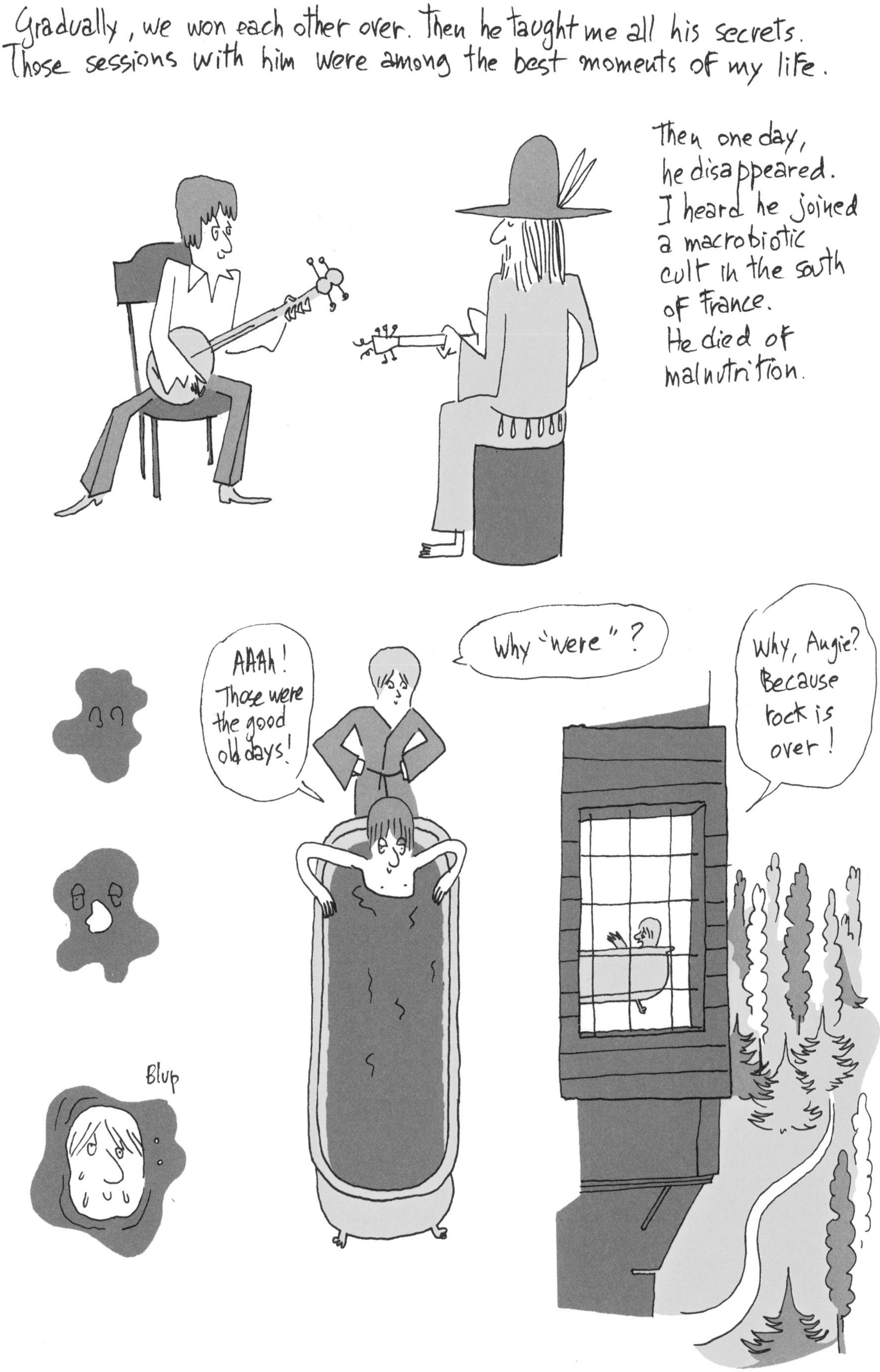
Gradually, we won each other over. Then he taught me all his secrets.
Those sessions with him were among the best moments of my life.
Then one day, he disappeared. I heard he joined a macrobiotic cult in the south of France. He died of malnutrition.
AAAh! Those were the good old days!
Why "were"?
Why, Angie? Because rock is over!
Blup

Why is England the land of Pop?

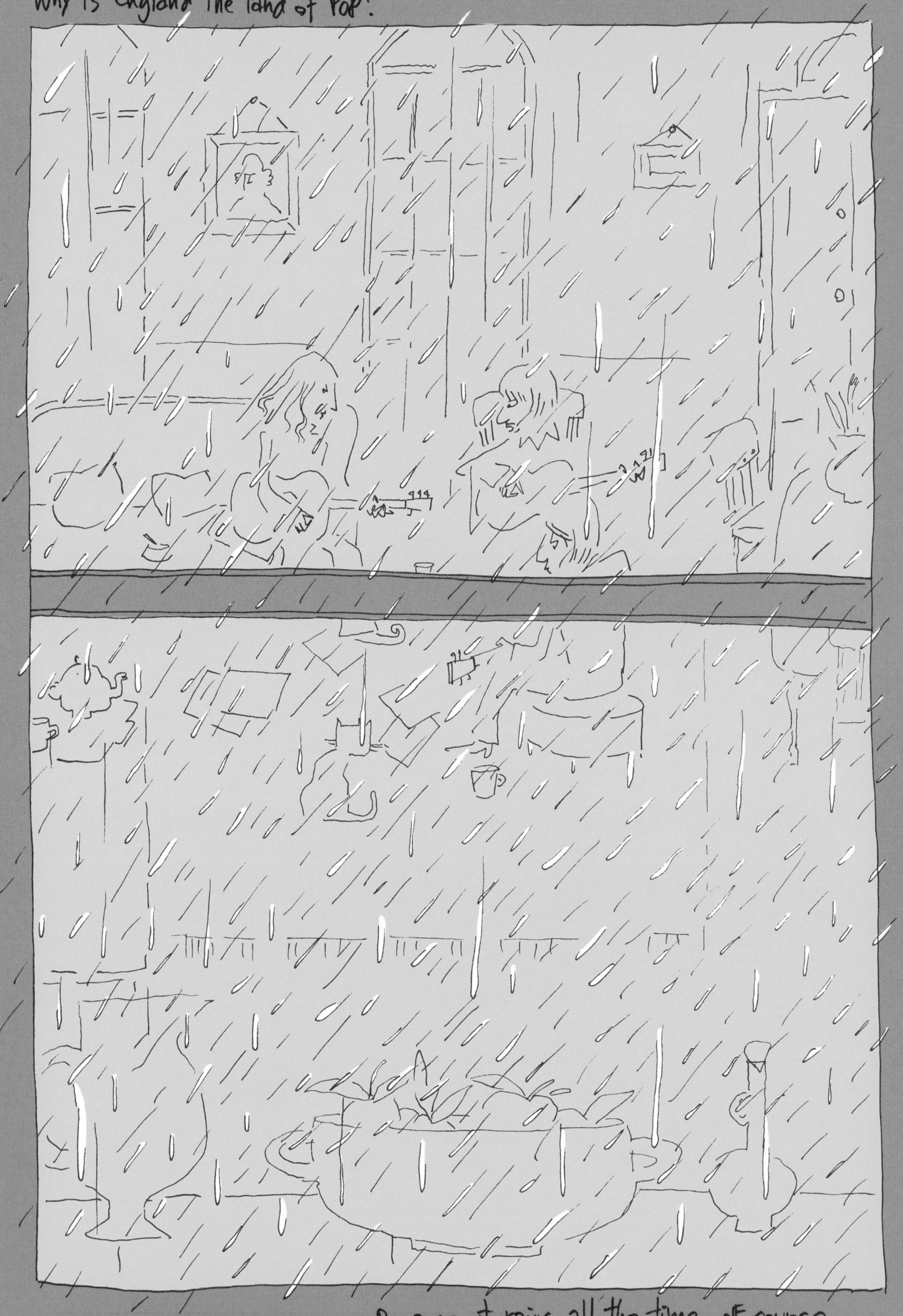

Because it rains all the time, of course.

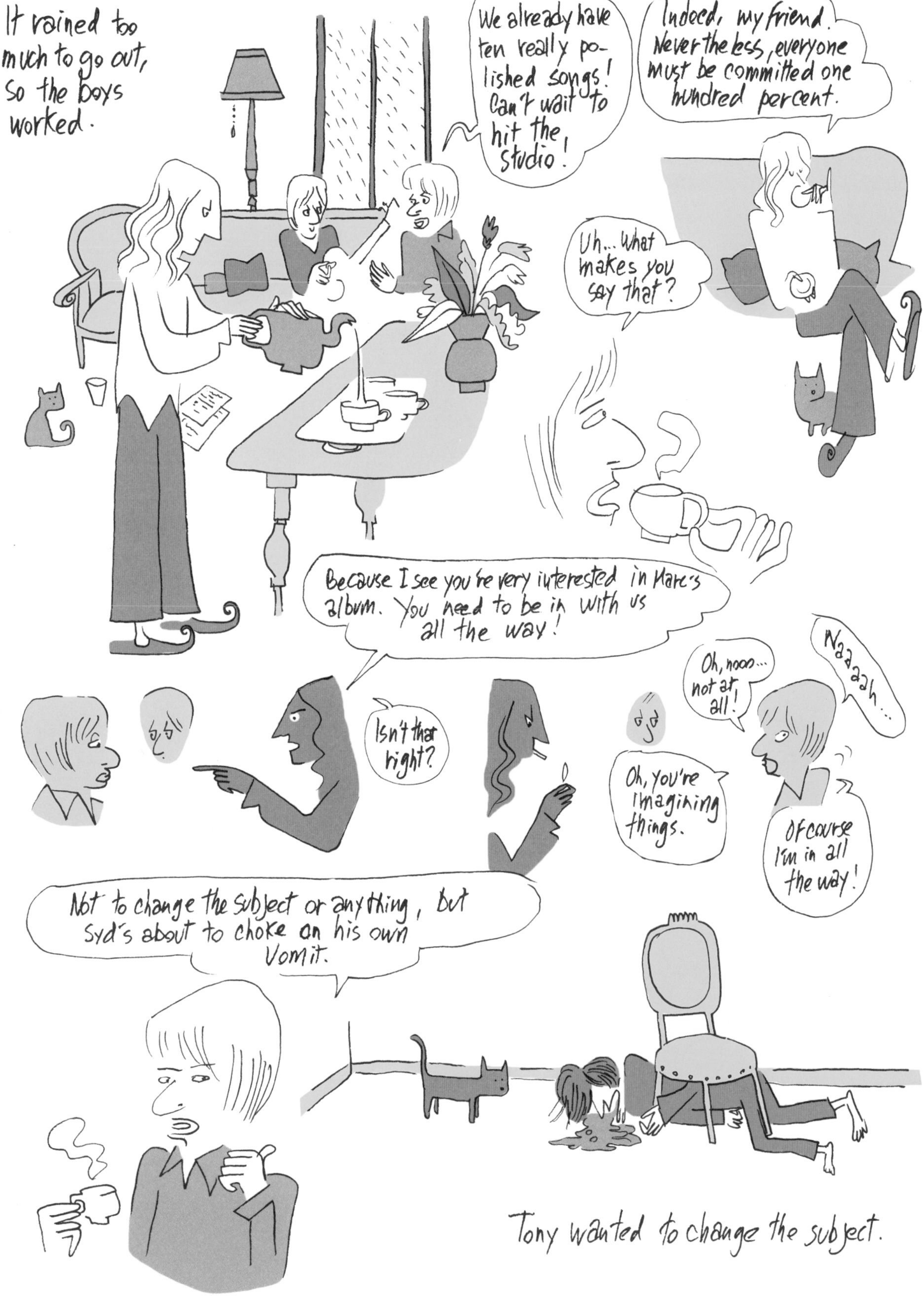
It rained too much to go out, so the boys worked.
We already have ten really polished songs! Can't wait to hit the studio!
Indeed, my friend. Nevertheless, everyone must be committed one hundred percent.
Uh... what makes you say that?
Because I see you're very interested in Marc's album. You need to be in with us all the way!
Isn't that right?
Oh, nooo... not at all!
Naaaaah...
Oh, you're imagining things.
Of course I'm in all the way!
Not to change the subject or anything, but Syd's about to choke on his own vomit.
Tony wanted to change the subject.

INTERMEZZO

Fashionista – a full-time job

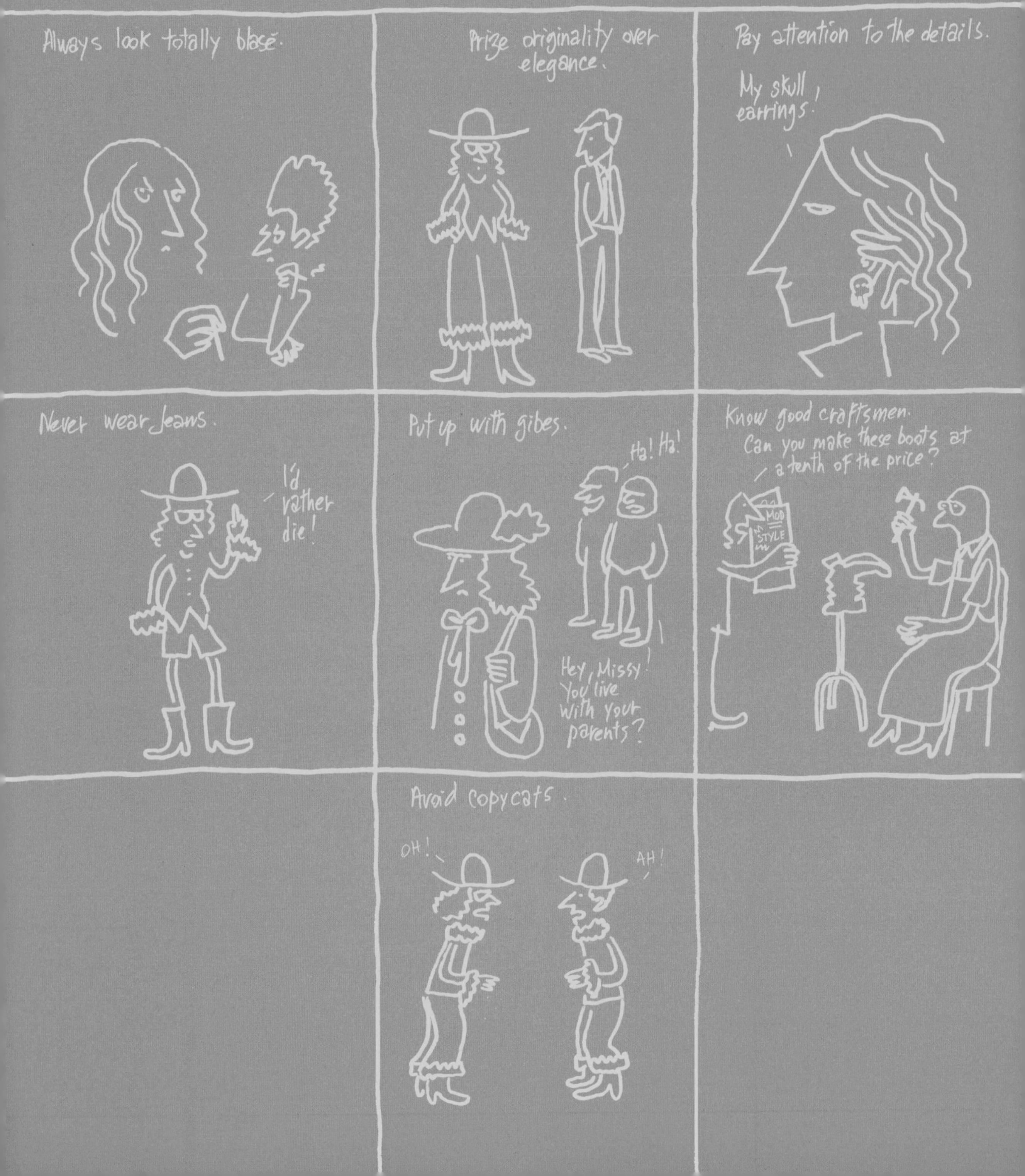
Always look totally blasé.
Prize originality over elegance.
Pay attention to the details.
My skull earrings!
Never wear jeans.
I'd rather die!
Put up with gibes.
Ha! Ha!
Hey, Missy! You live with your parents?
Know good craftsmen.
Can you make these boots at a tenth of the price?
MOD STYLE
Avoid copycats.
OH!
AH!

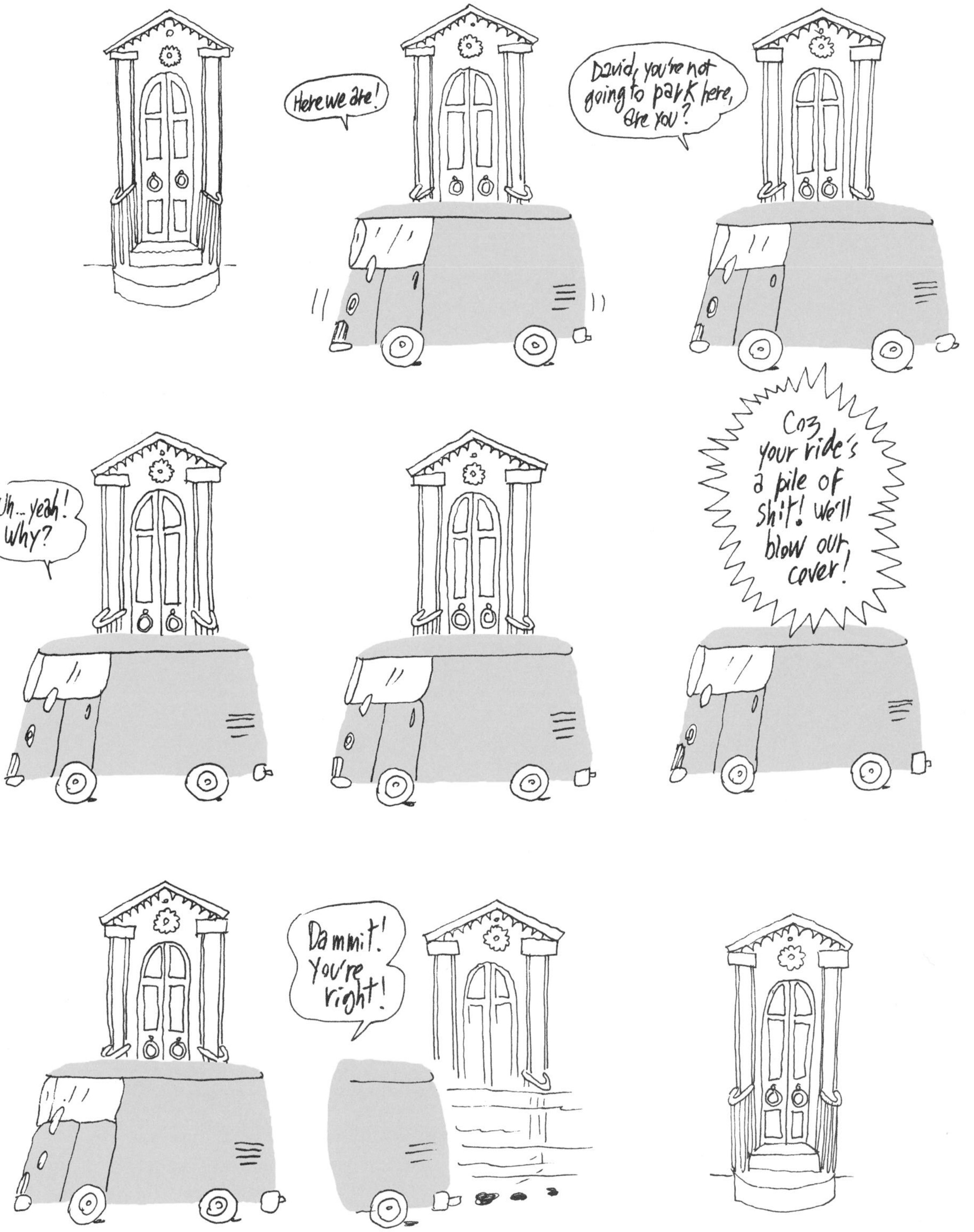
Here we are!
David, you're not going to park here, are you?
Uh... yeah! Why?
Coz your ride's a pile of shit! We'll blow our cover!
Dammit! You're right!

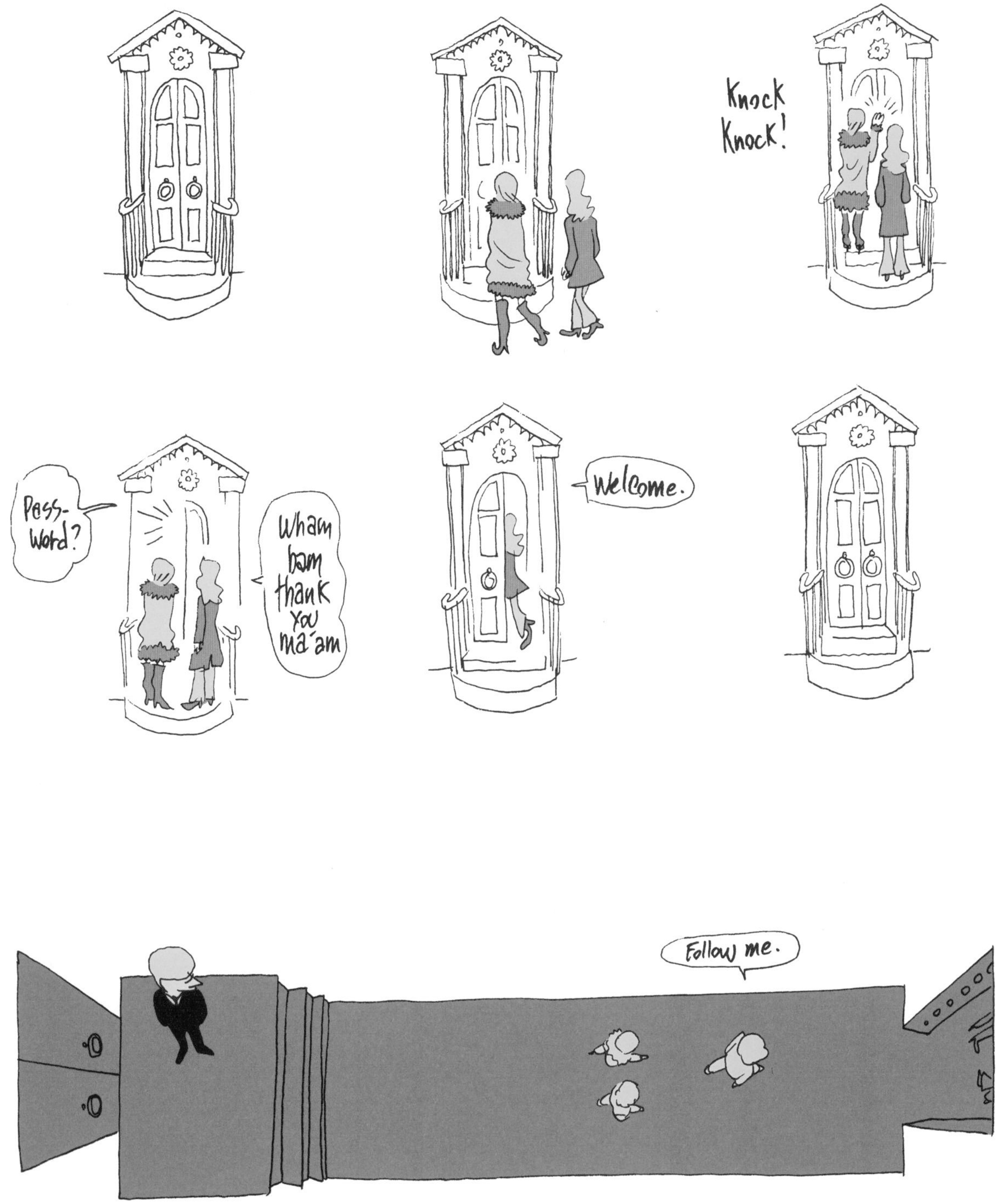
Knock Knock!
Pass-word?
Wham bam thank you ma'am
Welcome.
Follow me.

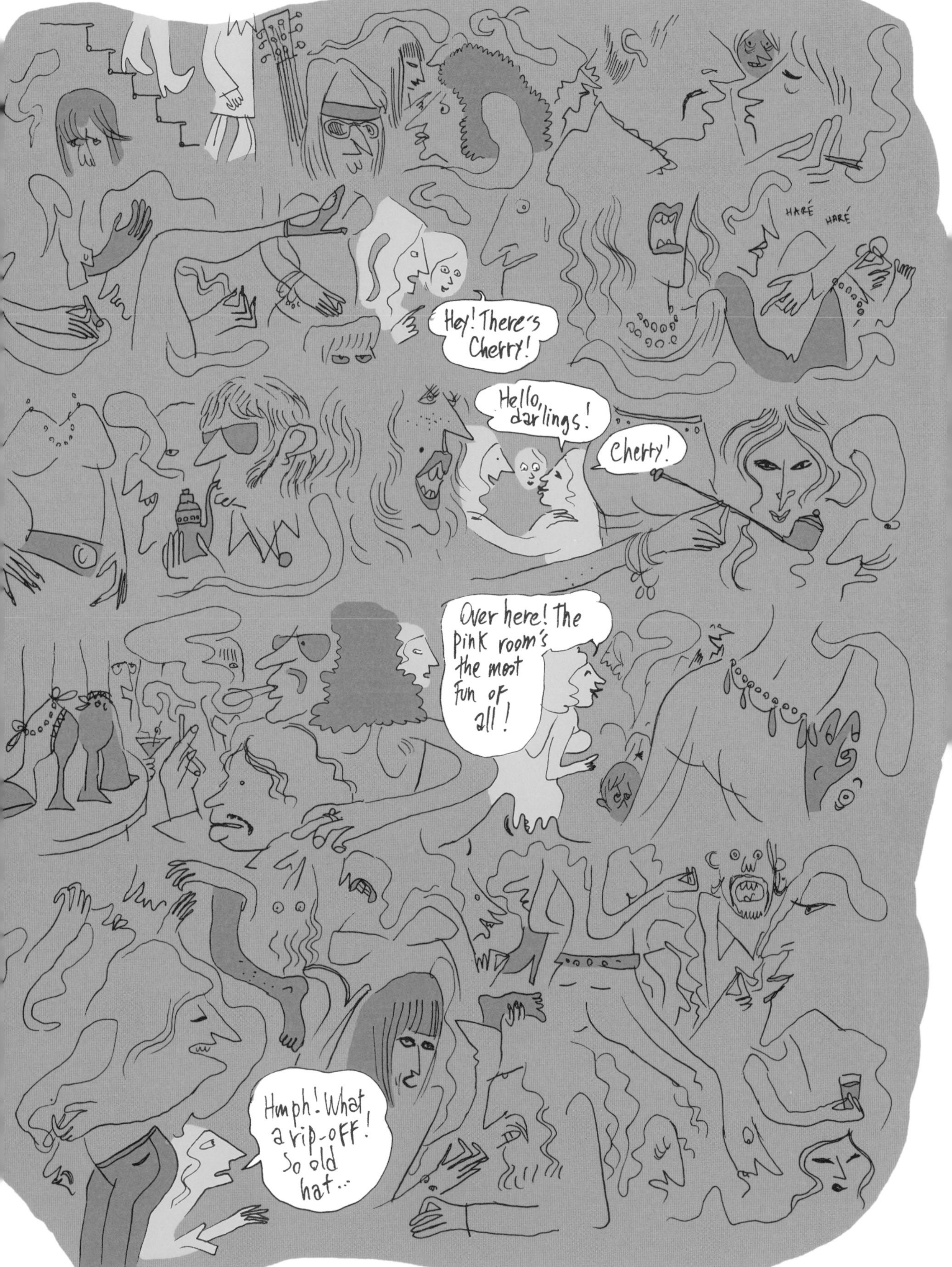
HARÉ HARÉ
Hey! There's Cherry!
Hello, darlings!
Cherry!
Over here! The pink room's the most fun of all!
Hmph! What a rip-off! So old hat...

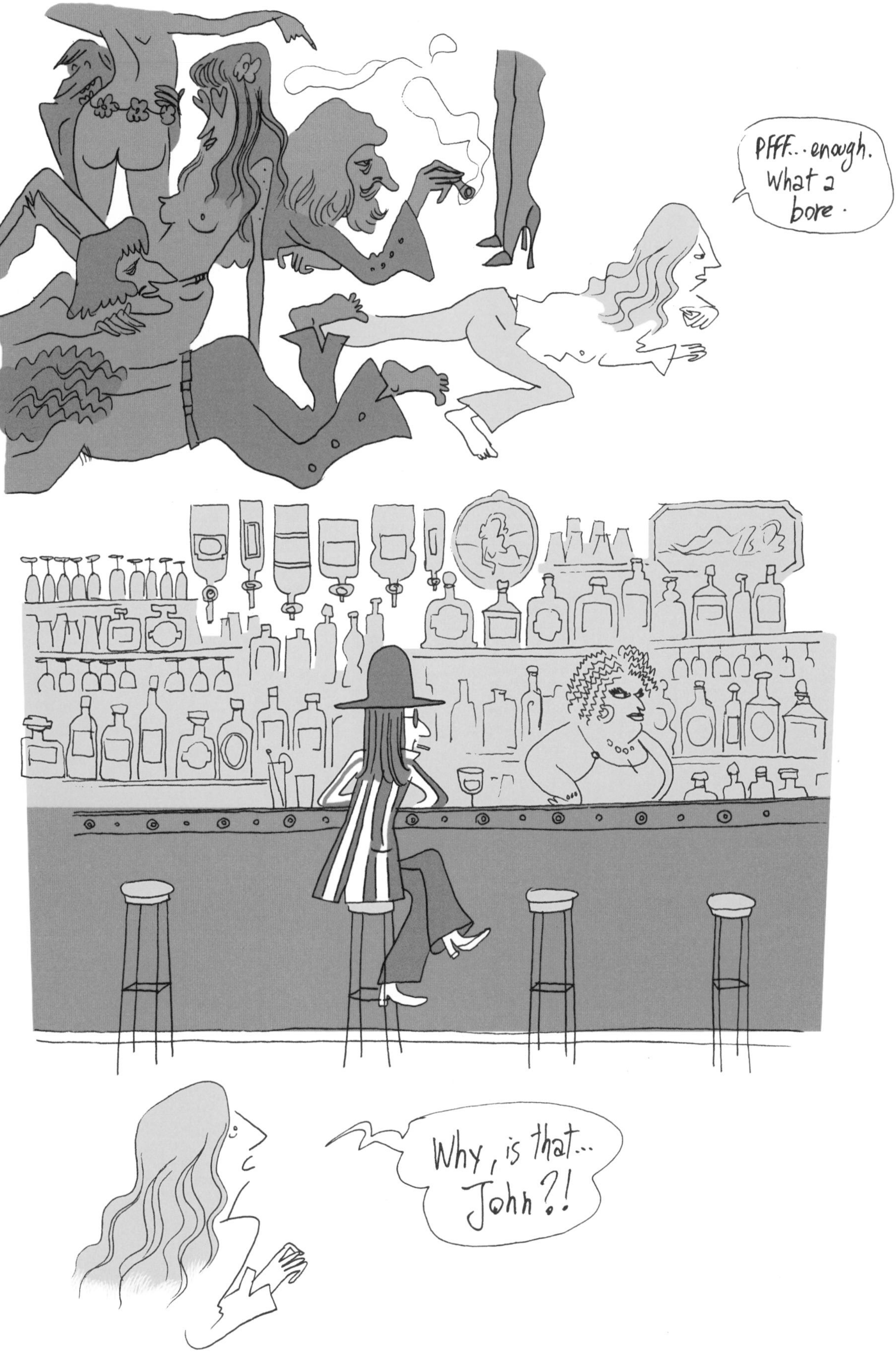
PFFF... enough. What a bore.
Why, is that... John?!

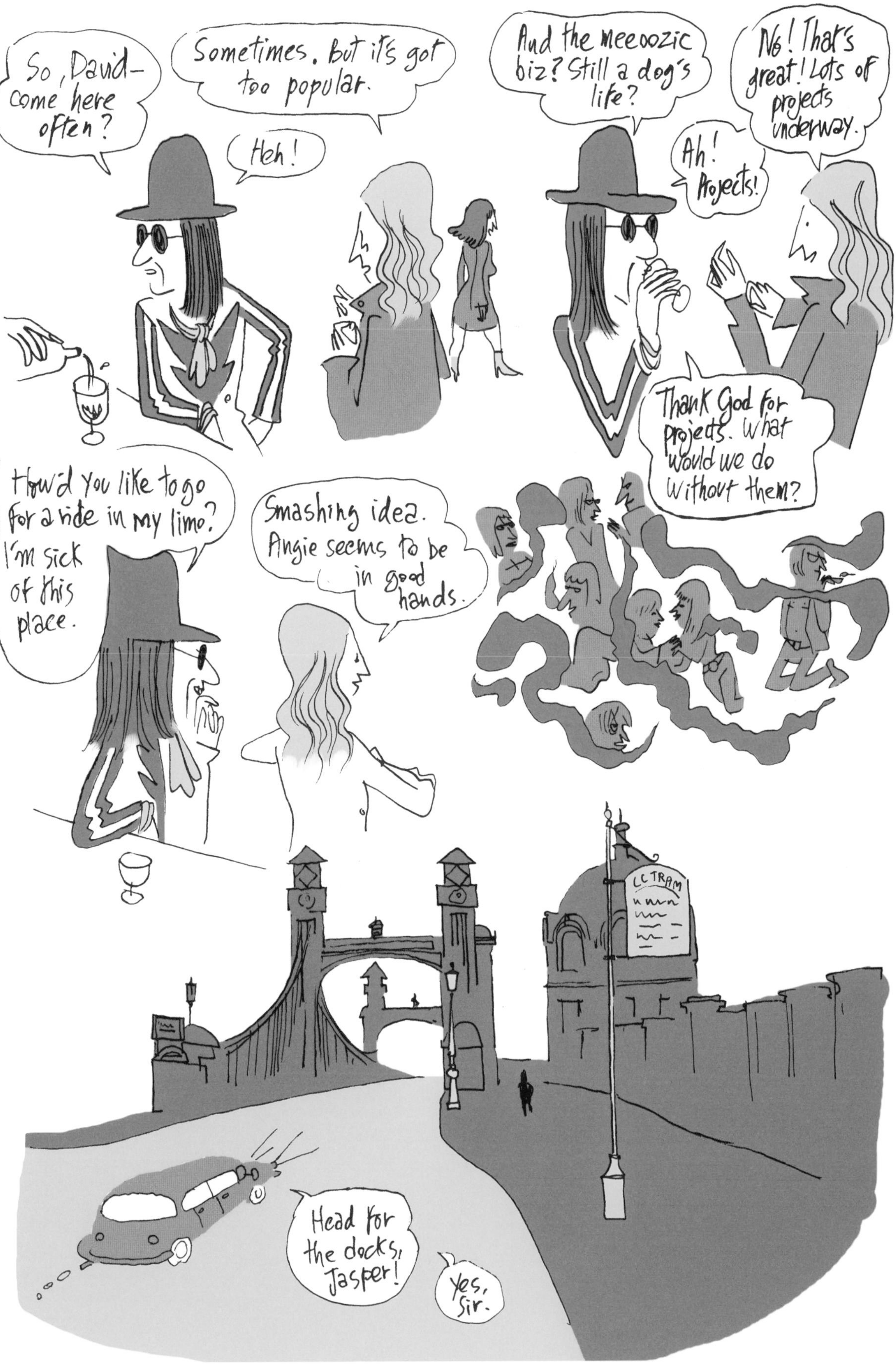
So, David- come here often?
Sometimes. But it's got too popular.
Heh!
And the meeoozic biz? Still a dog's life?
No! That's great! Lots of projects underway.
Ah! Projects!
Thank God for projects. What would we do without them?
How'd you like to go for a ride in my limo? I'm sick of this place.
Smashing idea. Angie seems to be in good hands.
LC TRAM
Head for the docks, Jasper!
Yes, sir.

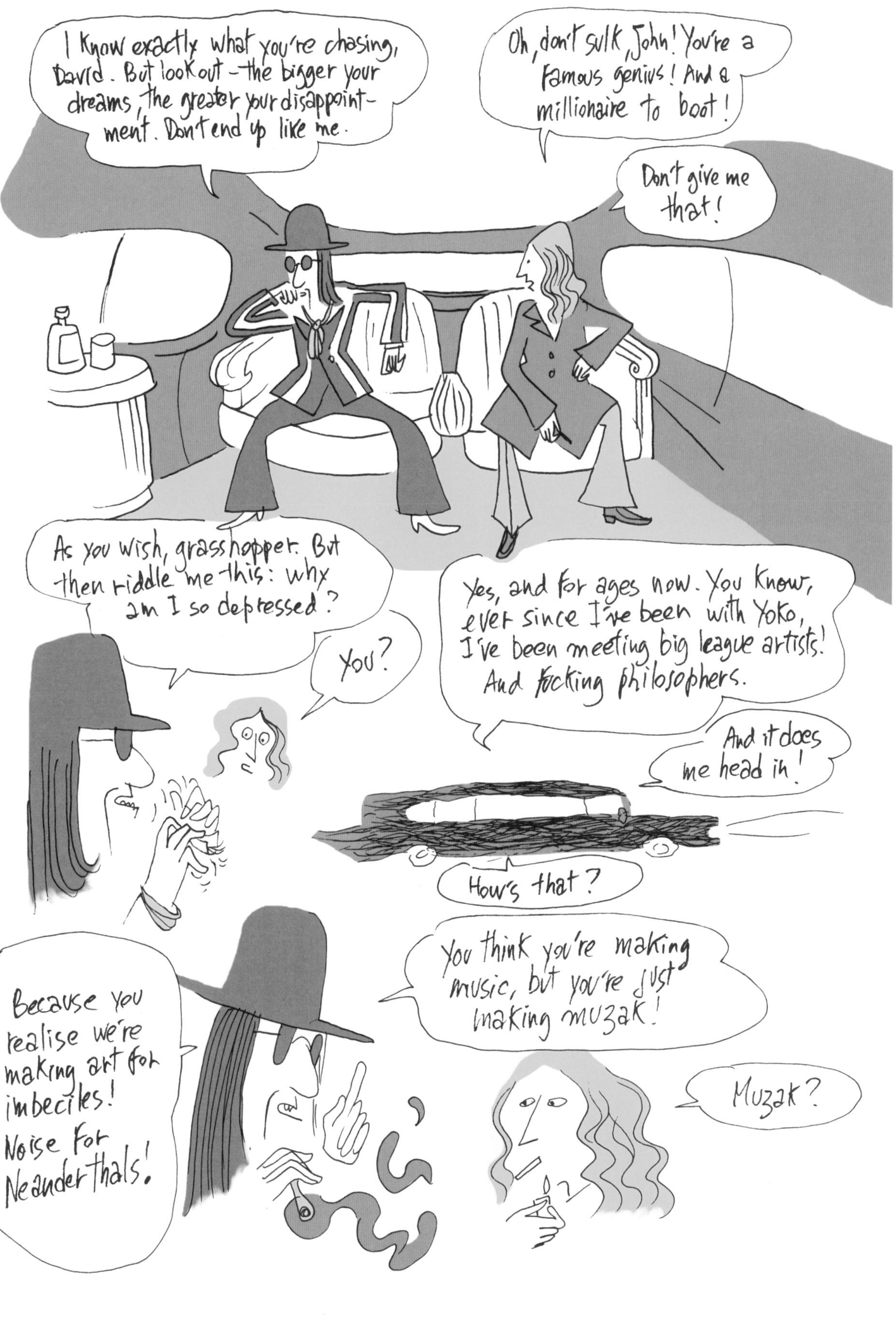
I Know exactly what you're chasing, David. But look out - the bigger your dreams, the greater your disappointment. Don't end up like me.
Oh, don't sulk, John! You're a famous genius! And a millionaire to boot!
Don't give me that!
As you wish, grasshopper. But then riddle me this: why am I so depressed?
You?
Yes, and for ages now. You know, ever since I've been with Yoko, I've been meeting big league artists! And fucking philosophers.
And it does me head in!
How's that?
Because you realise we're making art for imbeciles! Noise for Neanderthals!
You think you're making music, but you're just making muzak!
Muzak?

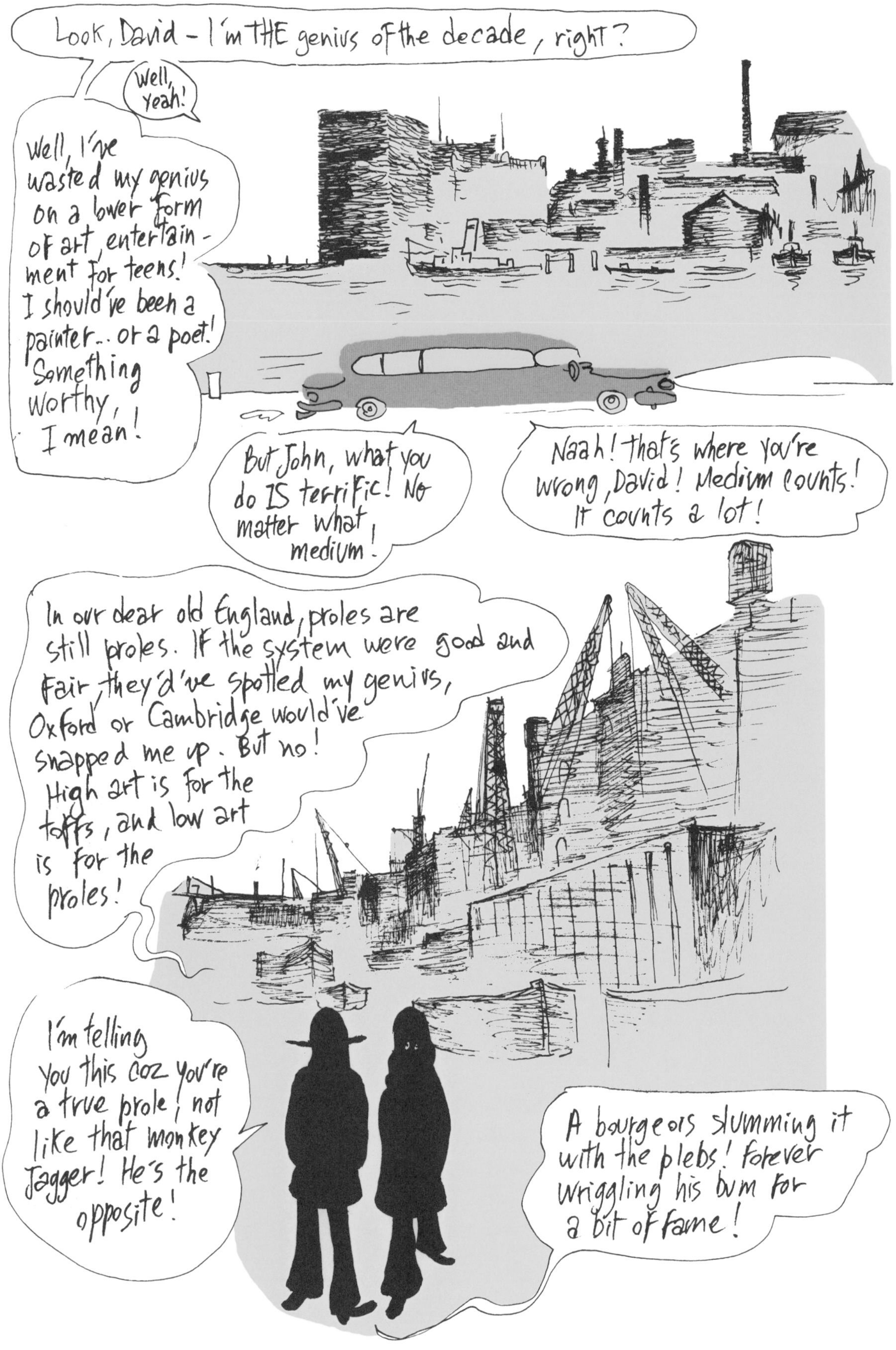
Look, David - I'm THE genius of the decade, right?
Well, Yeah!
Well, I've wasted my genius on a lower form of art, entertainment for teens! I should've been a painter.. or a poet! Something worthy, I mean!
But John, what you do IS terrific! No matter what medium!
Naah! that's where you're wrong, David! Medium counts! It counts a lot!
In our dear old England, proles are still proles. If the system were good and fair, they'd've spotted my genius, Oxford or Cambridge would've snapped me up. But no! High art is for the toffs, and low art is for the proles!
I'm telling you this coz you're a true prole, not like that monkey Jagger! He's the opposite!
A bourgeois slumming it with the plebs! Forever wriggling his bum for a bit of fame!

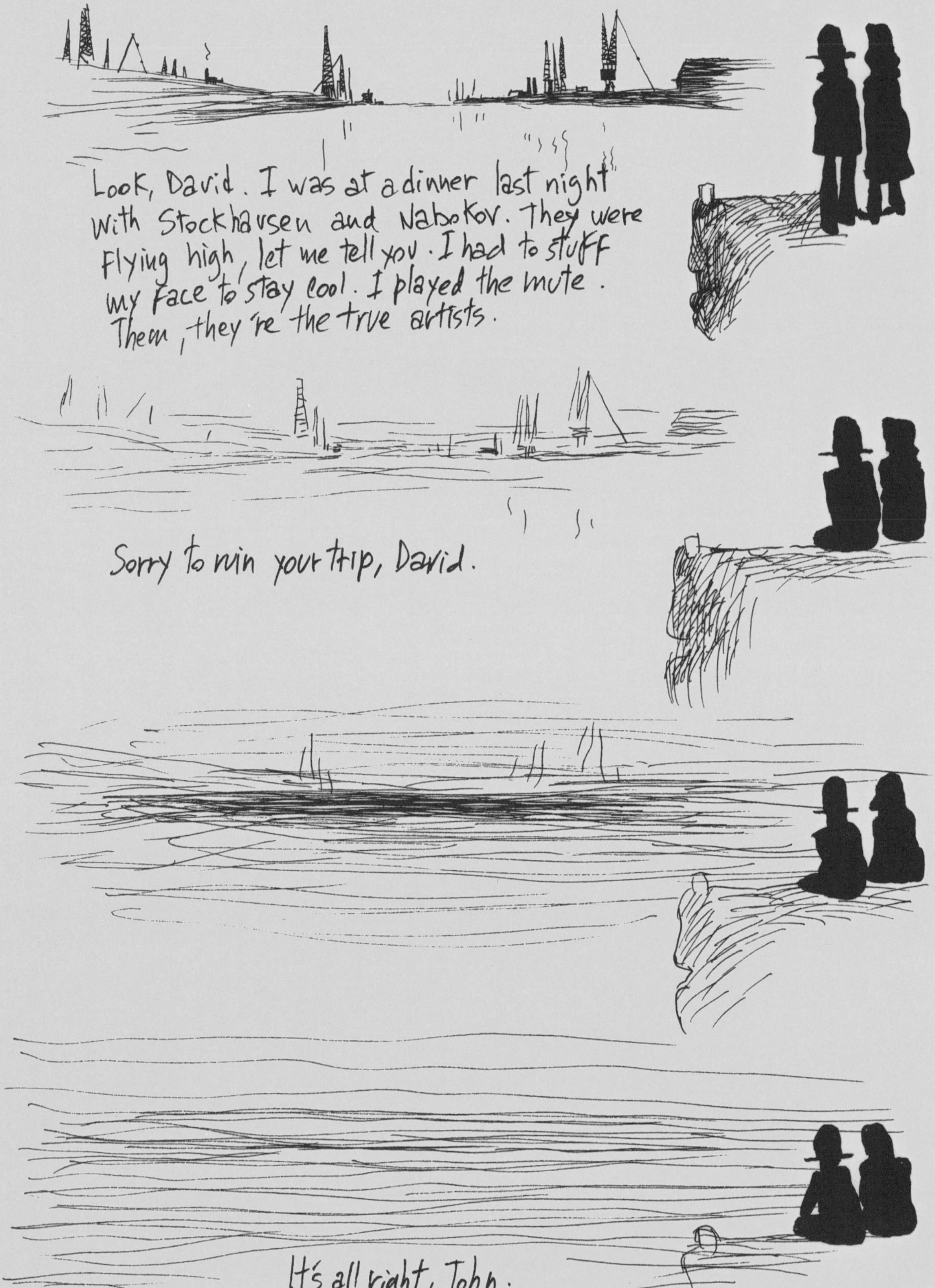
Look, David. I was at a dinner last night with Stockhausen and Nabokov. They were flying high, let me tell you. I had to stuff my face to stay cool. I played the mute. Them, they're the true artists.
Sorry to ruin your trip, David.
It's all right, John.

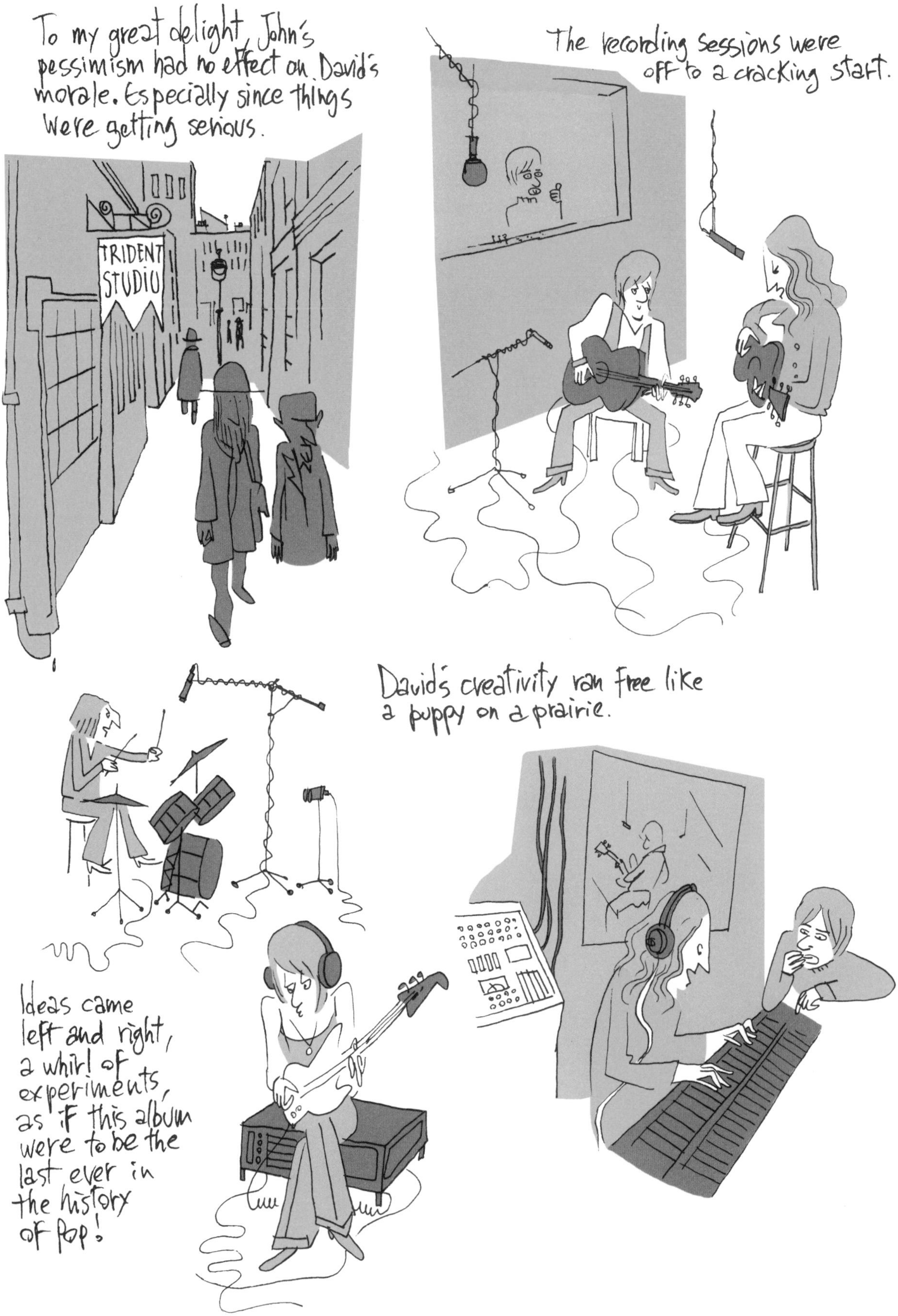
To my great delight, John's pessimism had no effect on David's morale. Especially since things were getting serious.
TRIDENT STUDIO
The recording sessions were off to a cracking start.
David's creativity ran free like a puppy on a prairie.
Ideas came left and right, a whirl of experiments, as if this album were to be the last ever in the history of pop!

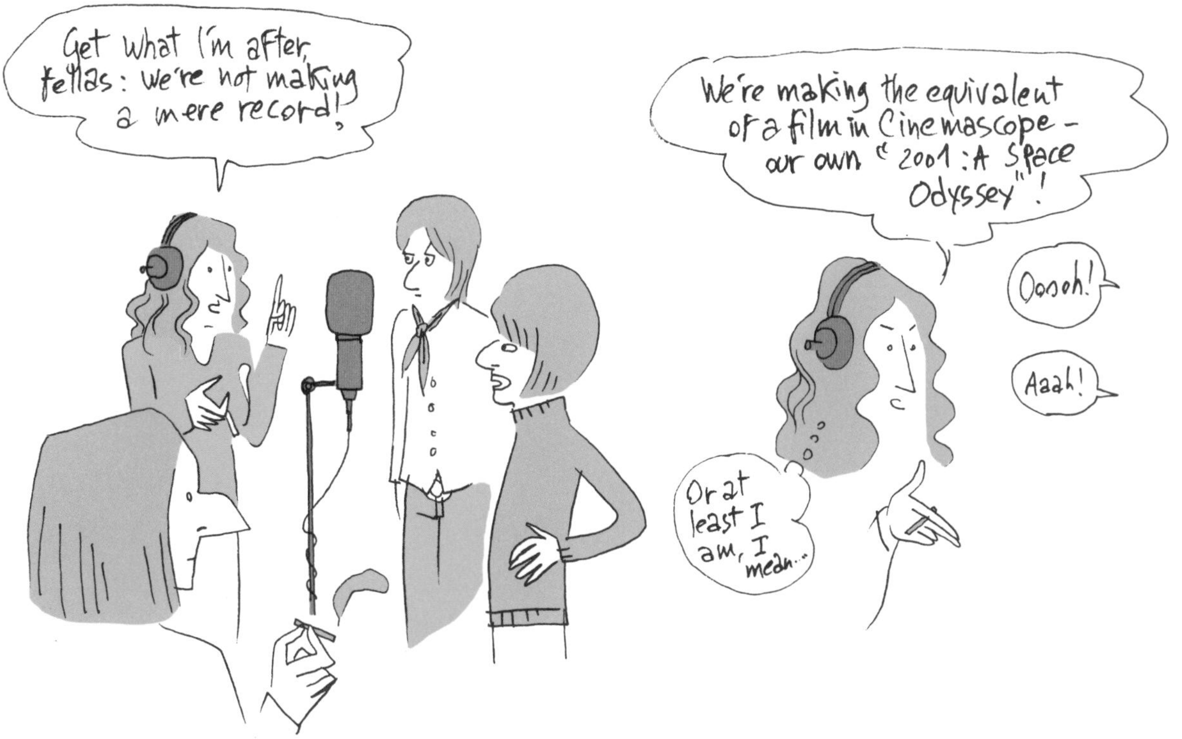
Get what I'm after, fellas: we're not making a mere record!
We're making the equivalent of a film in Cinemascope - our own "2001: A Space Odyssey"!
Ooooh!
Aaah!
Or at least I am, I mean...

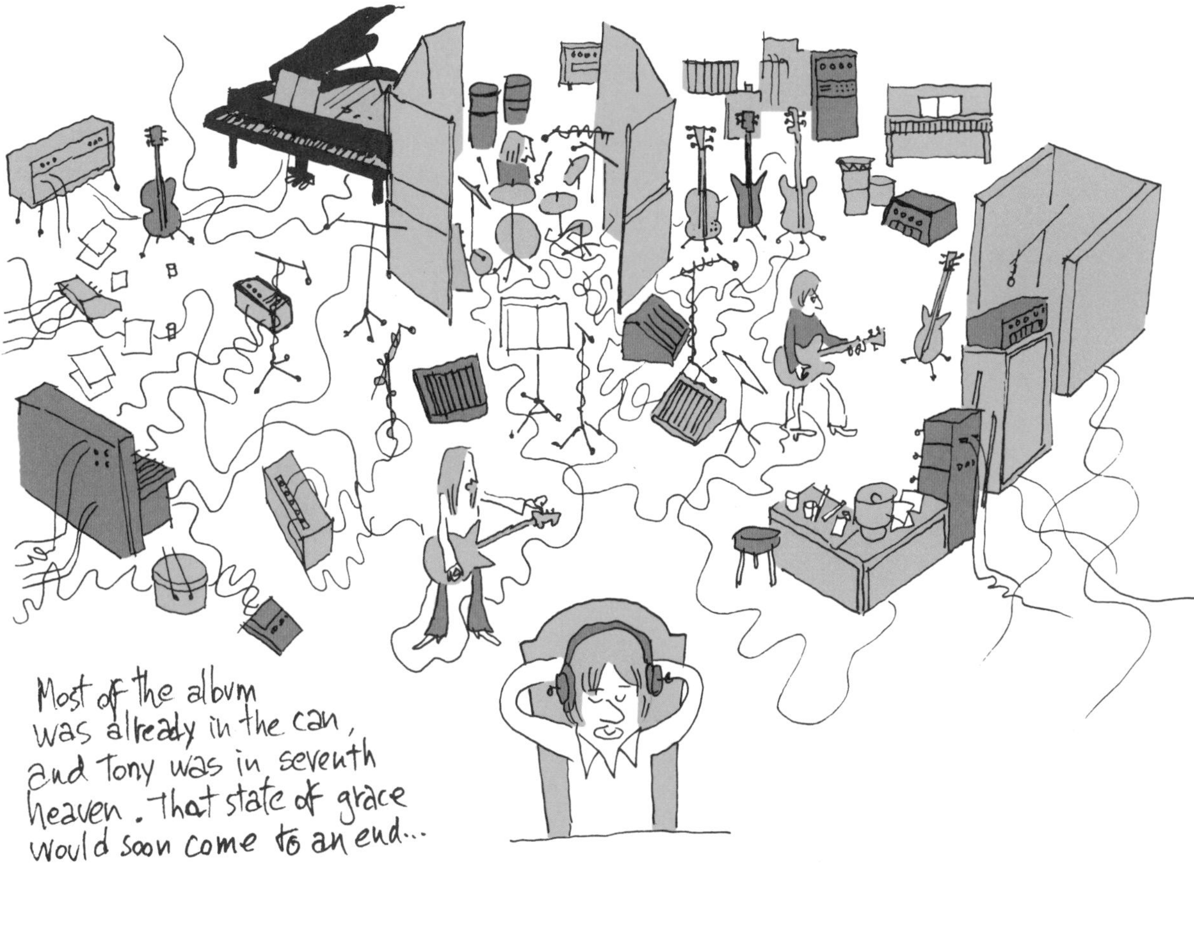
Most of the album was already in the can, and Tony was in seventh heaven. That state of grace would soon come to an end...

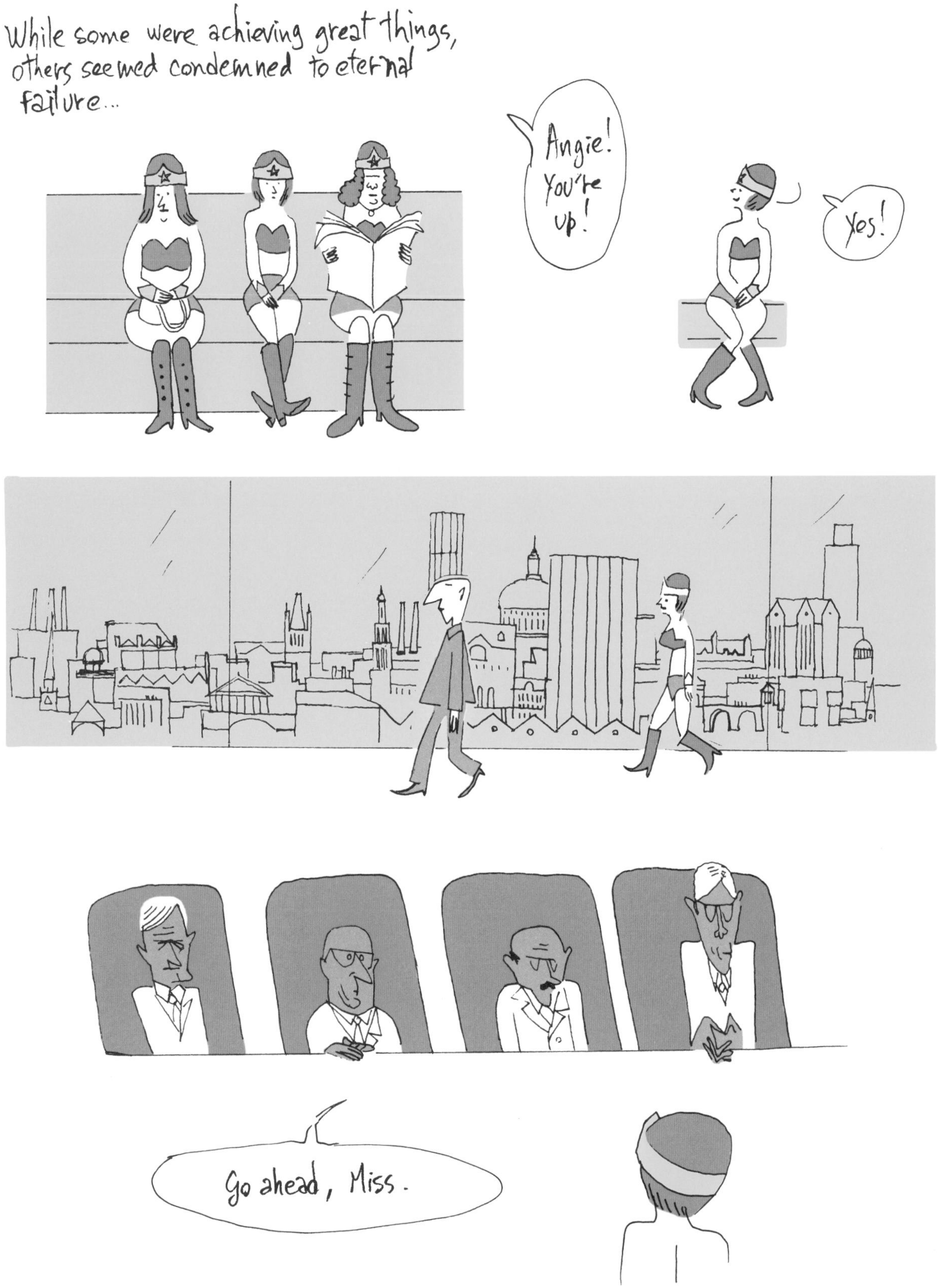
While some were achieving great things, others seemed condemned to eternal failure...
Angie! You're up!
Yes!
Go ahead, Miss.

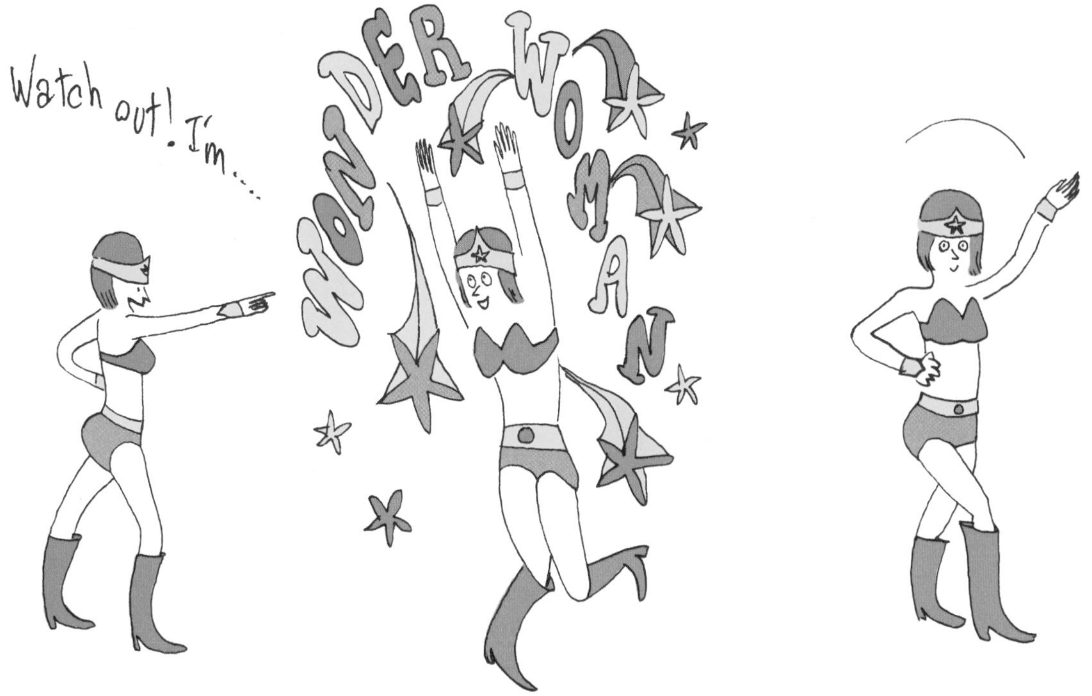
Watch out! I'm....
WONDER WOMAN

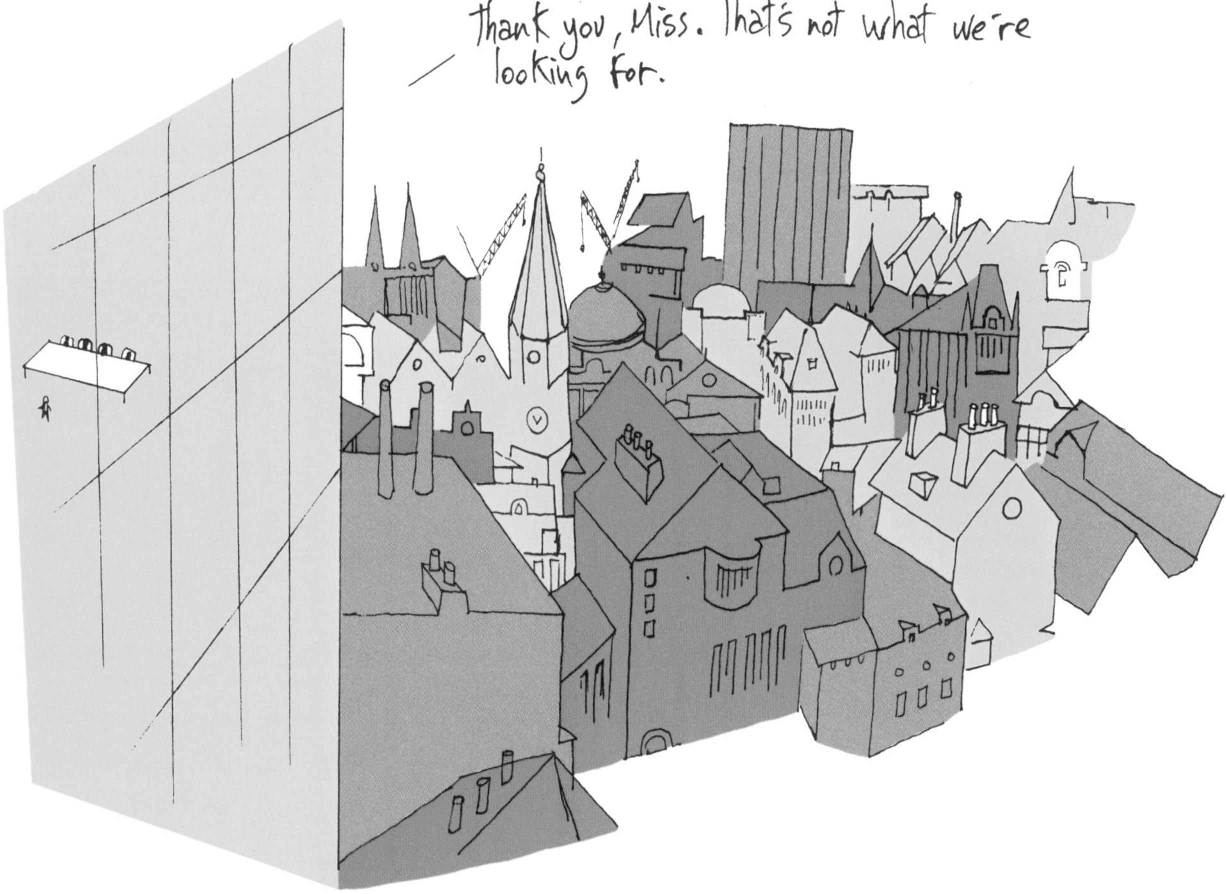
Thank you, Miss. That's not what we're looking for.

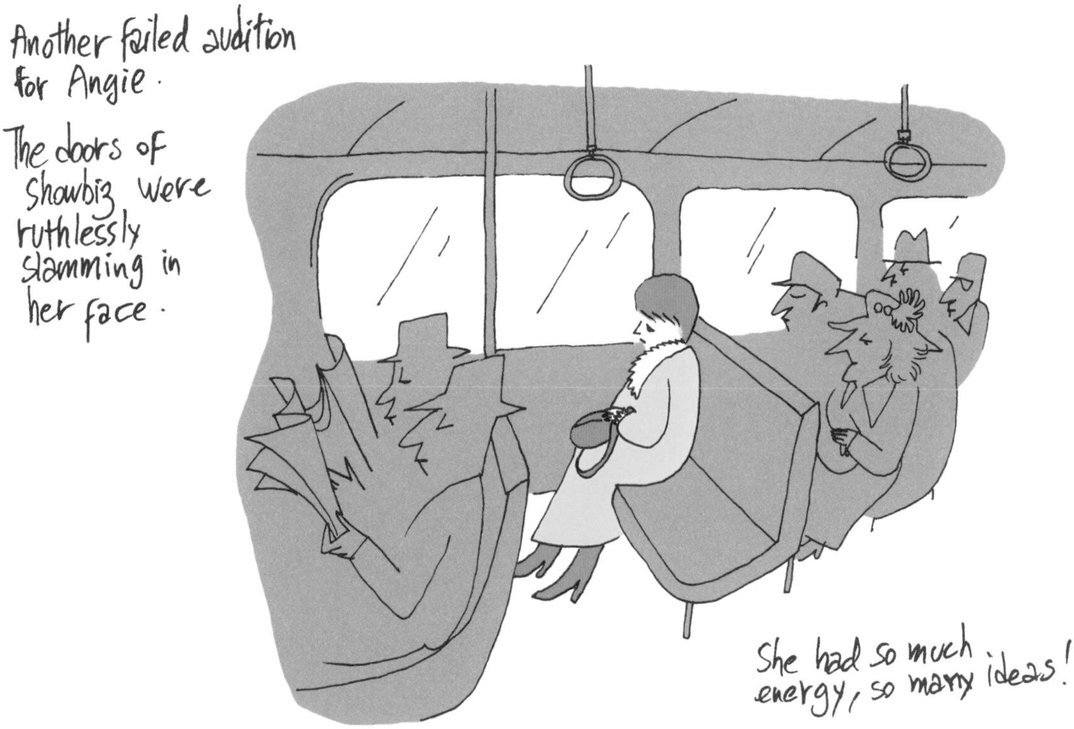
Another failed audition for Angie.
The doors of showbiz were ruthlessly slamming in her face.
She had so much energy, so many ideas!

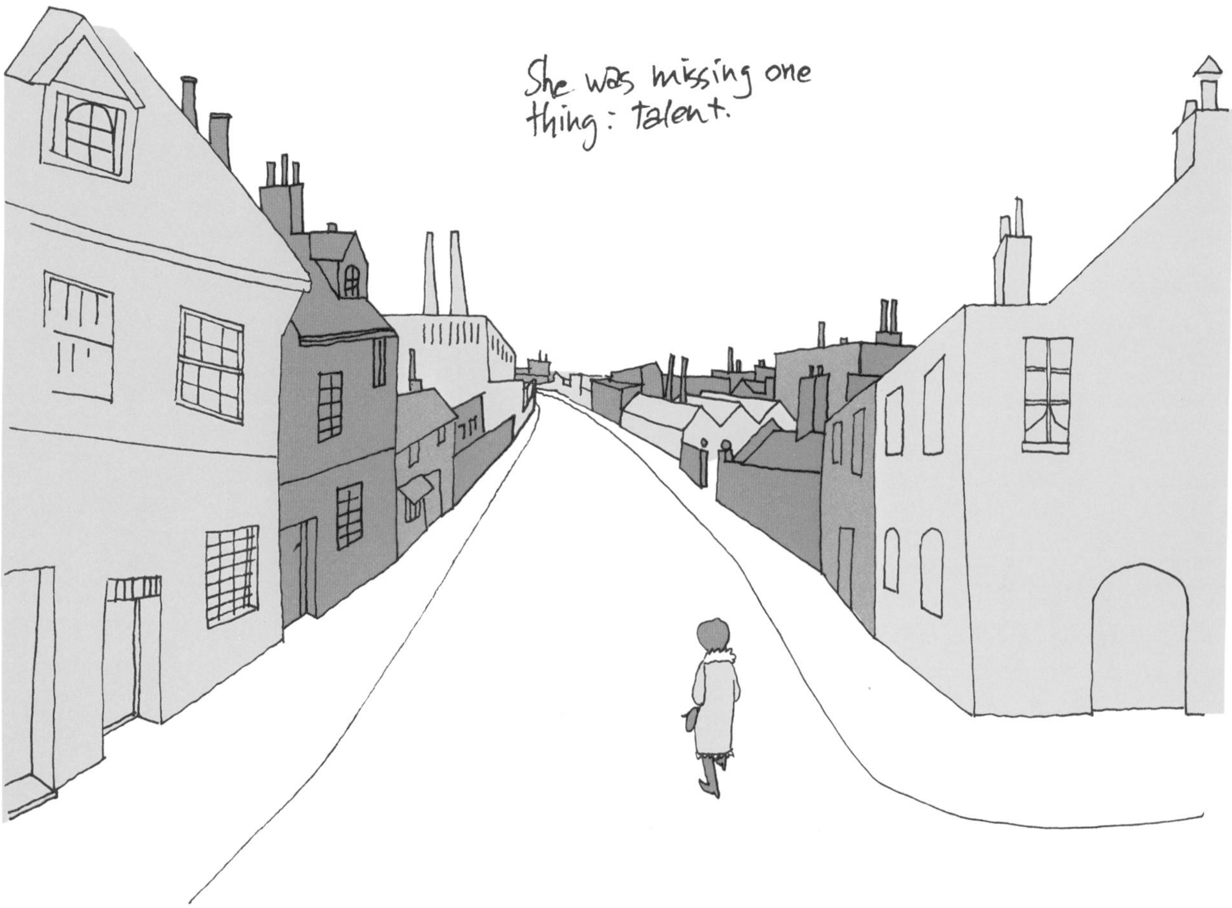
She was missing one thing: talent.

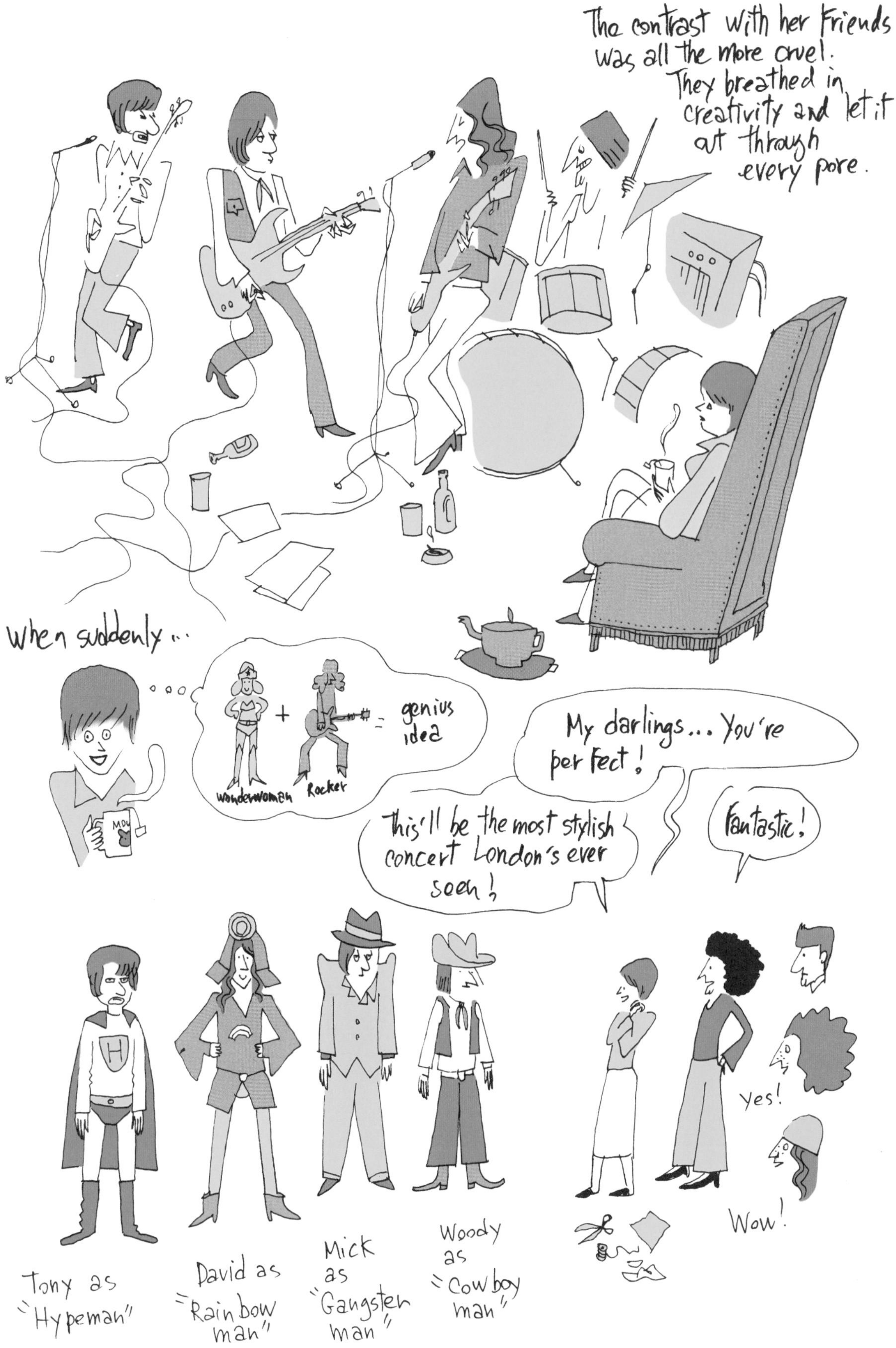
The contrast with her friends was all the more cruel.
They breathed in creativity and let it out through every pore.
When suddenly...
wonderwoman
Rocker
genius idea
My darlings... You're perfect!
This'll be the most stylish concert London's ever seen!
Fantastic!
Yes!
Wow!
Tony as "Hypeman"
David as "Rainbow man"
Mick as "Gangster man"
Woody as "Cowboy man"

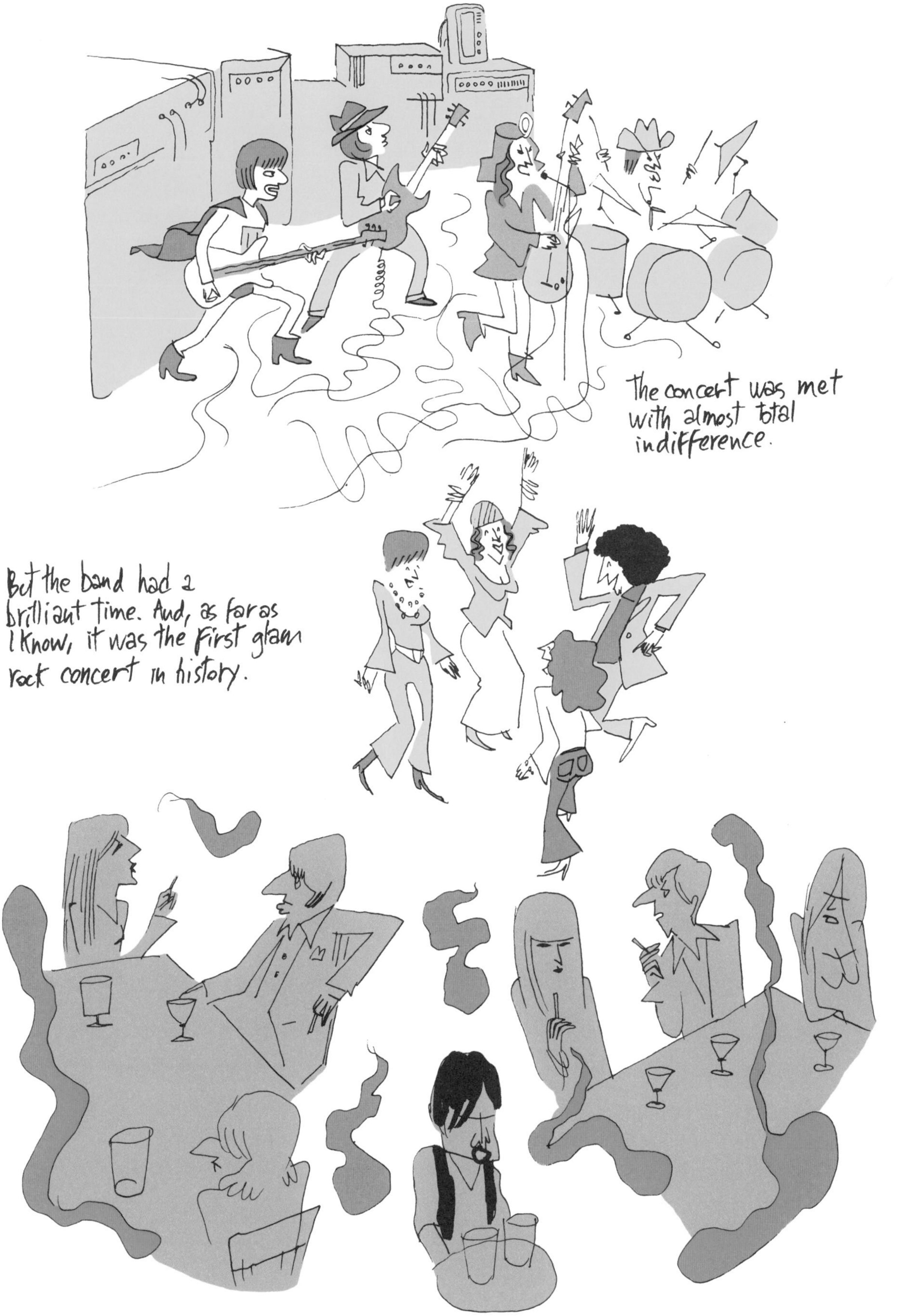
The concert was met with almost total indifference.
But the band had a brilliant time. And, as far as I know, it was the first glam rock concert in history.

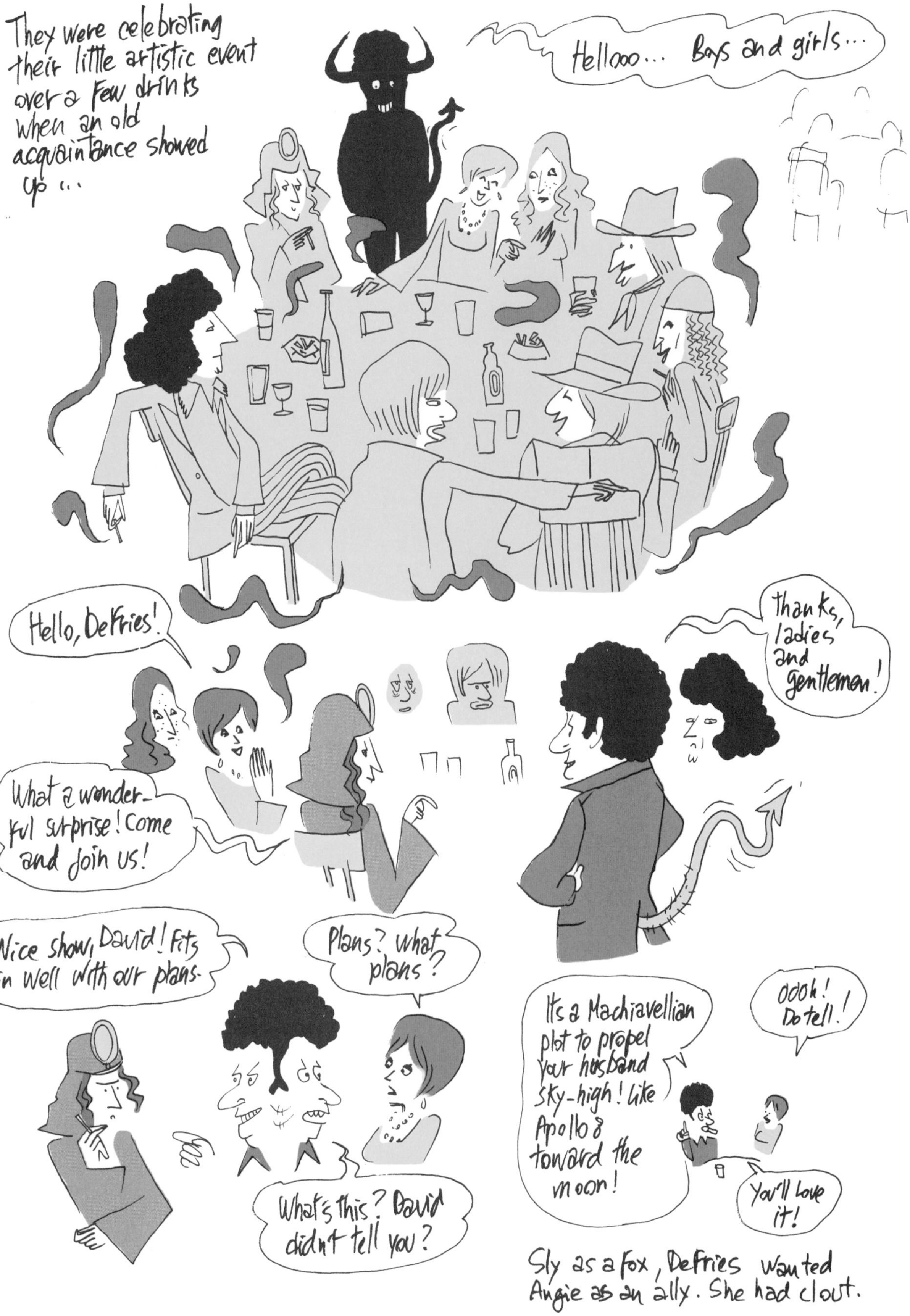
They were celebrating their little artistic event over a few drinks when an old acquaintance showed up ...
Helloo... Boys and girls...
Hello, DeFries!
Thanks, ladies and gentlemen!
What a wonderful surprise! Come and join us!
Nice show, David! Fits in well with our plans.
Plans? What plans?
What's this? David didn't tell you?
It's a Machiavellian plot to propel your husband sky-high! Like Apollo 8 toward the moon!
Oooh! Do tell!
You'll love it!
Sly as a fox, DeFries wanted Angie as an ally. She had clout.

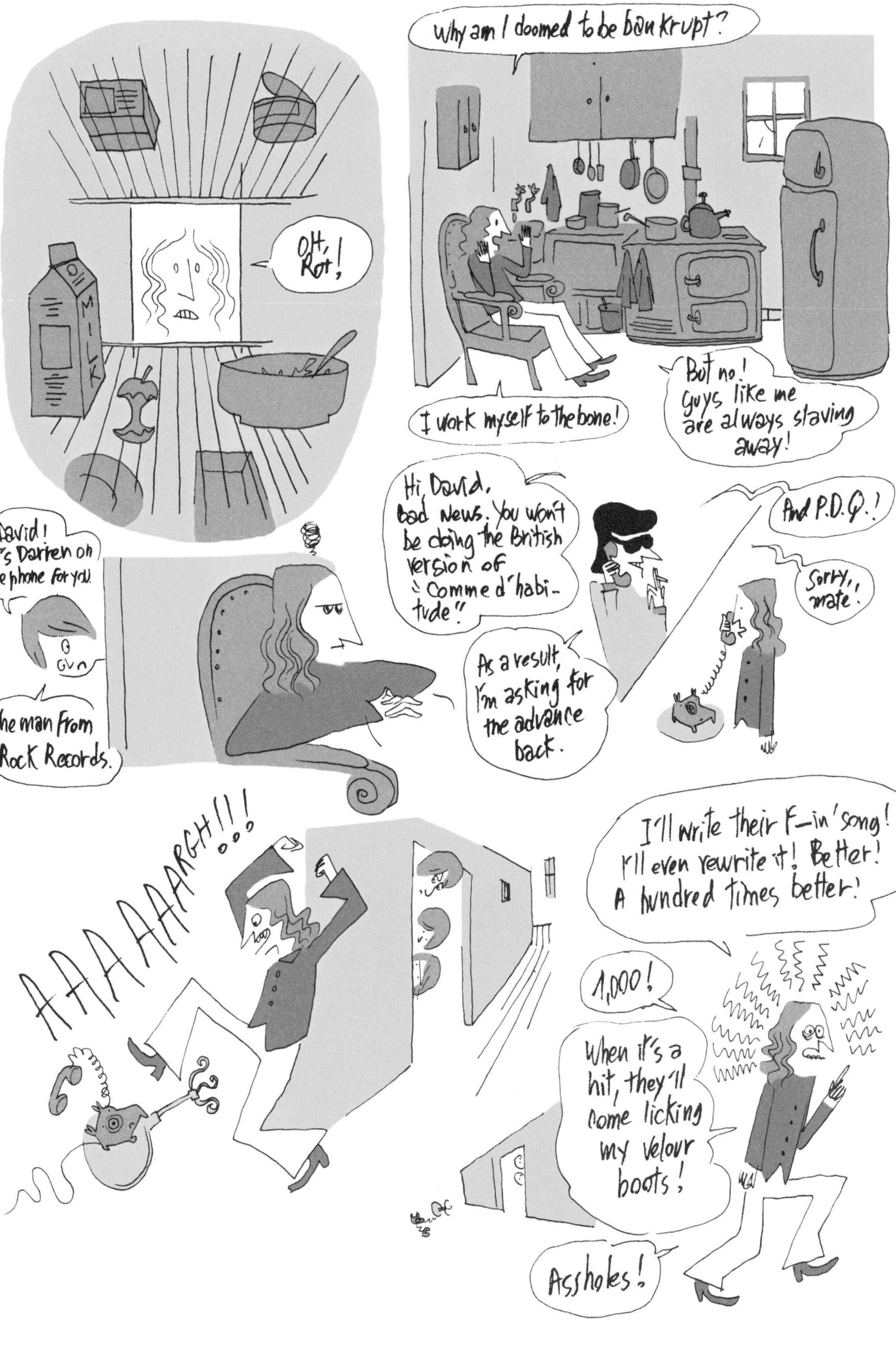
OH, Rot!
Why am I doomed to be bankrupt?
I work myself to the bone!
But no! Guys like me are always slaving away!
David! It's Darren on the phone for you.
The man from Rock Records.
Hi, David. Bad News. You won't be doing the British version of "Comme d'habitude"!
As a result, I'm asking for the advance back.
And P.D.Q.!
Sorry, mate!
AAAAAARGH!!!
I'll write their F—in' song! I'll even rewrite it! Better! A hundred times better!
1,000!
When it's a hit, they'll come licking my velour boots!
Assholes!

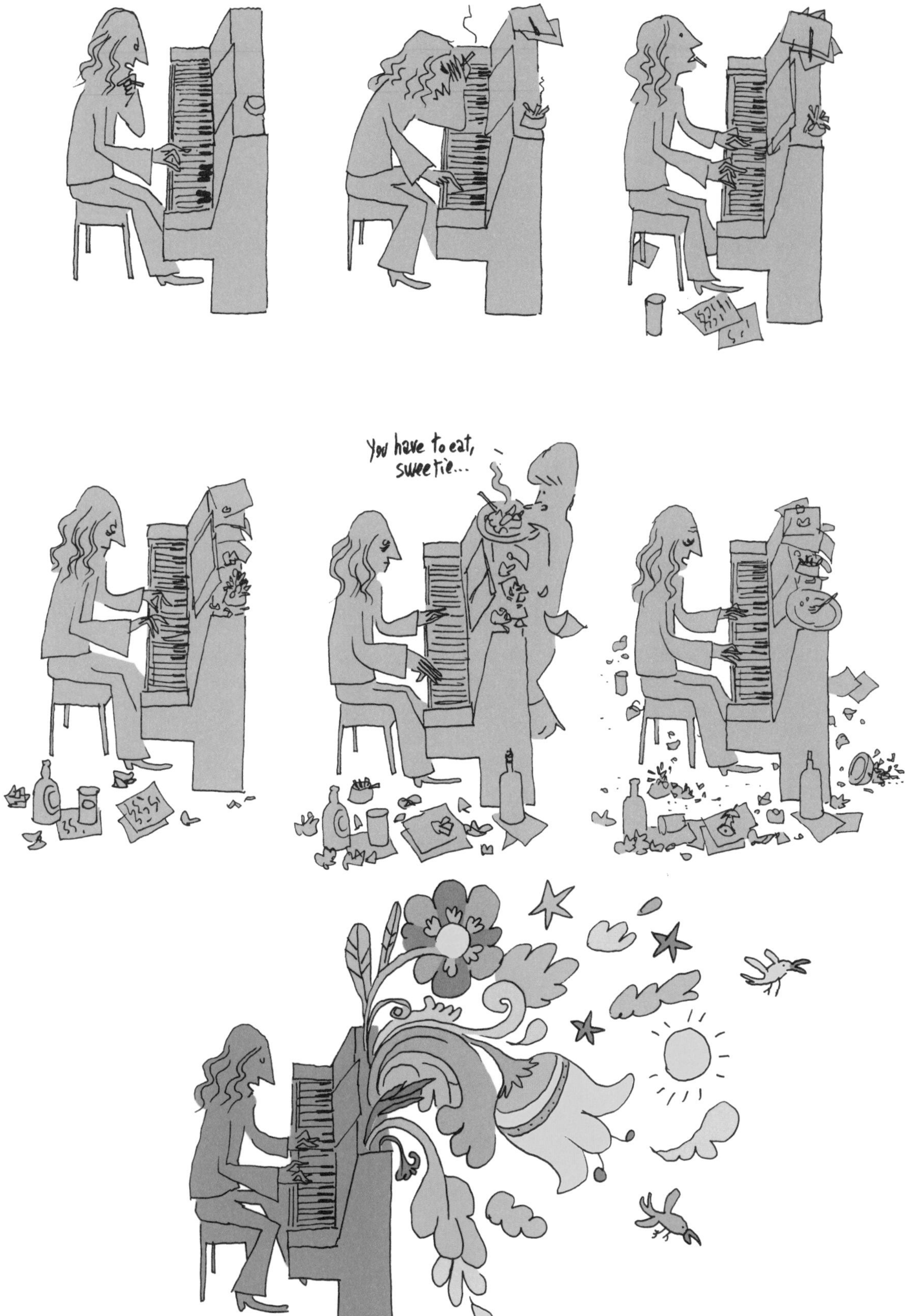
You have to eat, sweetie...

That day, inside me, it was "Life on Mars".

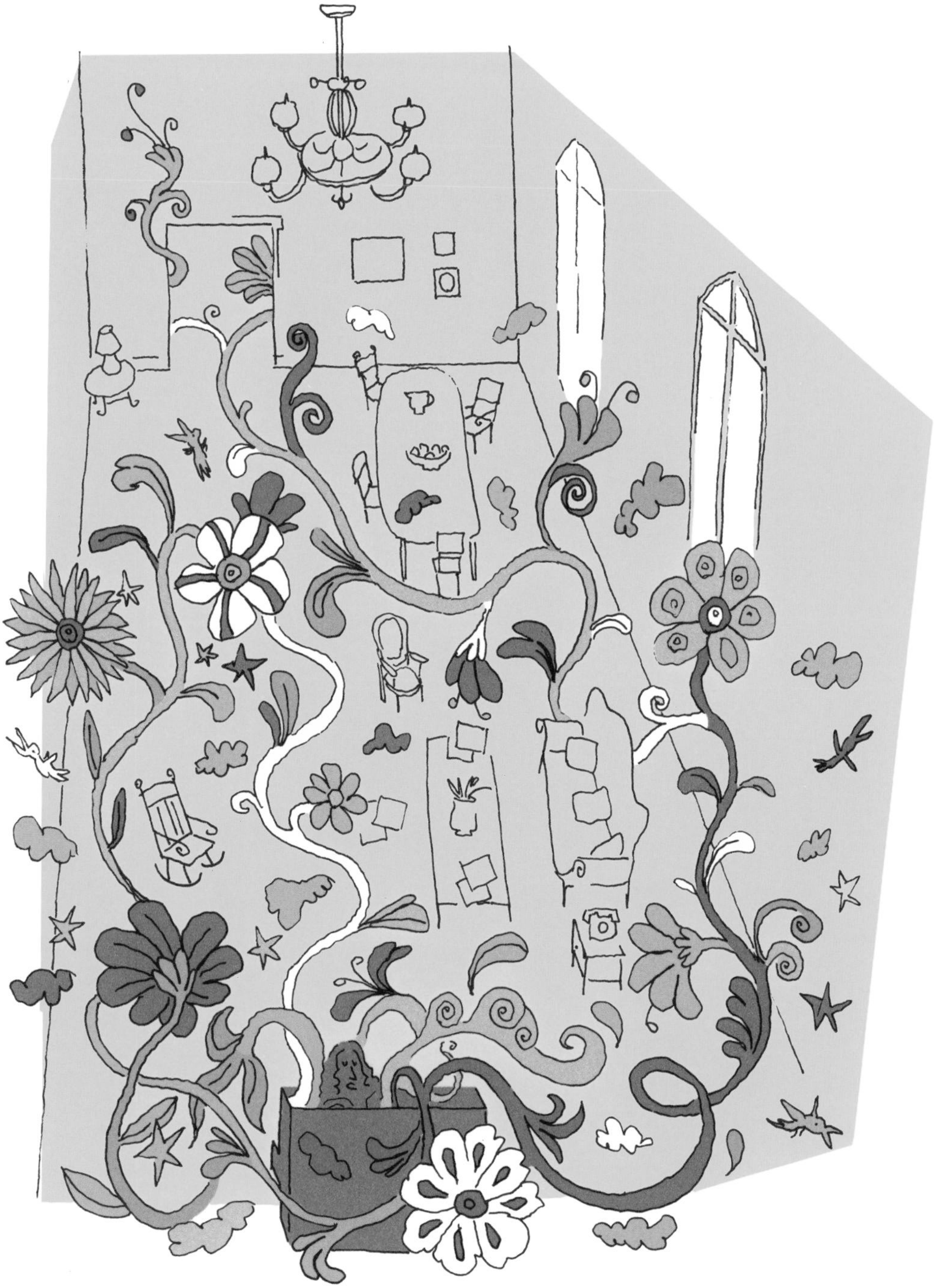

Artists are by nature
dissatisfied creatures.
And yet, sometimes
they surprise themselves
with moments of
bliss.

But quick as it comes,
this feeling deserts them.

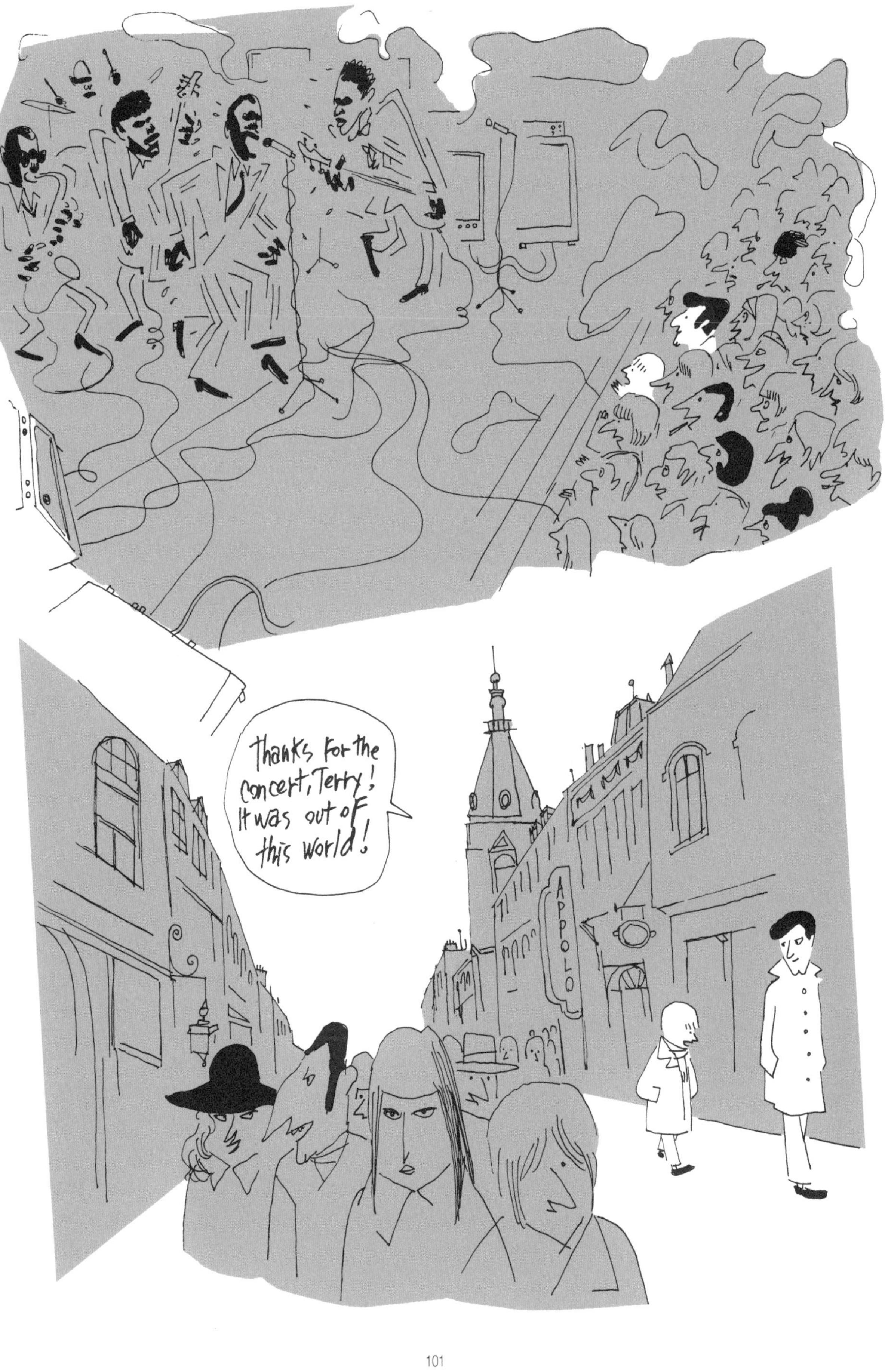
Thanks for the concert, Terry! It was out of this world!
APPOLO

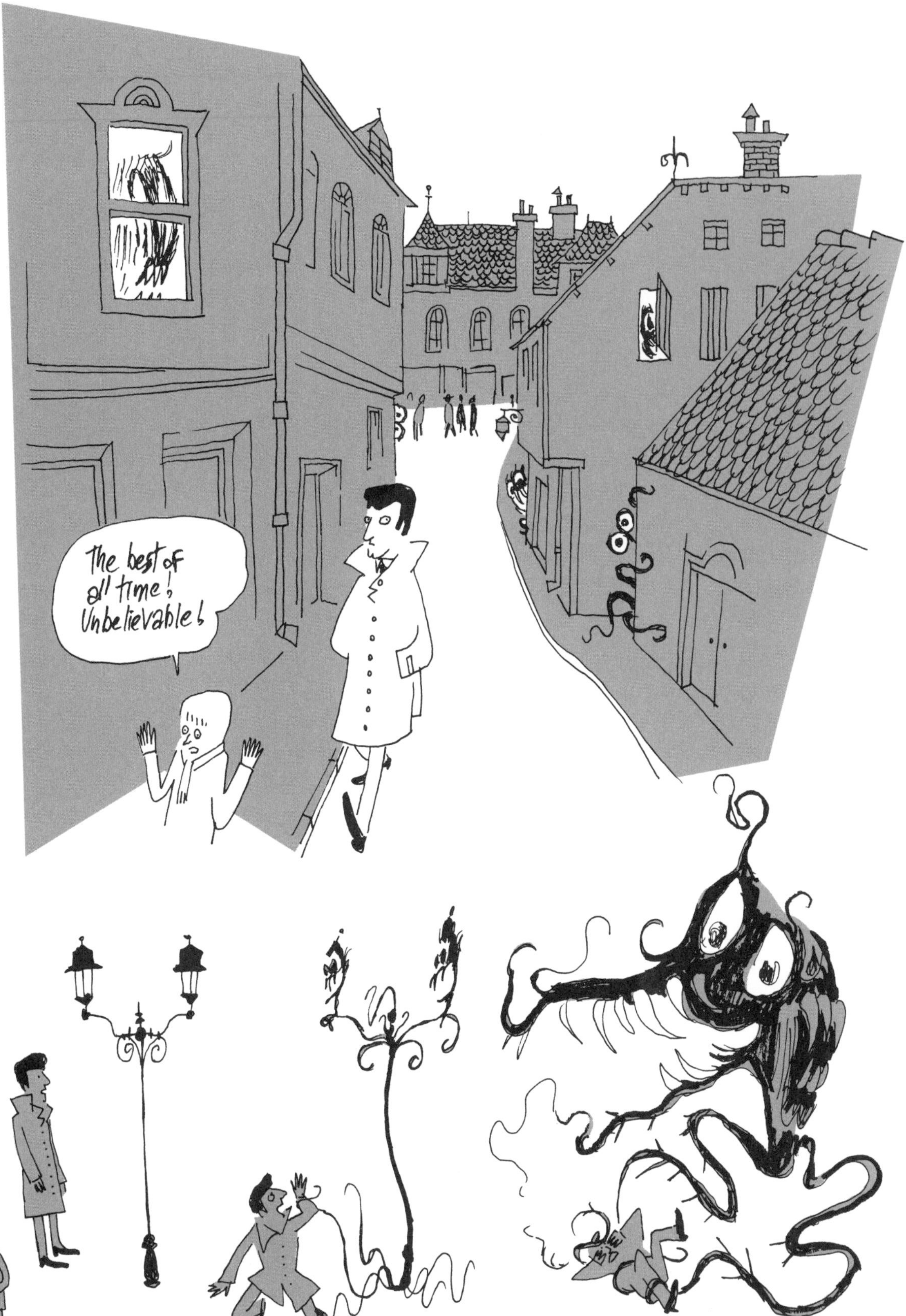
The best of all time! Unbelievable!
♫

It was Terry's first attack of schizophrenia. And David was on hand to witness it.

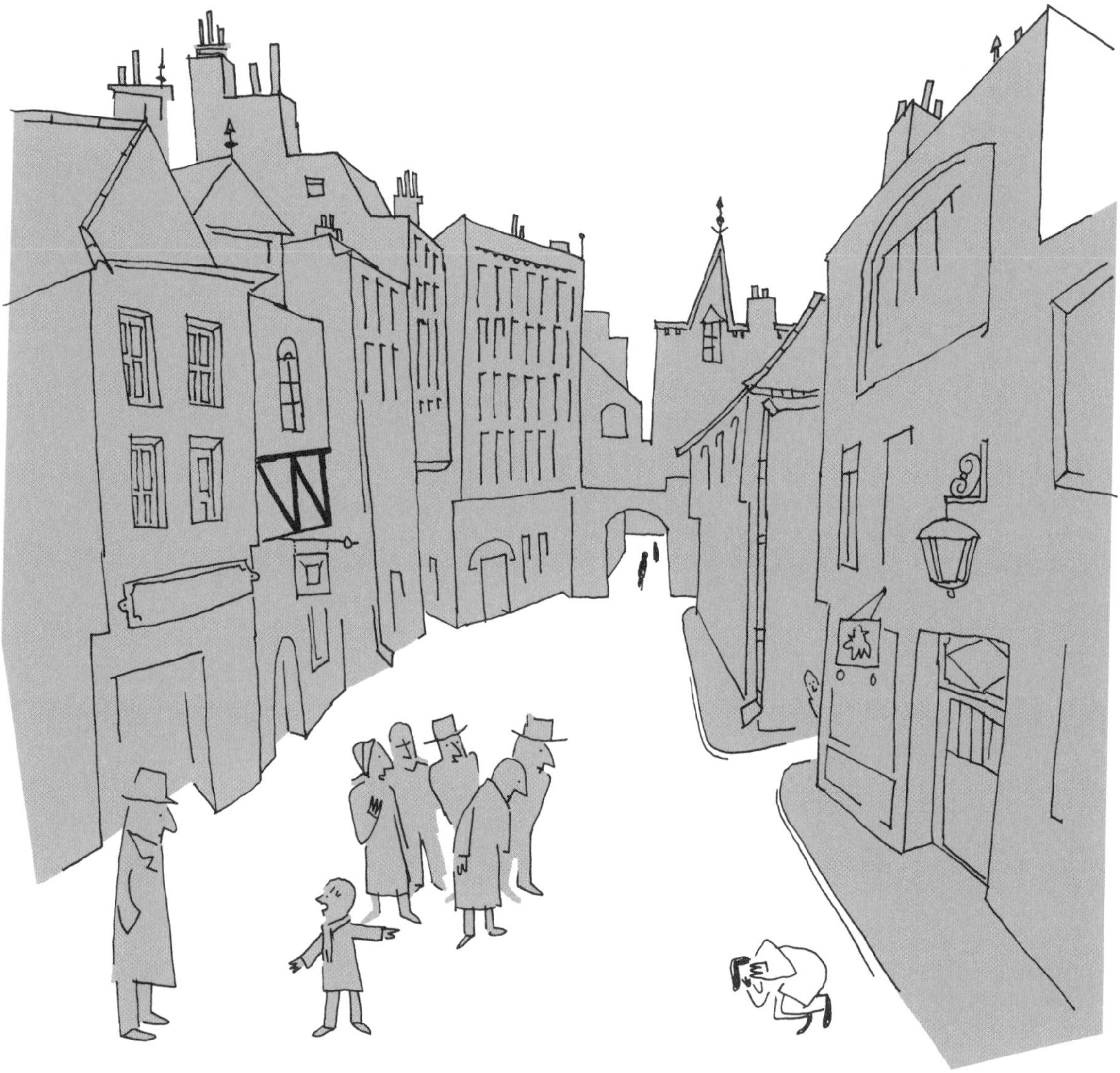

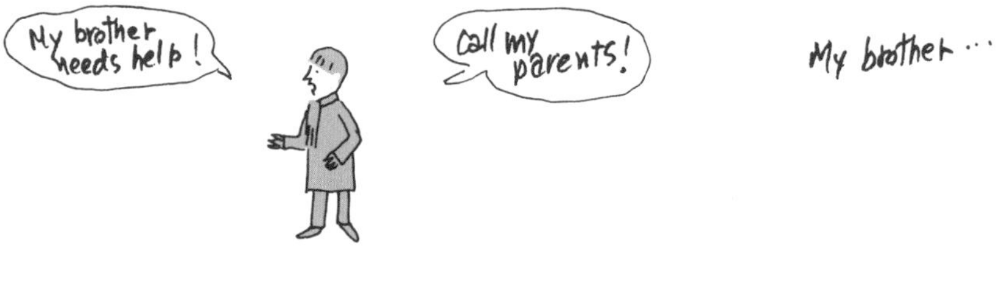

My brother needs help!
Call my parents!
My brother...

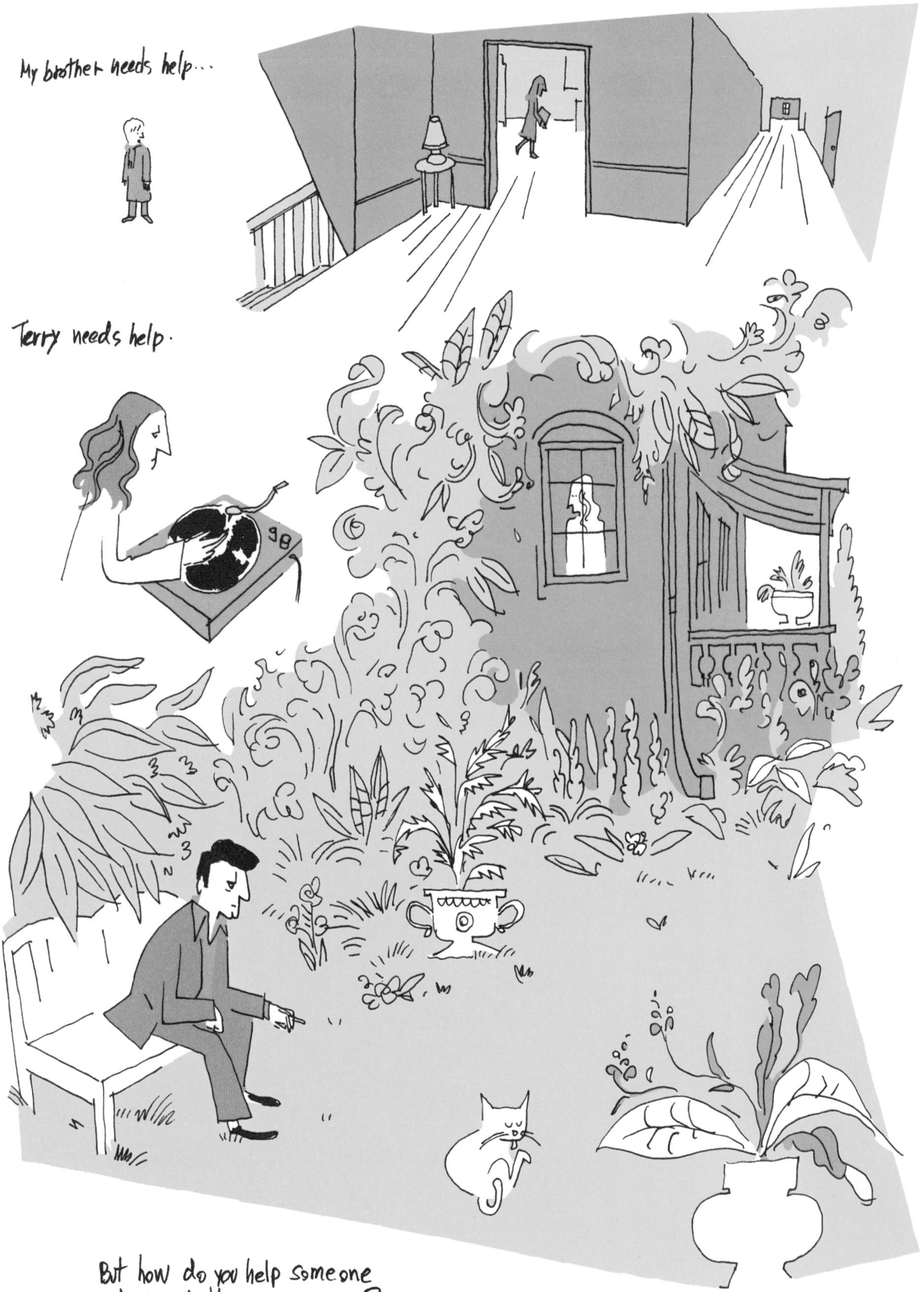
My brother needs help...
Terry needs help.
But how do you help someone who's not there any more?

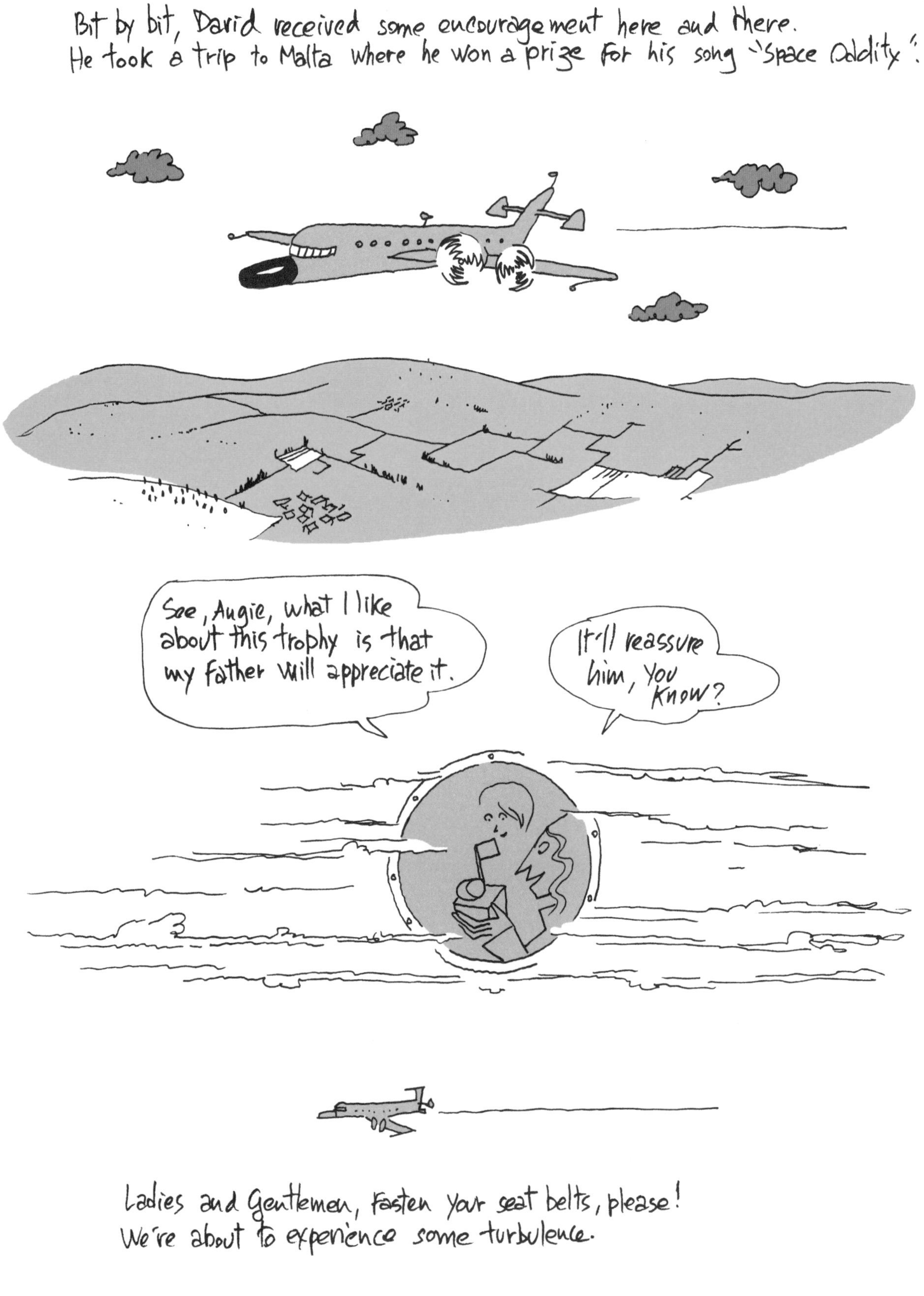
Bit by bit, David received some encouragement here and there.
He took a trip to Malta where he won a prize for his song "Space Oddity".
See, Angie, what I like about this trophy is that my father will appreciate it.
It'll reassure him, you know?
Ladies and Gentlemen, fasten your seat belts, please!
We're about to experience some turbulence.

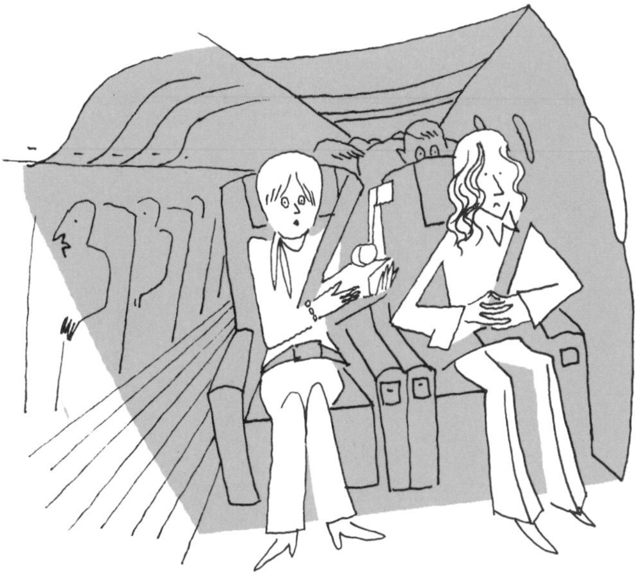

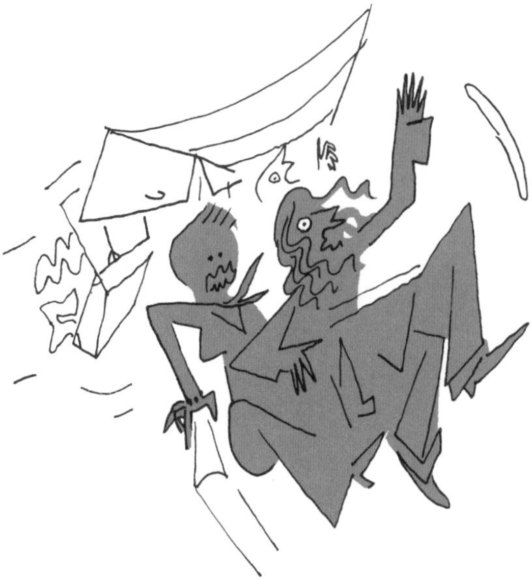

The turbulence turned out to be a terrifying storm.

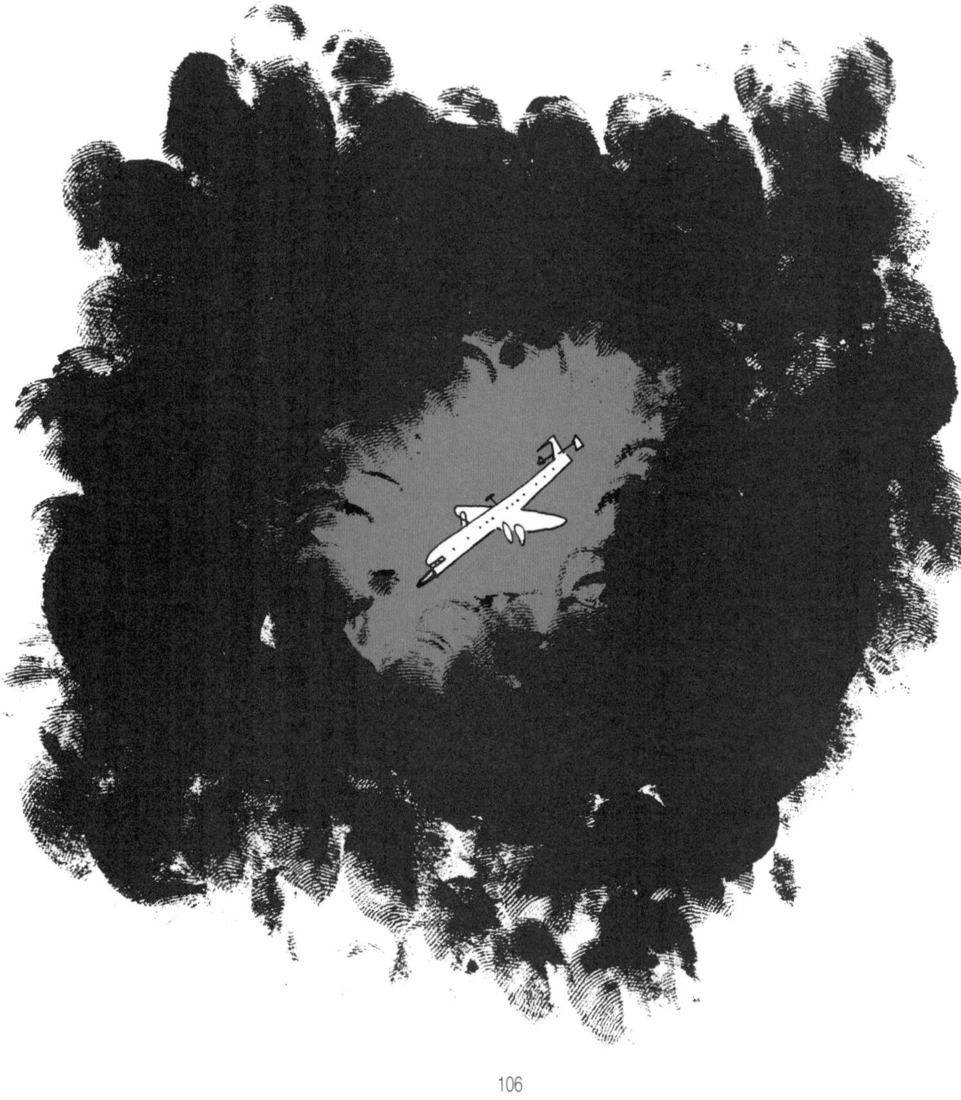

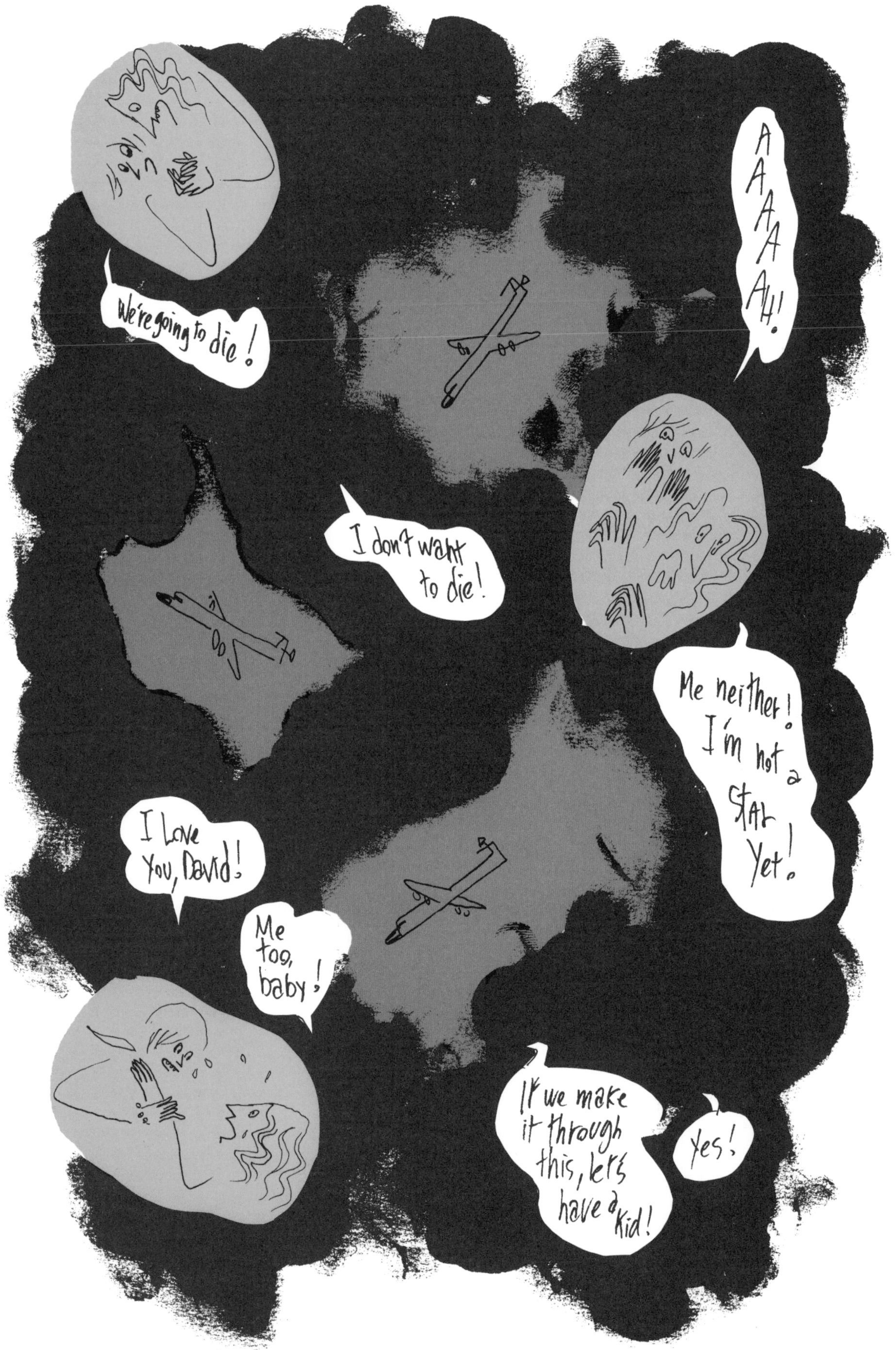
We're going to die!
AAAAAH!
I don't want to die!
Me neither! I'm not a STAR yet!
I Love You, David!
Me too, baby!
If we make it through this, let's have a kid!
Yes!

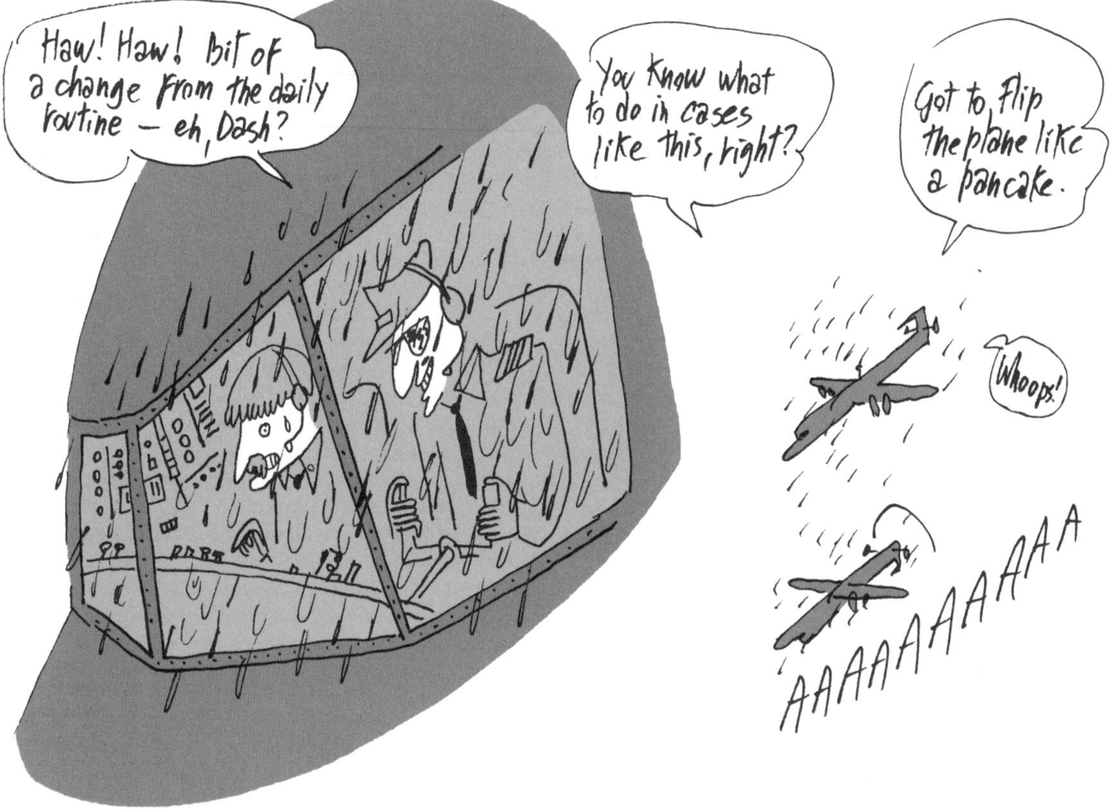
Haw! Haw! Bit of a change from the daily routine – eh, Dash?
You know what to do in cases like this, right?
Got to flip the plane like a pancake.
Whoops!
AAAAAAAAAAA

The experience left David with a long-lasting fear of flying.

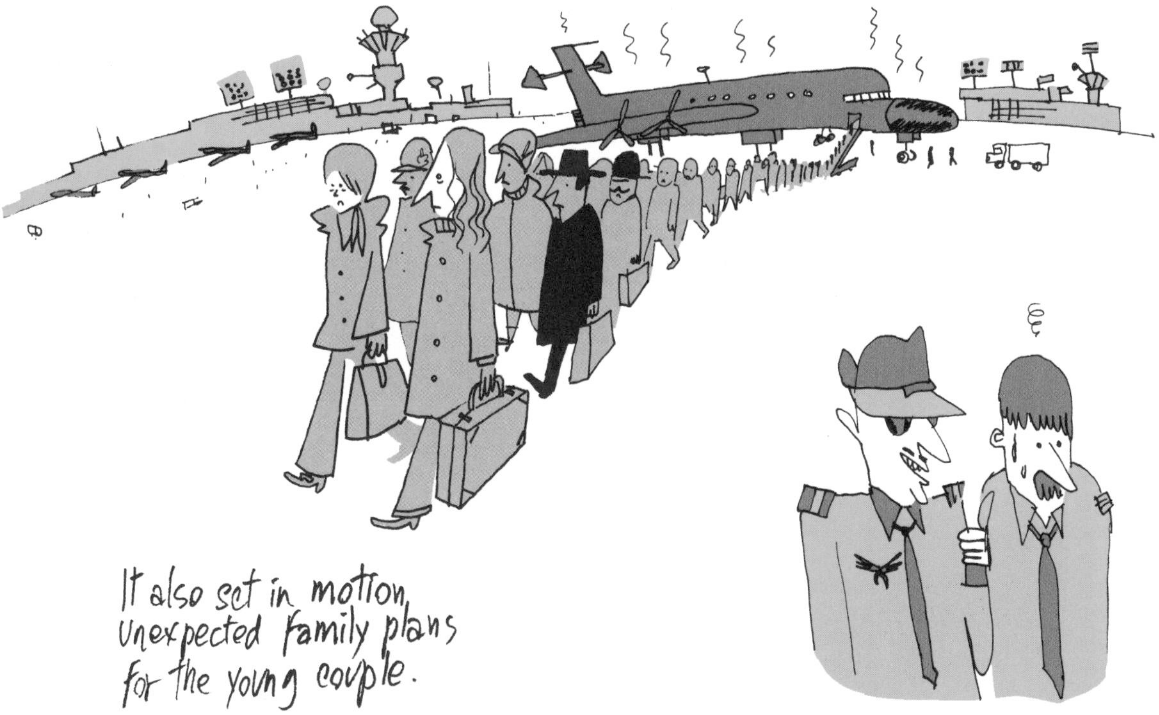

It also set in motion unexpected family plans for the young couple.

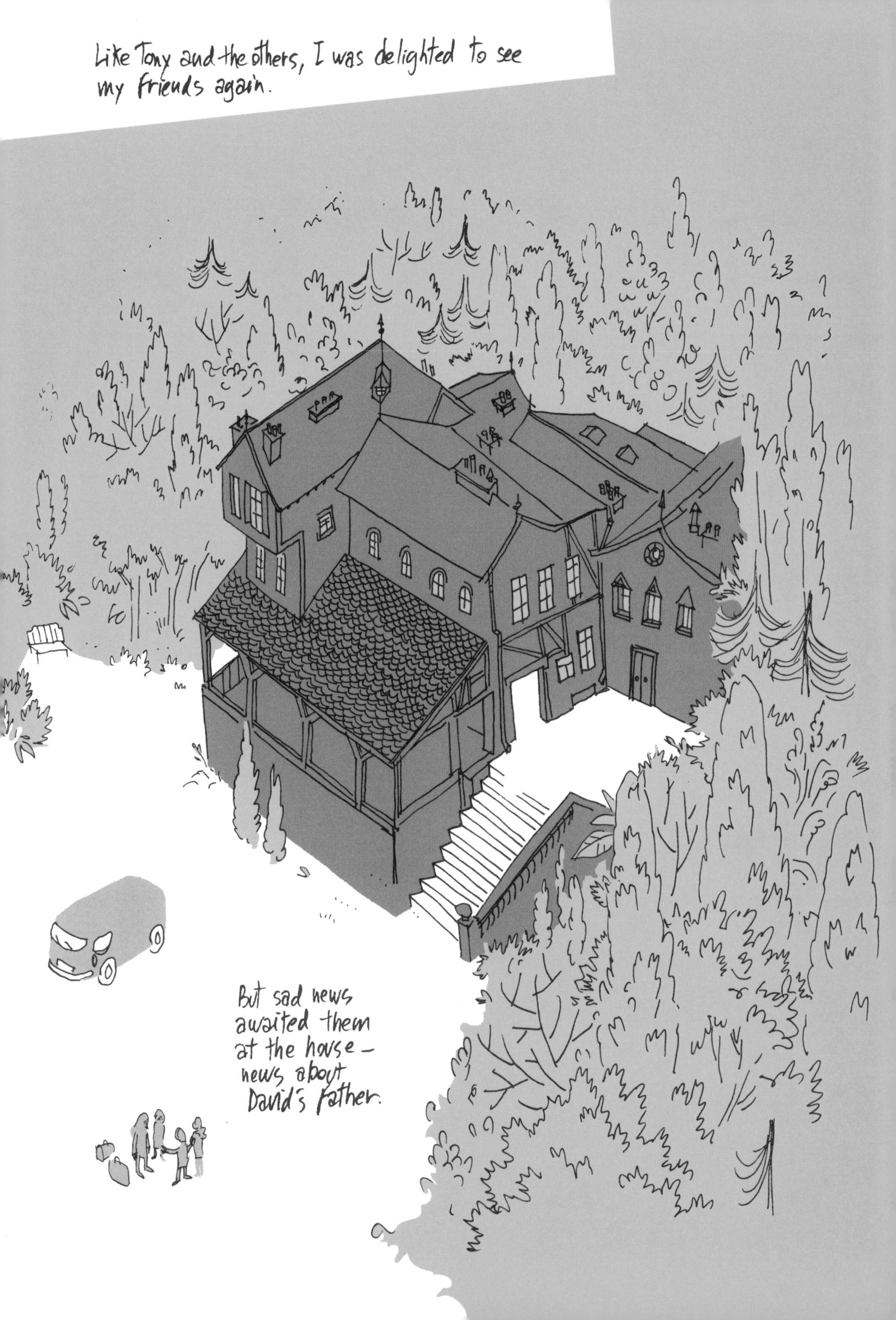
Like Tony and the others, I was delighted to see my friends again.
But sad news awaited them at the house – news about David's father.

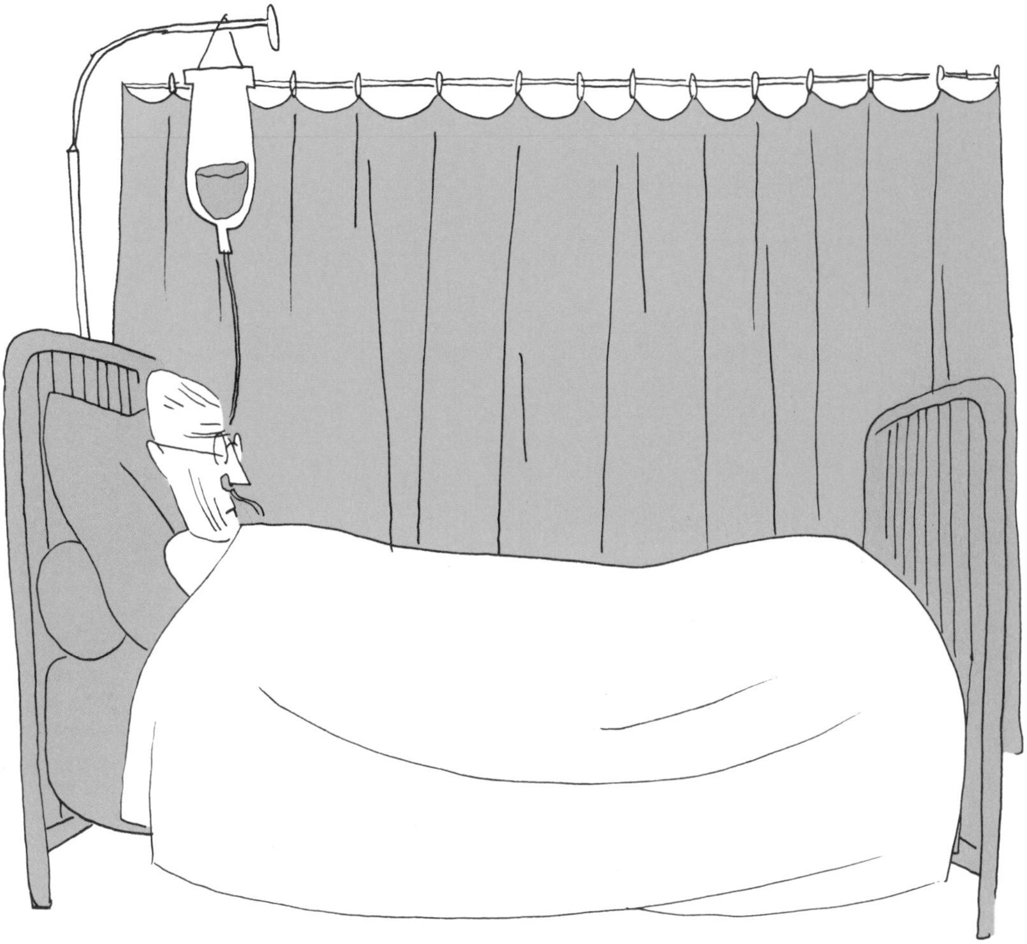

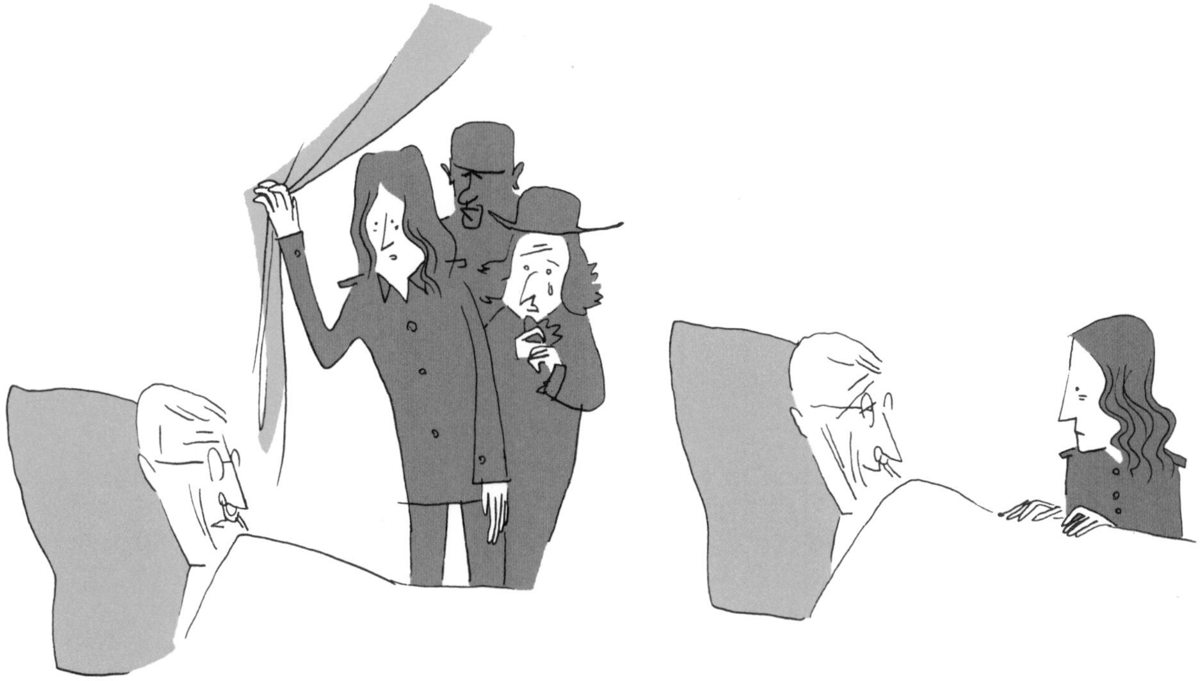

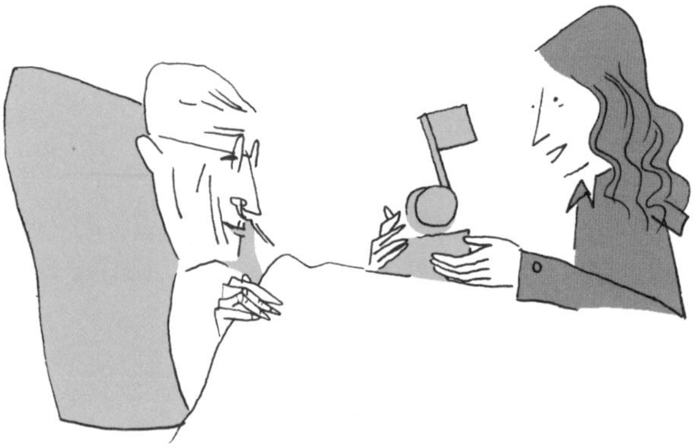

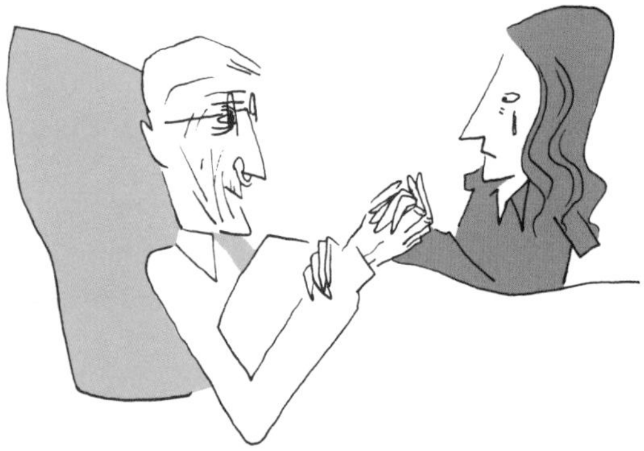

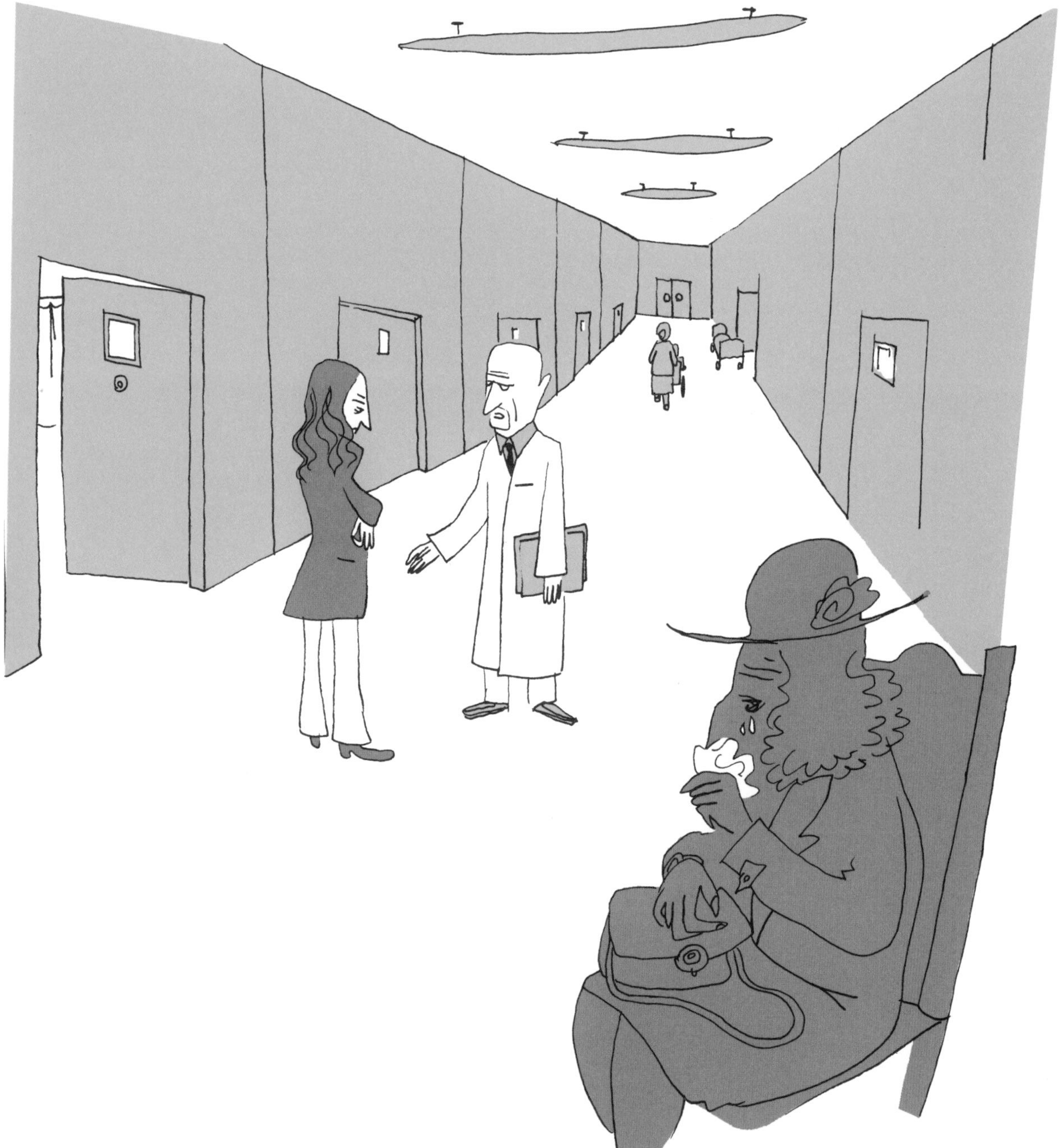

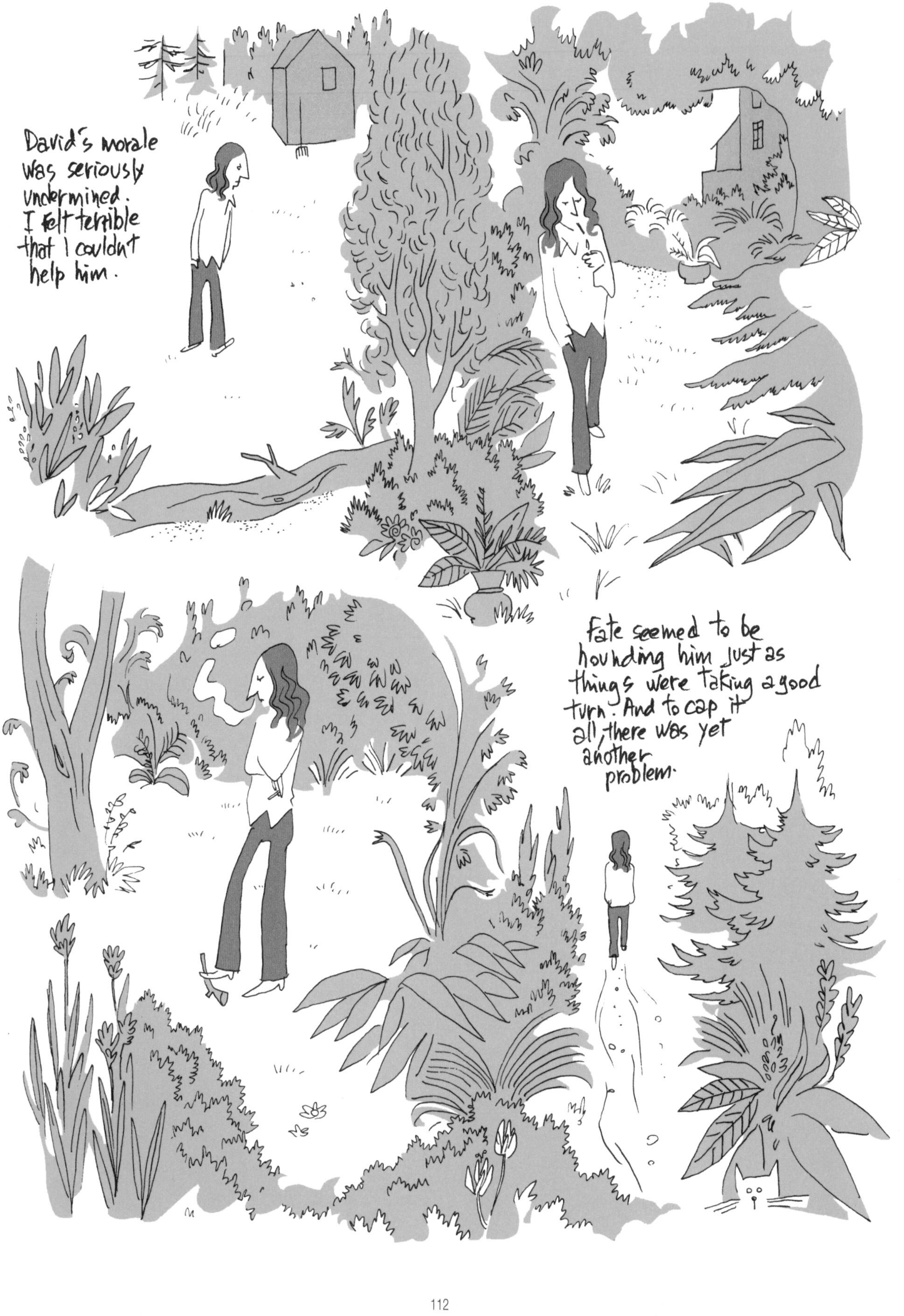
David's morale was seriously undermined. I felt terrible that I couldn't help him.
Fate seemed to be hounding him just as things were taking a good turn. And to cap it all, there was yet another problem.

How to break
the news to
Terry?

INTERMEZZO

Terry's Days

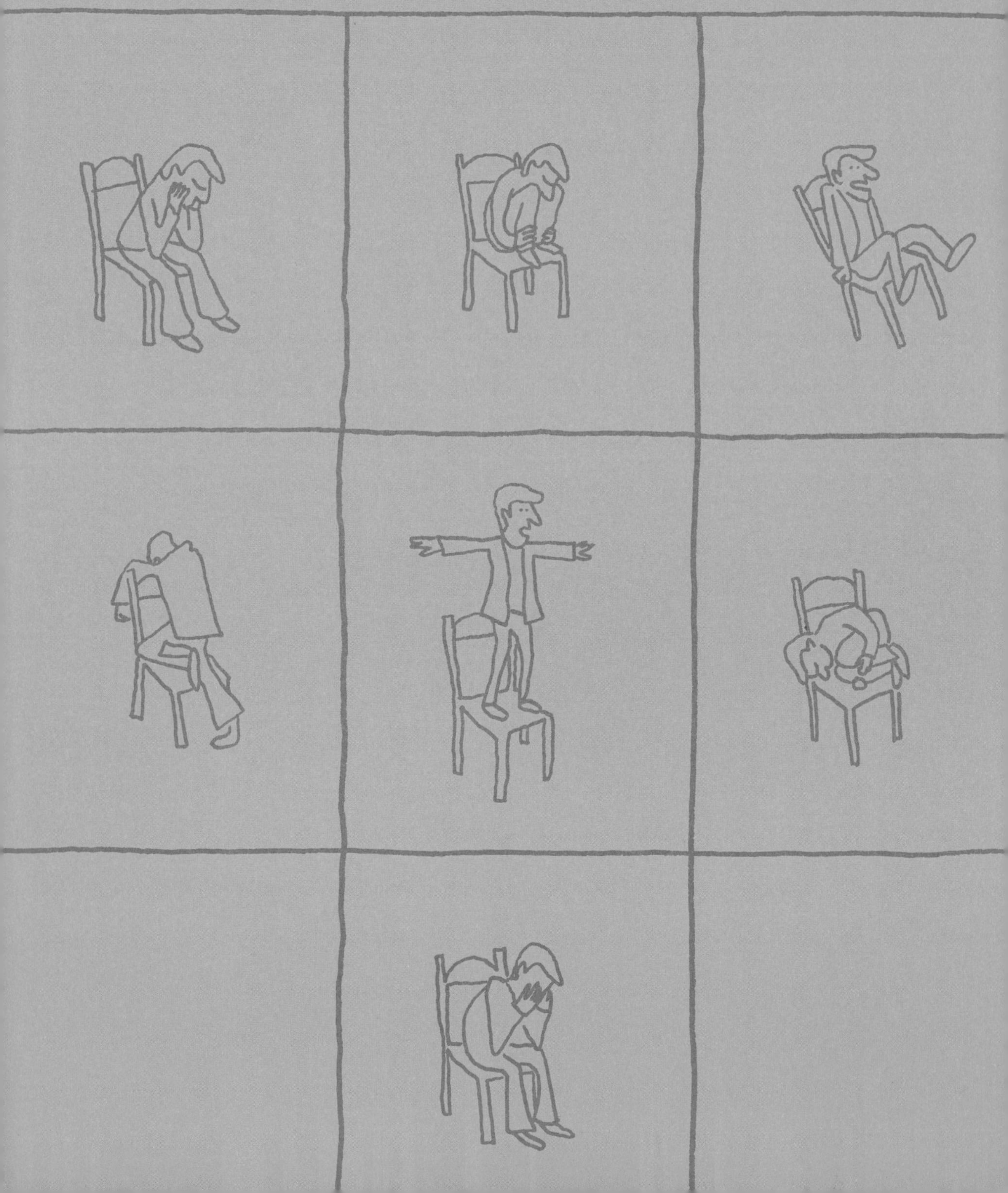

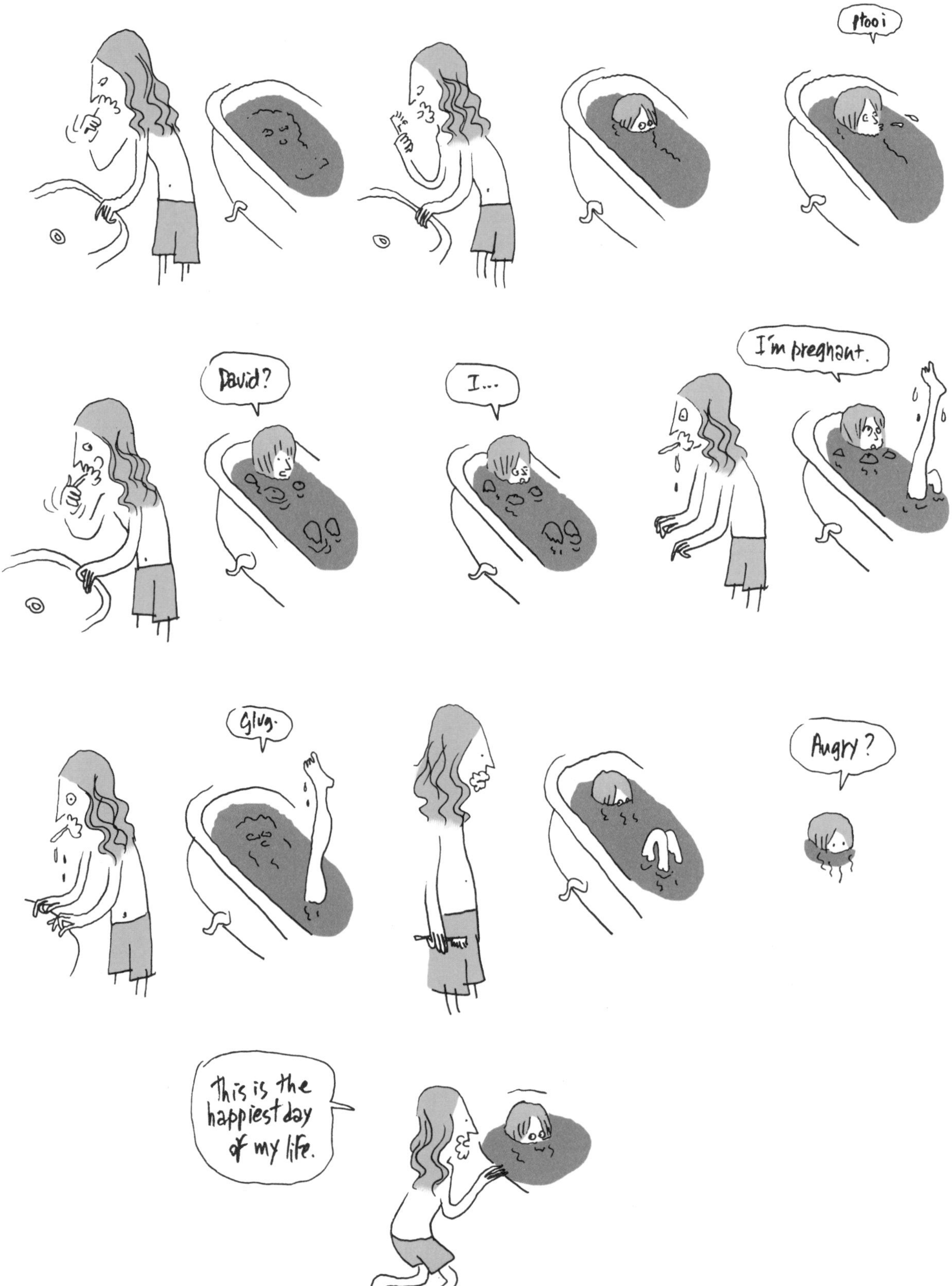
ptooi
David?
I...
I'm pregnant.
Glug.
Angry?
This is the happiest day of my life.

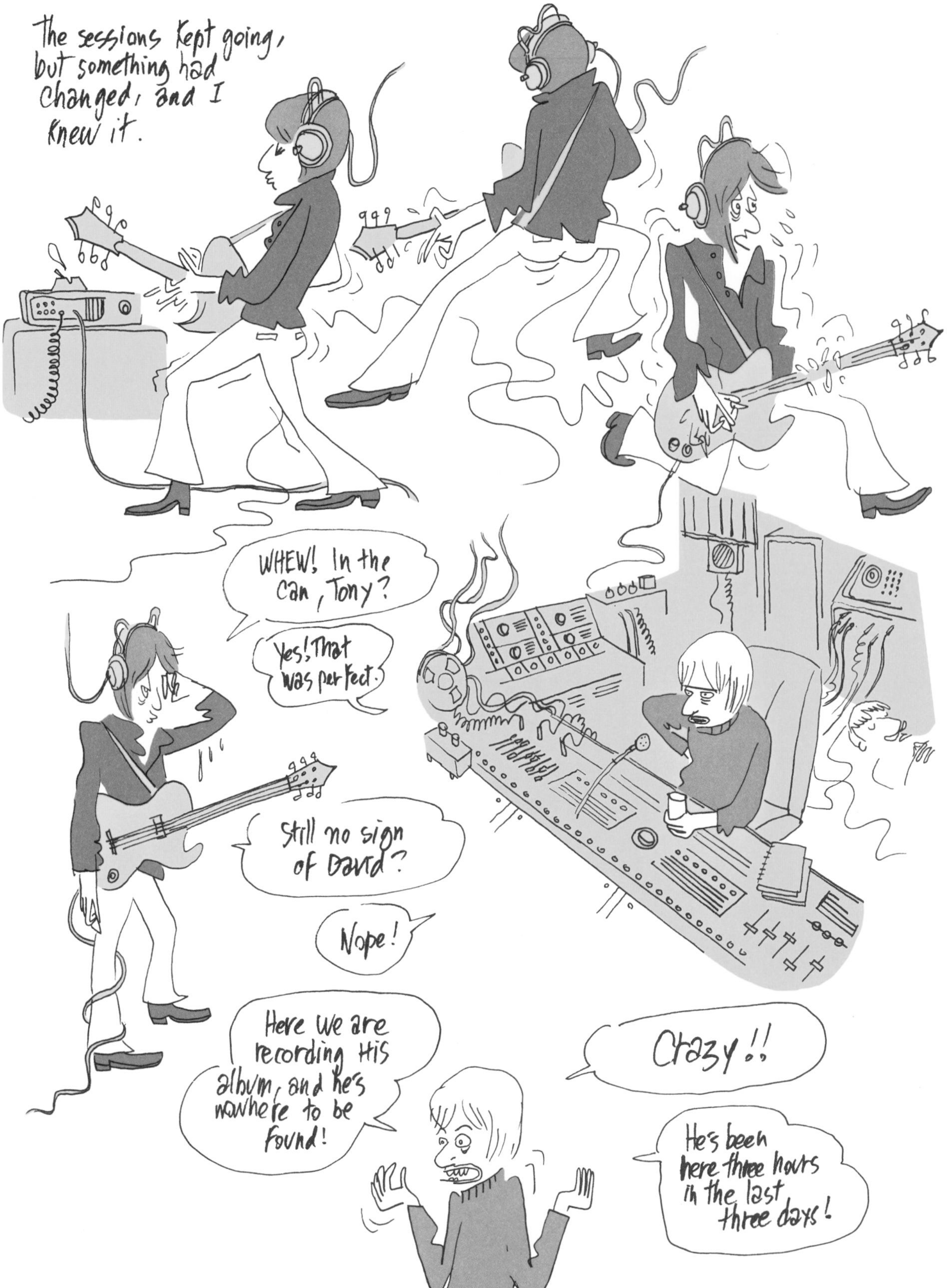
The sessions kept going, but something had changed, and I knew it.
WHEW! In the can, Tony?
Yes! That was perfect.
Still no sign of David?
Nope!
Here we are recording his album, and he's nowhere to be found!
Crazy!!
He's been here three hours in the last three days!

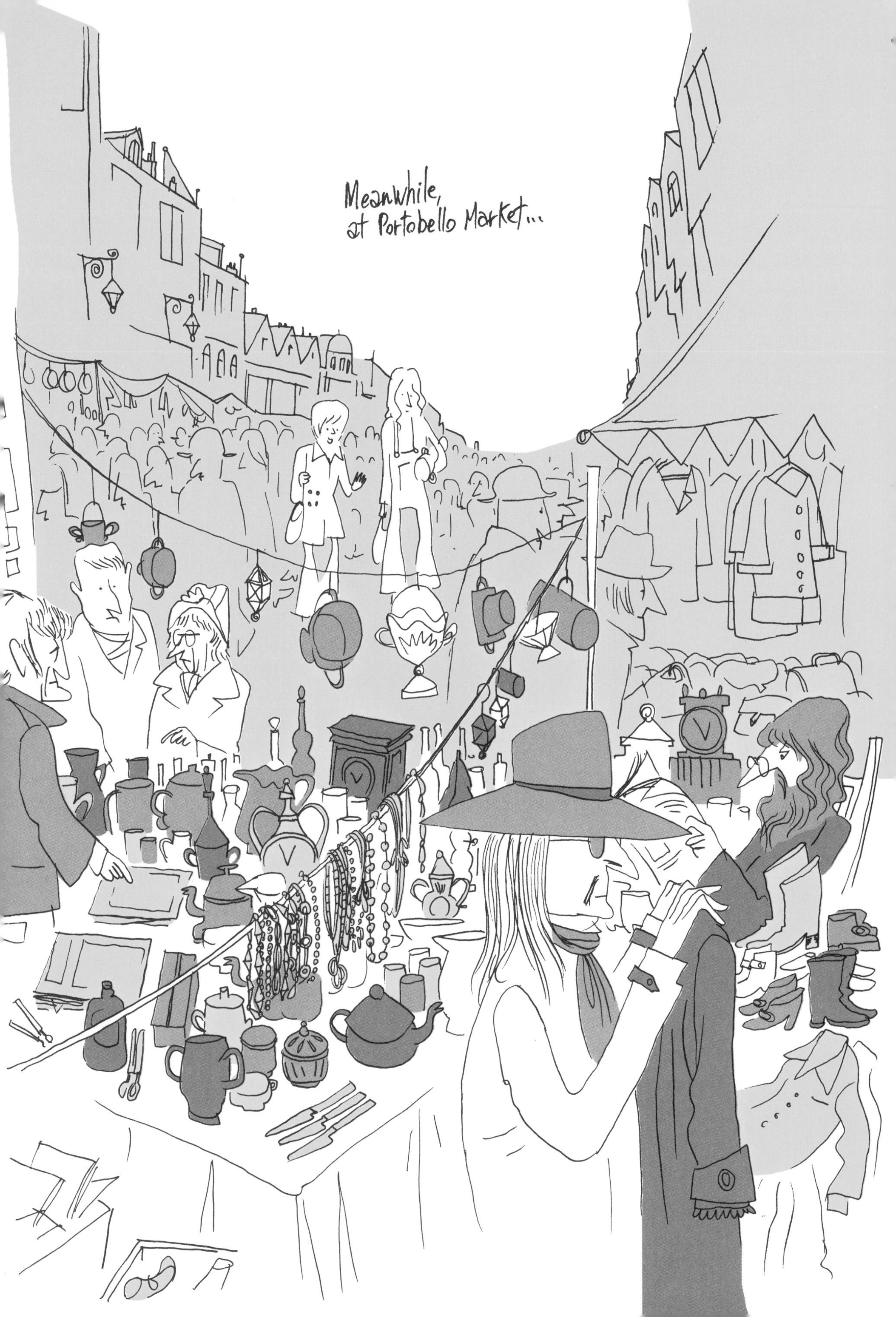
Meanwhile,
at Portobello Market...

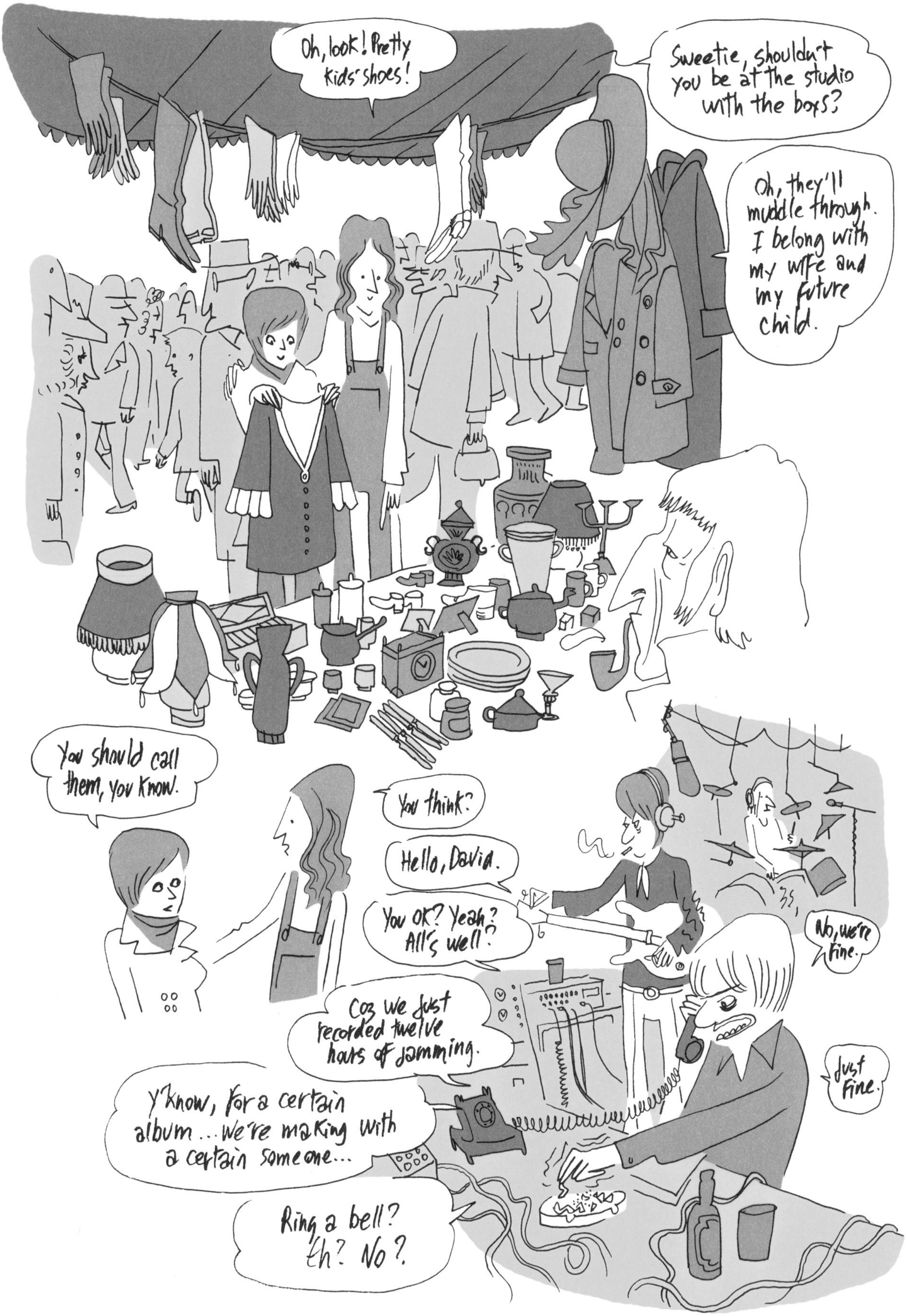

Oh, look! Pretty kids' shoes!
Sweetie, shouldn't you be at the studio with the boys?
Oh, they'll muddle through. I belong with my wife and my future child.
You should call them, you know.
You think?
Hello, David.
You OK? Yeah? All's well?
No, we're fine.
Coz we just recorded twelve hours of jamming.
Just fine.
Y'know, for a certain album... we're making with a certain someone...
Ring a bell? Eh? No?

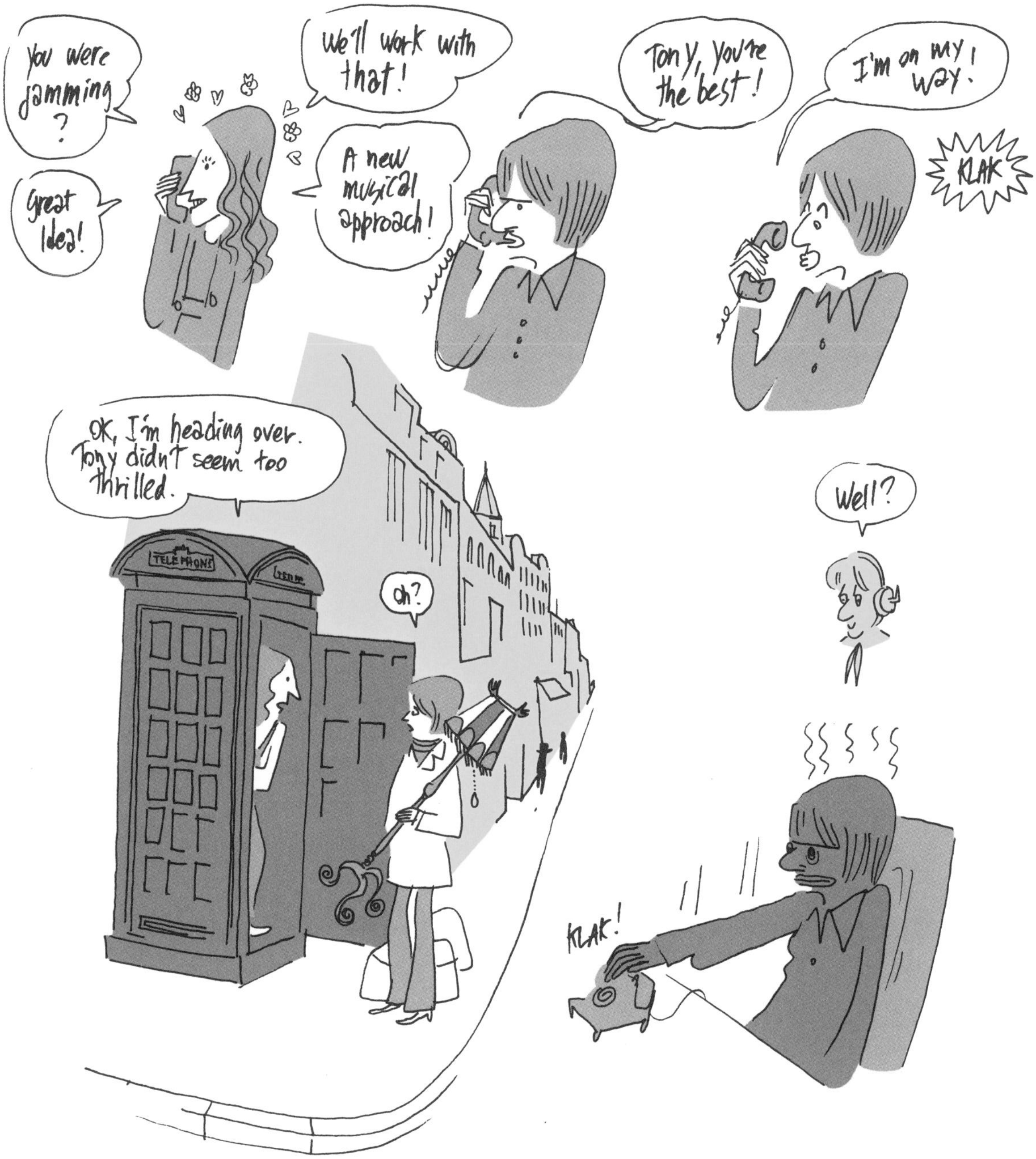
You were jamming?
Great idea!
We'll work with that!
A new musical approach!
Tony, you're the best!
I'm on my way!
KLAK
OK, I'm heading over. Tony didn't seem too thrilled.
Oh?
Well?
KLAK!
TELEPHONE

The final songs were wrapped up in an icy atmosphere.

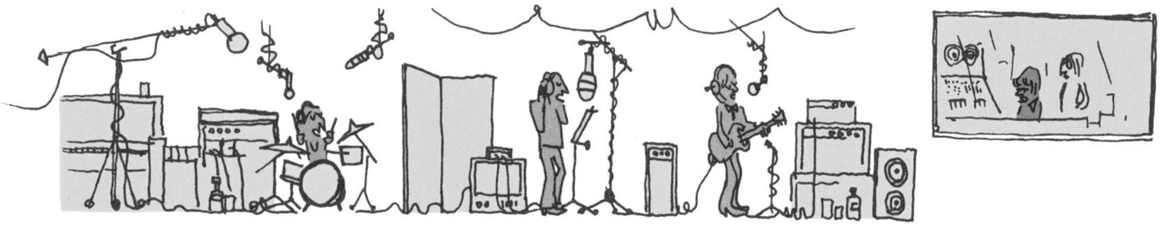

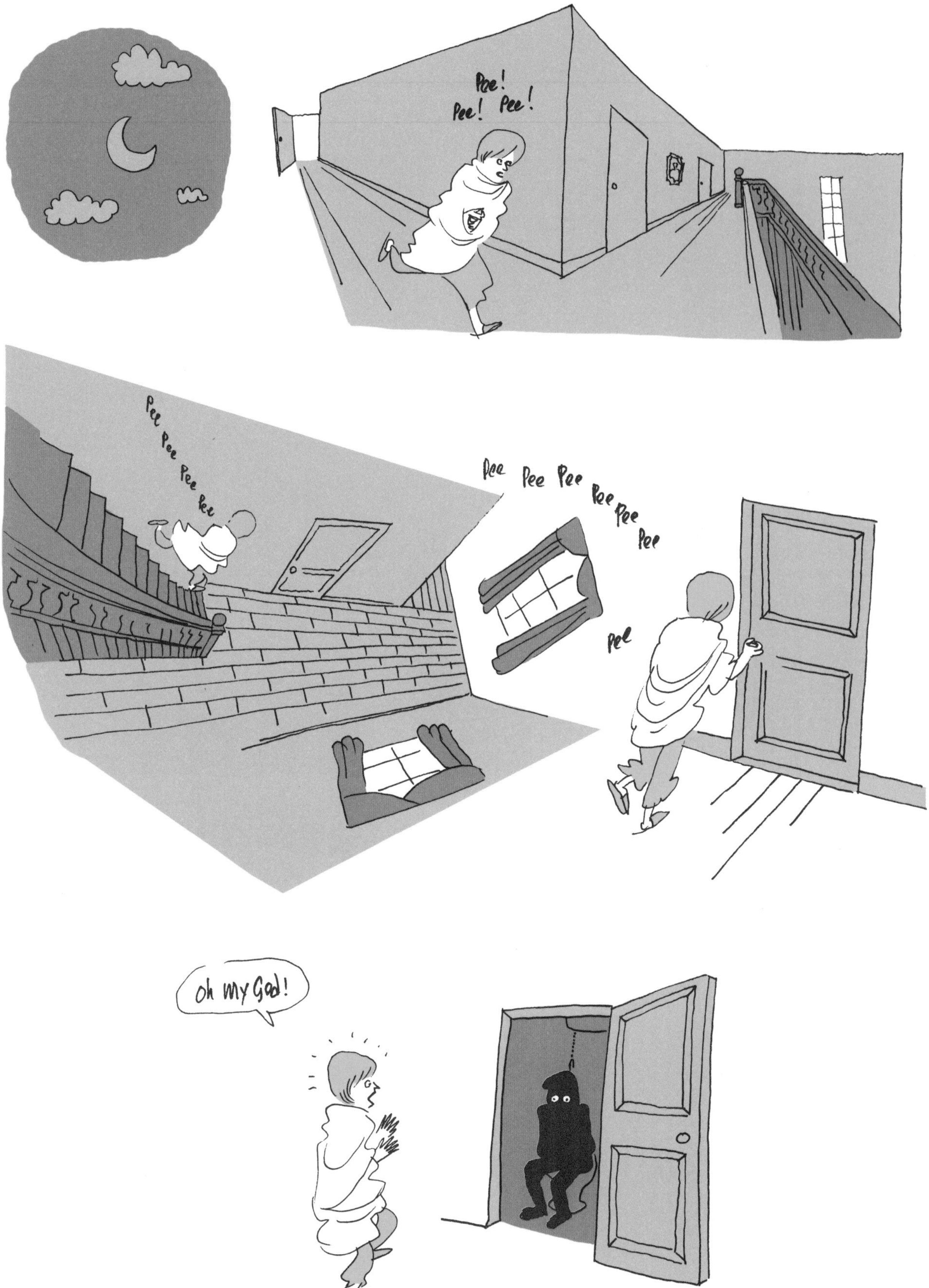
Pee!
Pee! Pee!
Pee
Pee
Pee
Pee
Pee Pee Pee Pee Pee Pee Pee
Pee
oh my God!

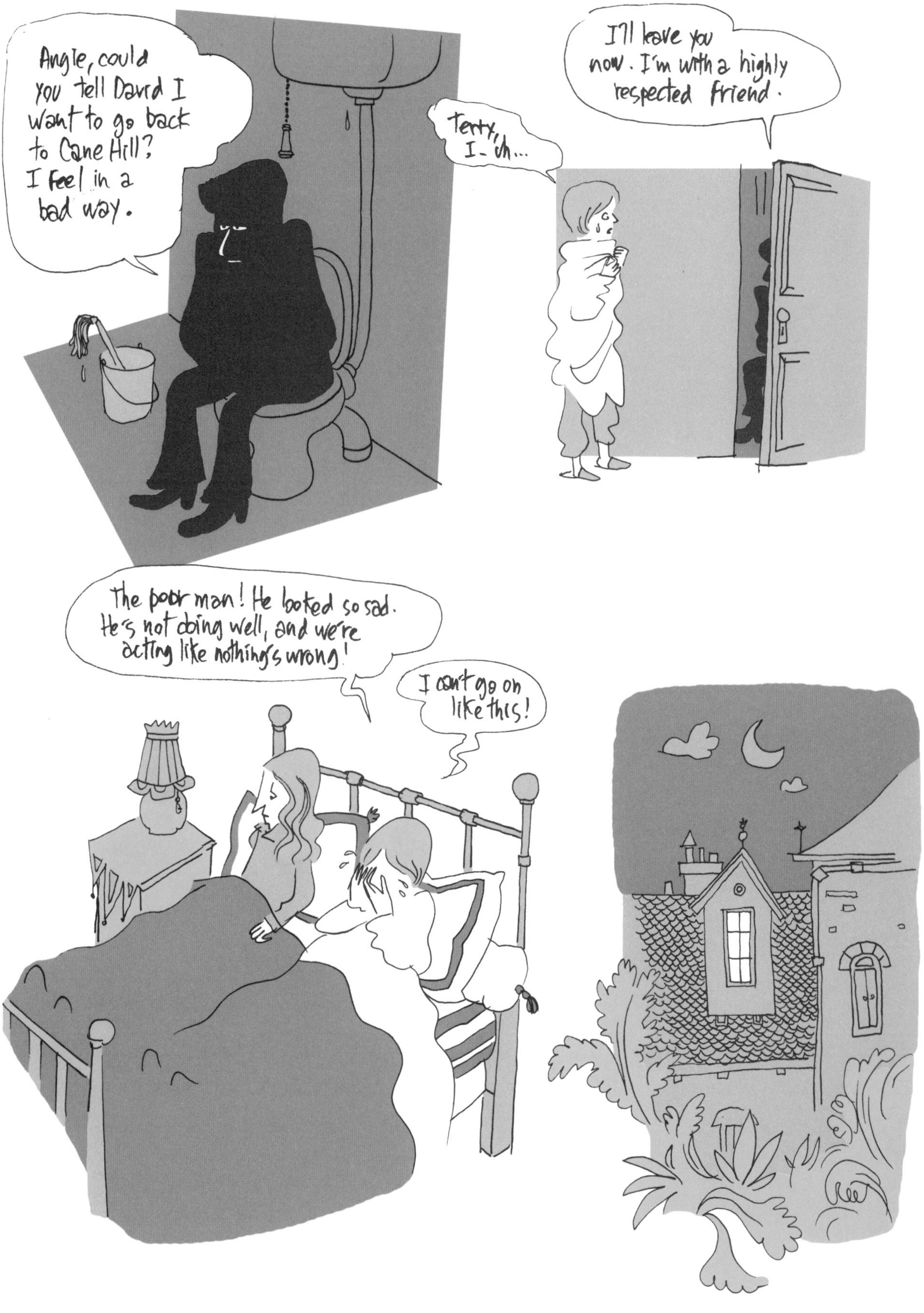
Angie, could you tell David I want to go back to Cane Hill? I feel in a bad way.
Terry, I- uh...
I'll leave you now. I'm with a highly respected friend.
The poor man! He looked so sad. He's not doing well, and we're acting like nothing's wrong!
I can't go on like this!

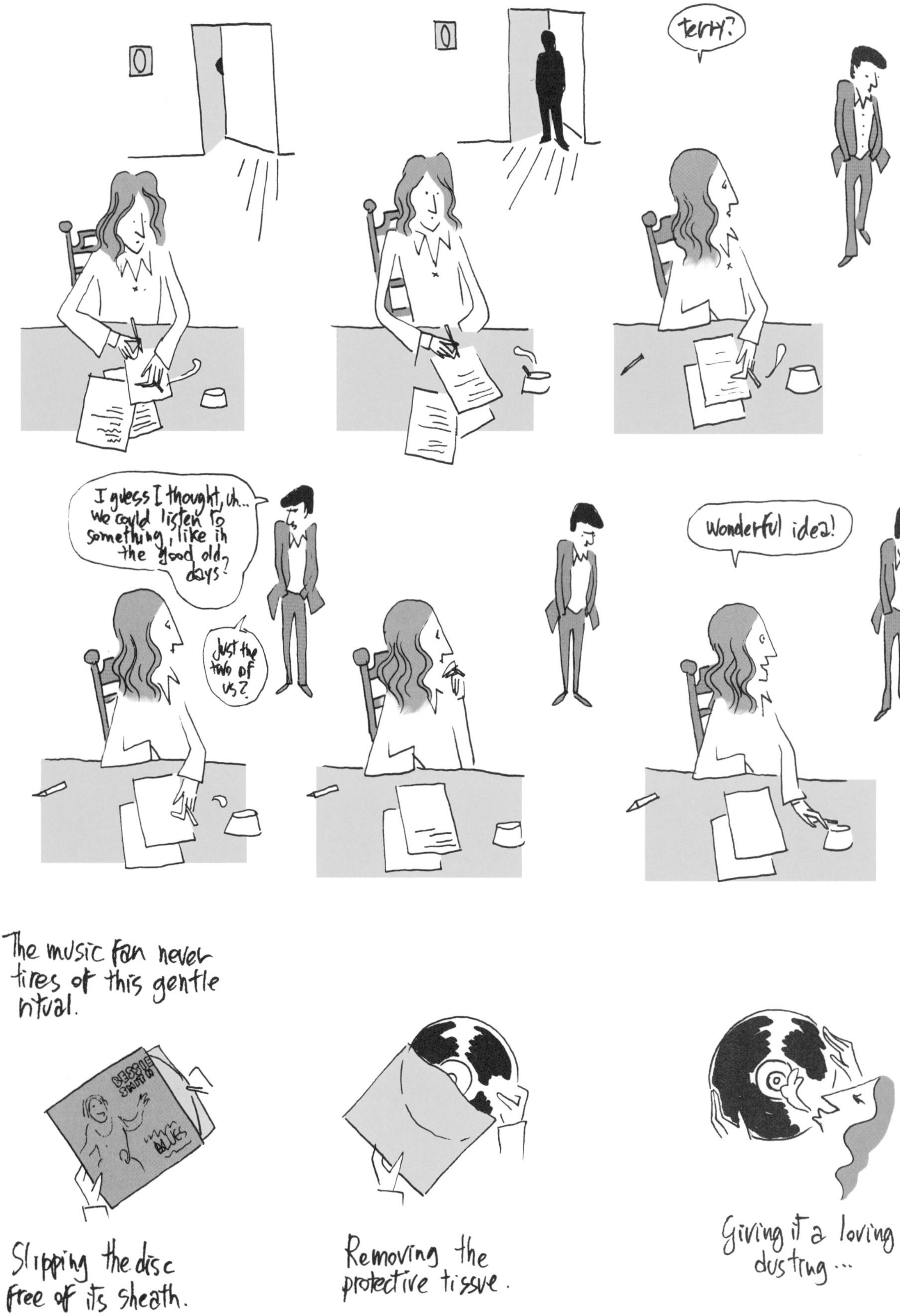
terry?
I guess I thought, uh... we could listen to something, like in the good old days?
Just the two of us?
Wonderful idea!
The music fan never tires of this gentle ritual.
Slipping the disc free of its sheath.
Removing the protective tissue.
Giving it a loving dusting...

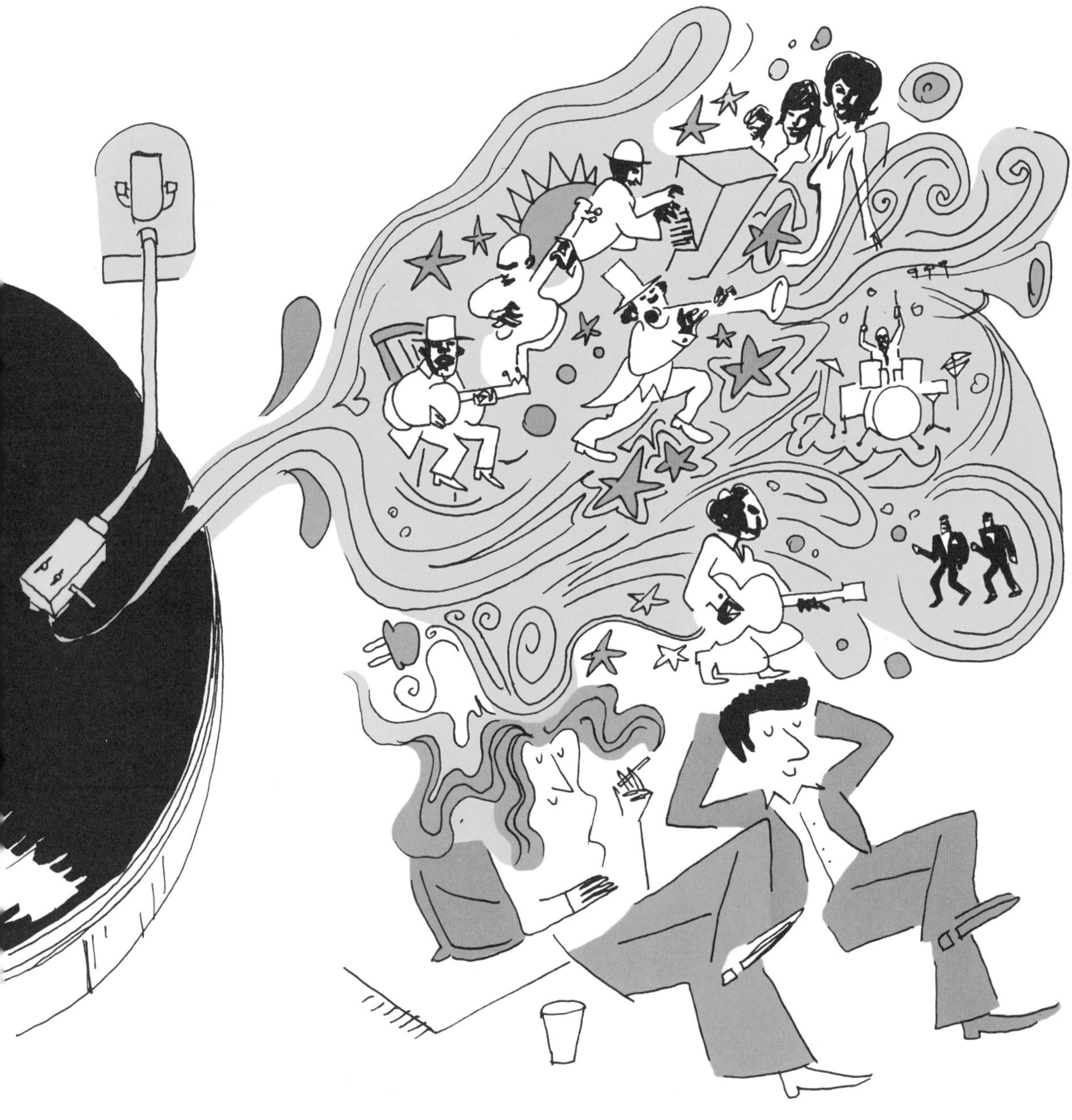

... and leaving this grey world far behind.

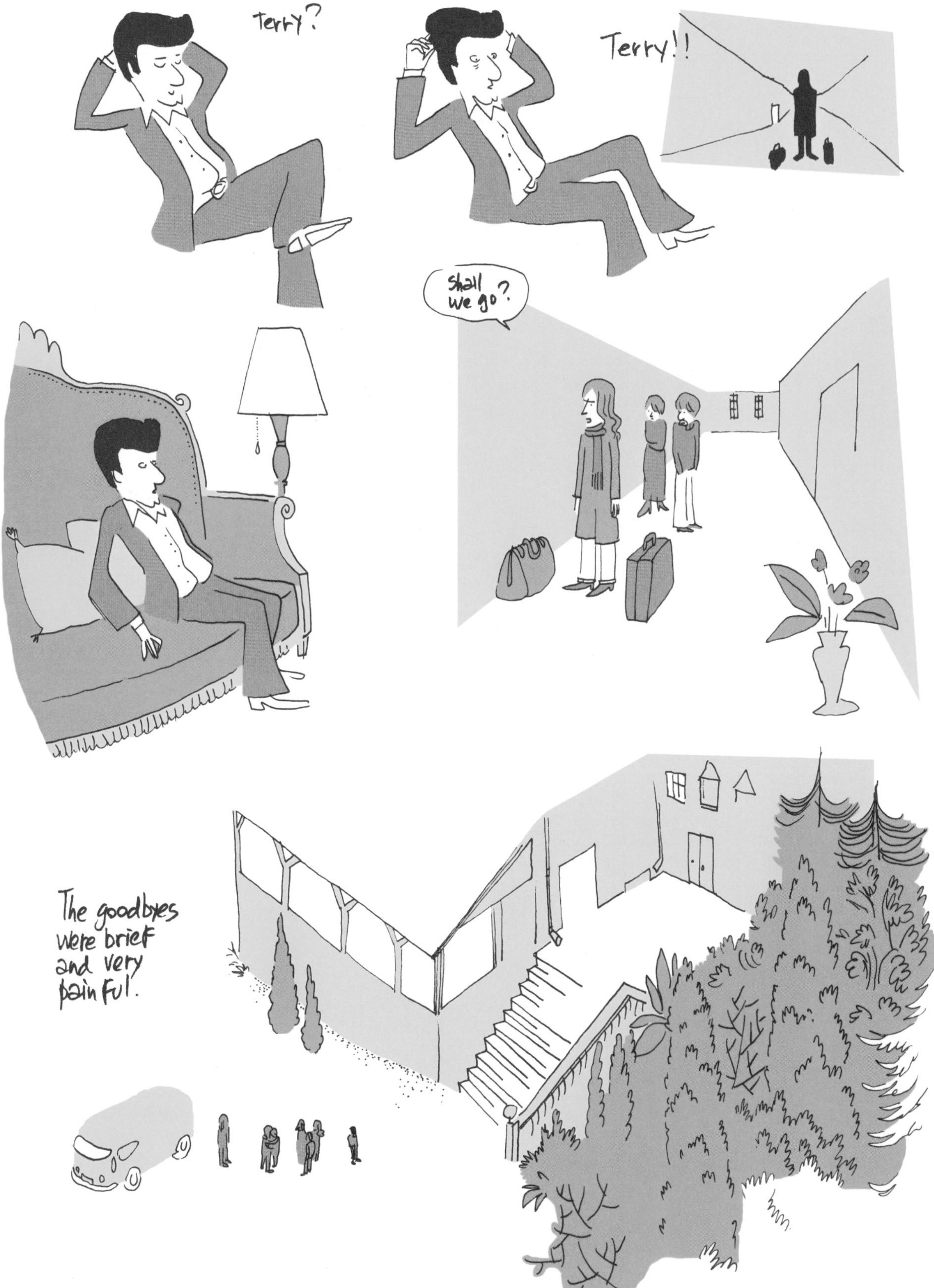
Terry?
Terry!!
Shall we go?
The goodbyes were brief and very painful.

INTERMEZZO

How to be a music snob

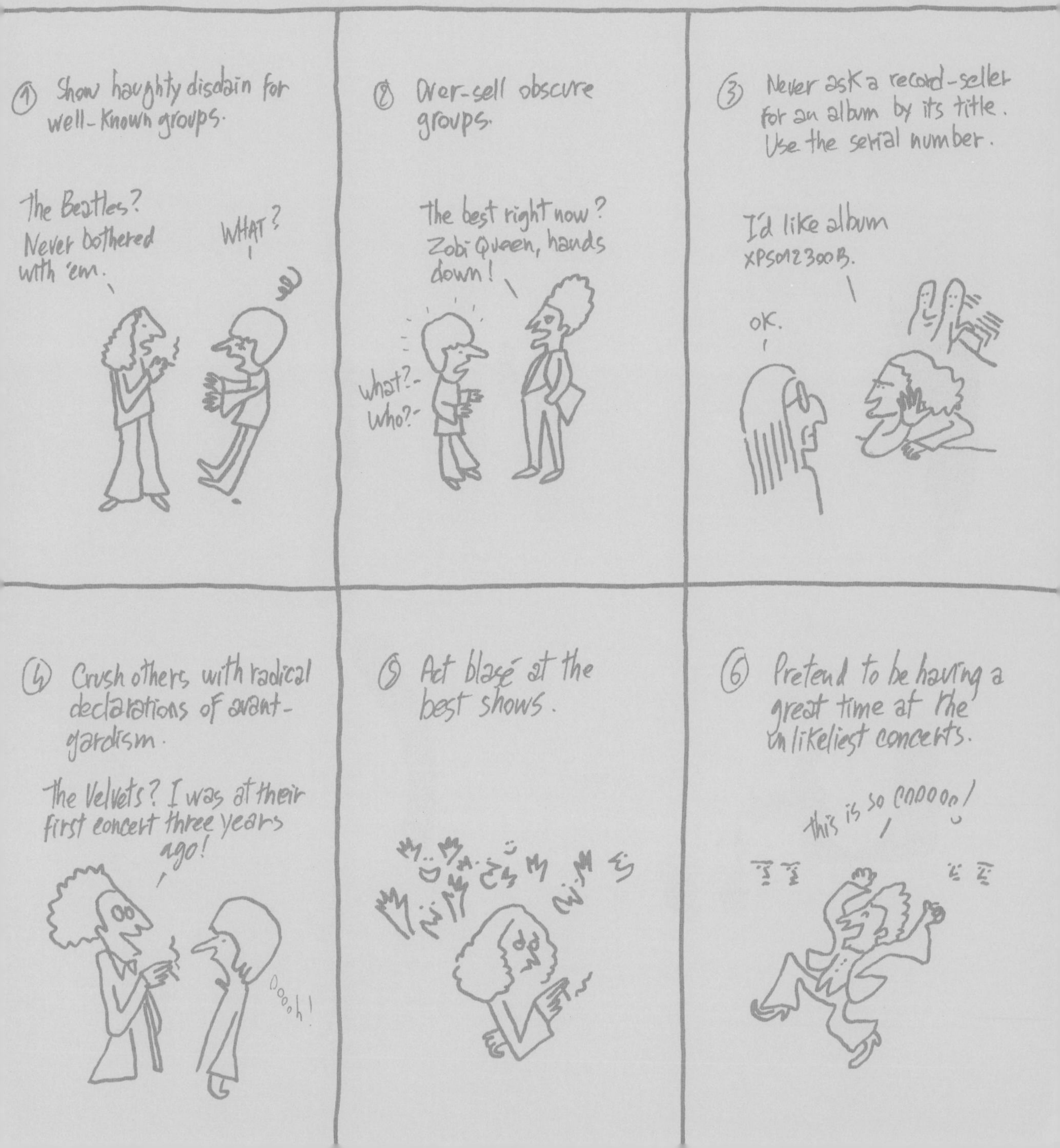

1 Show haughty disdain for well-known groups.
The Beatles? Never bothered with 'em.
WHAT?
2 Over-sell obscure groups.
The best right now? Zobi Queen, hands down!
what?- who?-
3 Never ask a record-seller for an album by its title. Use the serial number.
I'd like album XPS012300B.
OK.
4 Crush others with radical declarations of avant-gardism.
The Velvets? I was at their first concert three years ago!
Ooooh!
5 Act blasé at the best shows.
6 Pretend to be having a great time at the unlikeliest concerts.
This is so cooooo!

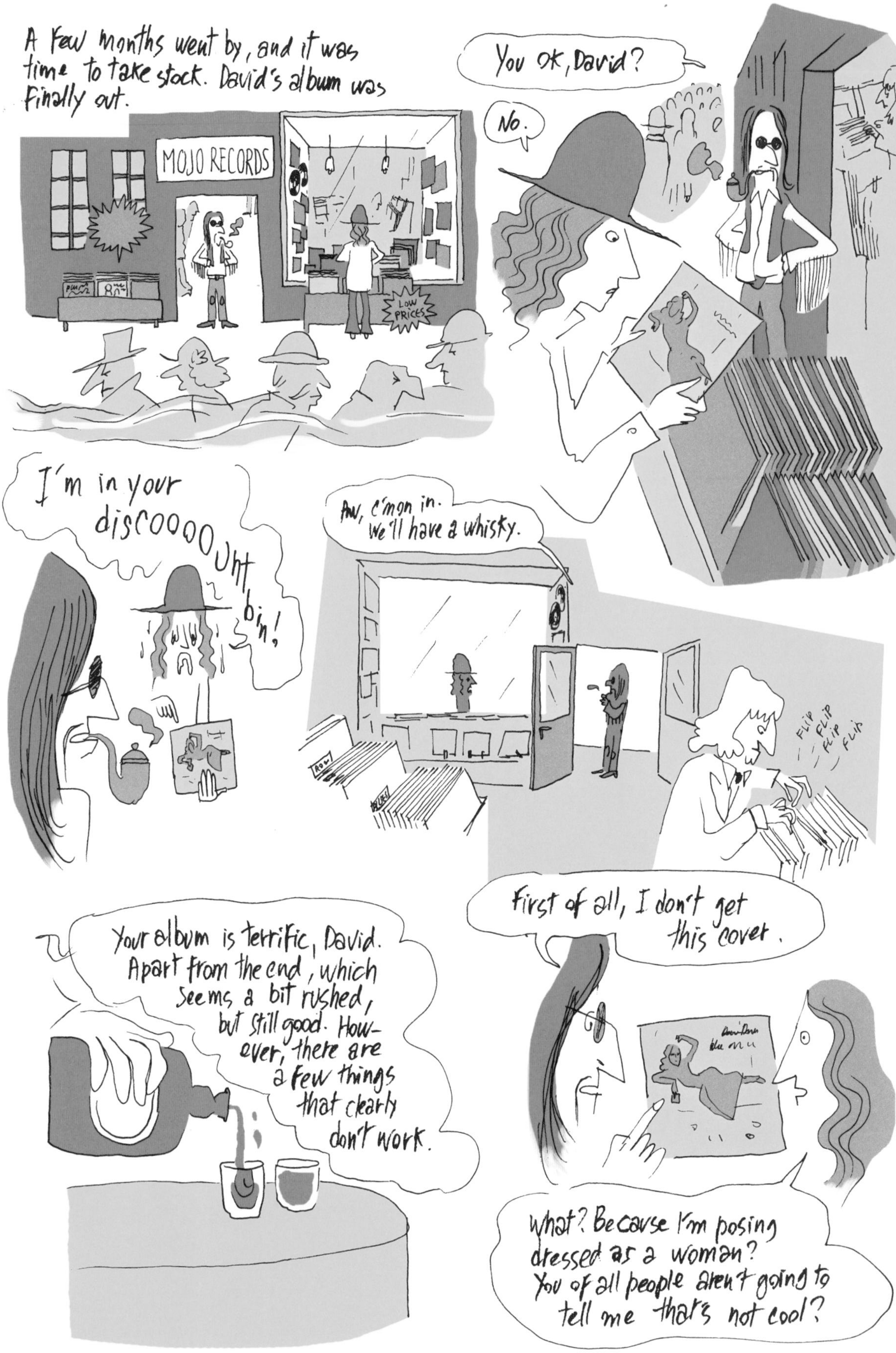

A few months went by, and it was time to take stock. David's album was finally out.
MOJO RECORDS
LOW PRICES
You ok, David?
No.
I'm in your discooooouht bin!
Aw, c'mon in. We'll have a whisky.
FLIP FLIP FLIP FLIP
Your album is terrific, David. Apart from the end, which seems a bit rushed, but still good. However, there are a few things that clearly don't work.
First of all, I don't get this cover.
What? Because I'm posing dressed as a woman? You of all people aren't going to tell me that's not cool?

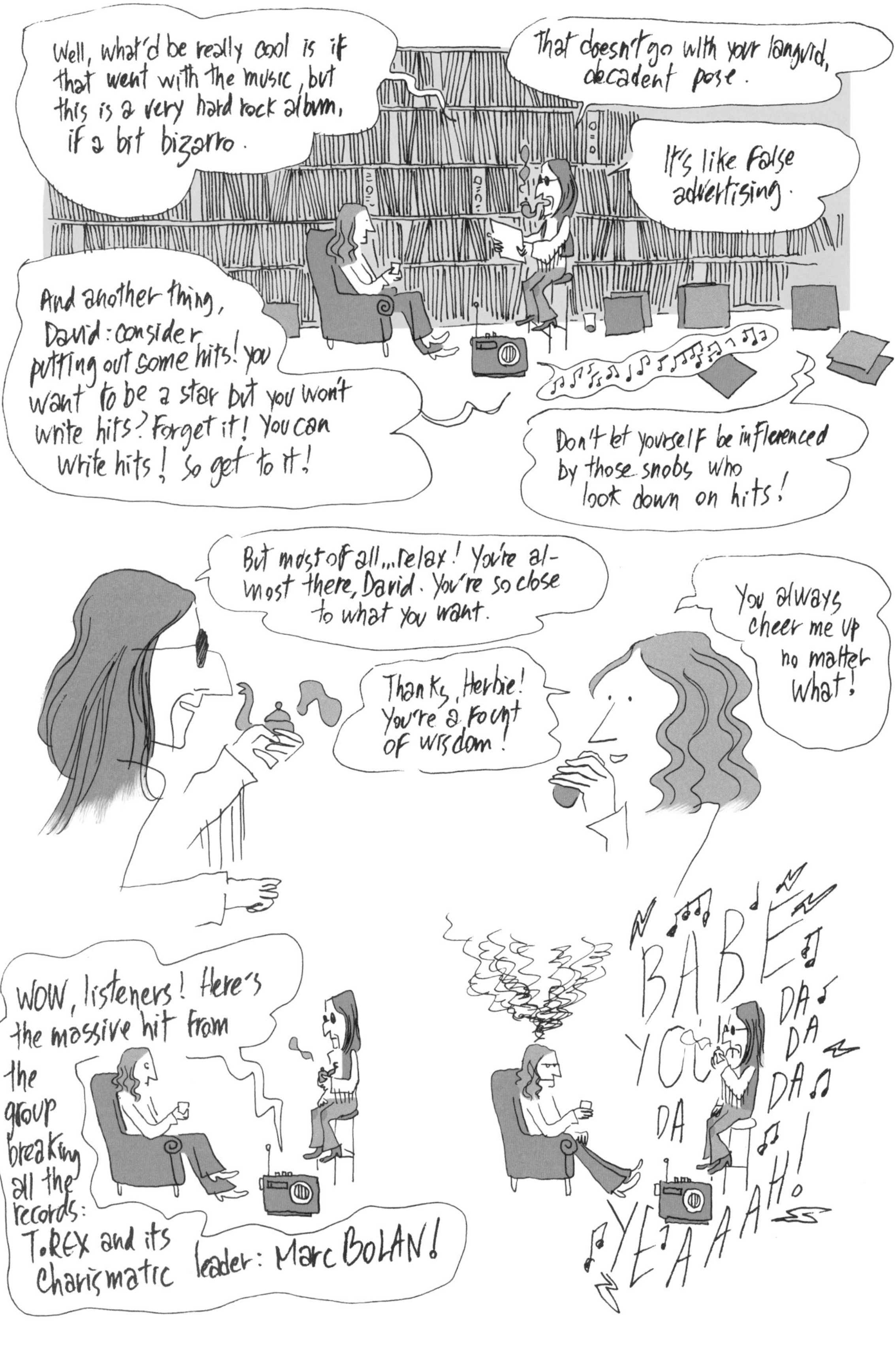
Well, what'd be really cool is if that went with the music, but this is a very hard rock album, if a bit bizarro.
That doesn't go with your languid, decadent pose.
It's like false advertising.
And another thing, David: consider putting out some hits! You want to be a star but you won't write hits? Forget it! You can write hits! So get to it!
Don't let yourself be influenced by those snobs who look down on hits!
But most of all... relax! You're almost there, David. You're so close to what you want.
Thanks, Herbie! You're a fount of wisdom!
You always cheer me up no matter what!
WOW, listeners! Here's the massive hit from the group breaking all the records: T.REX and its charismatic leader: Marc BOLAN!
BABE
YOU
DA
DA
DA
DA
DA
YEAAAH!

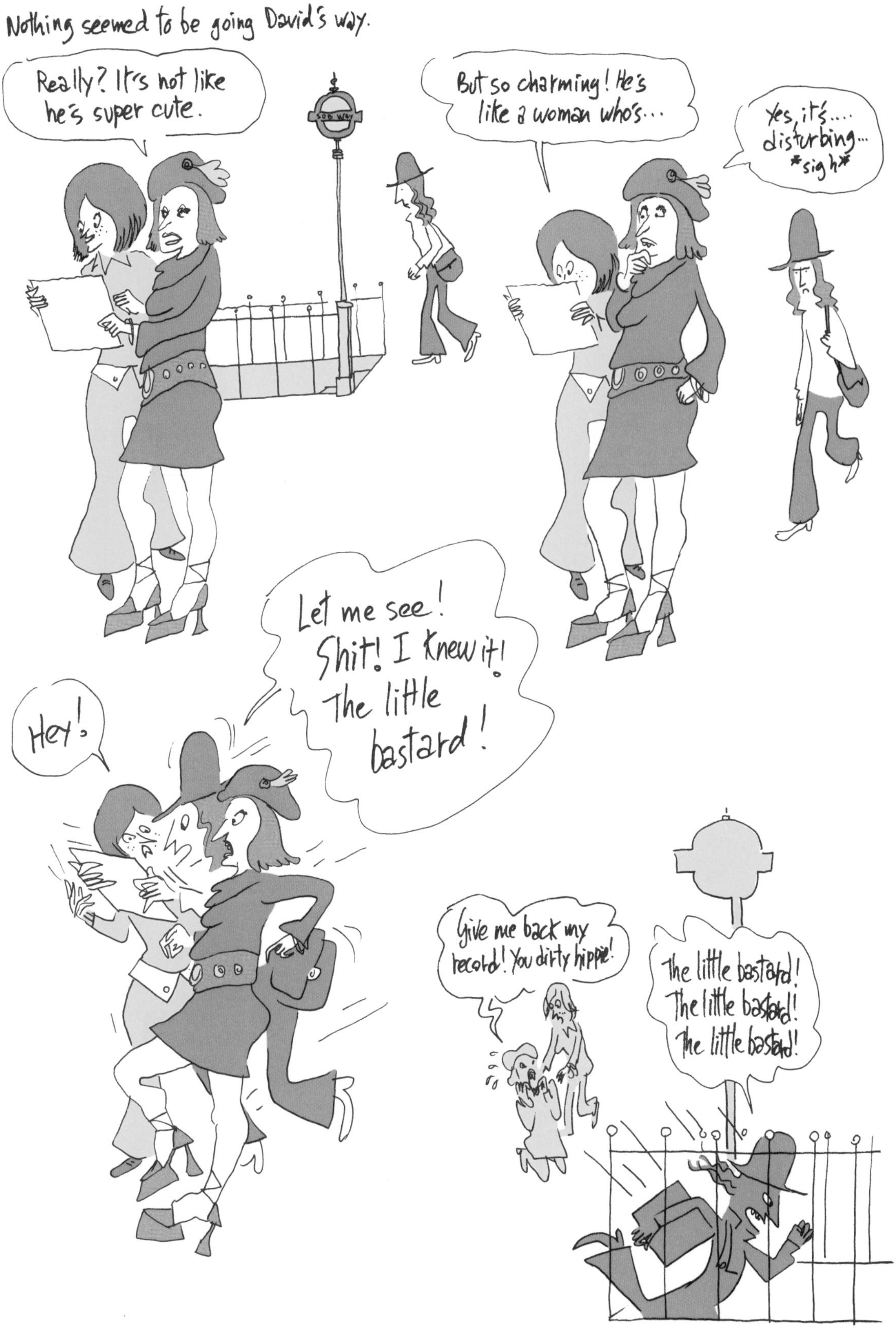
Nothing seemed to be going David's way.
Really? It's not like he's super cute.
SUB WAY
But so charming! He's like a woman who's...
Yes, it's.... disturbing... *sigh*
Hey!
Let me see! Shit! I knew it! The little bastard!
Give me back my record! You dirty hippie!
The little bastard! The little bastard! The little bastard!

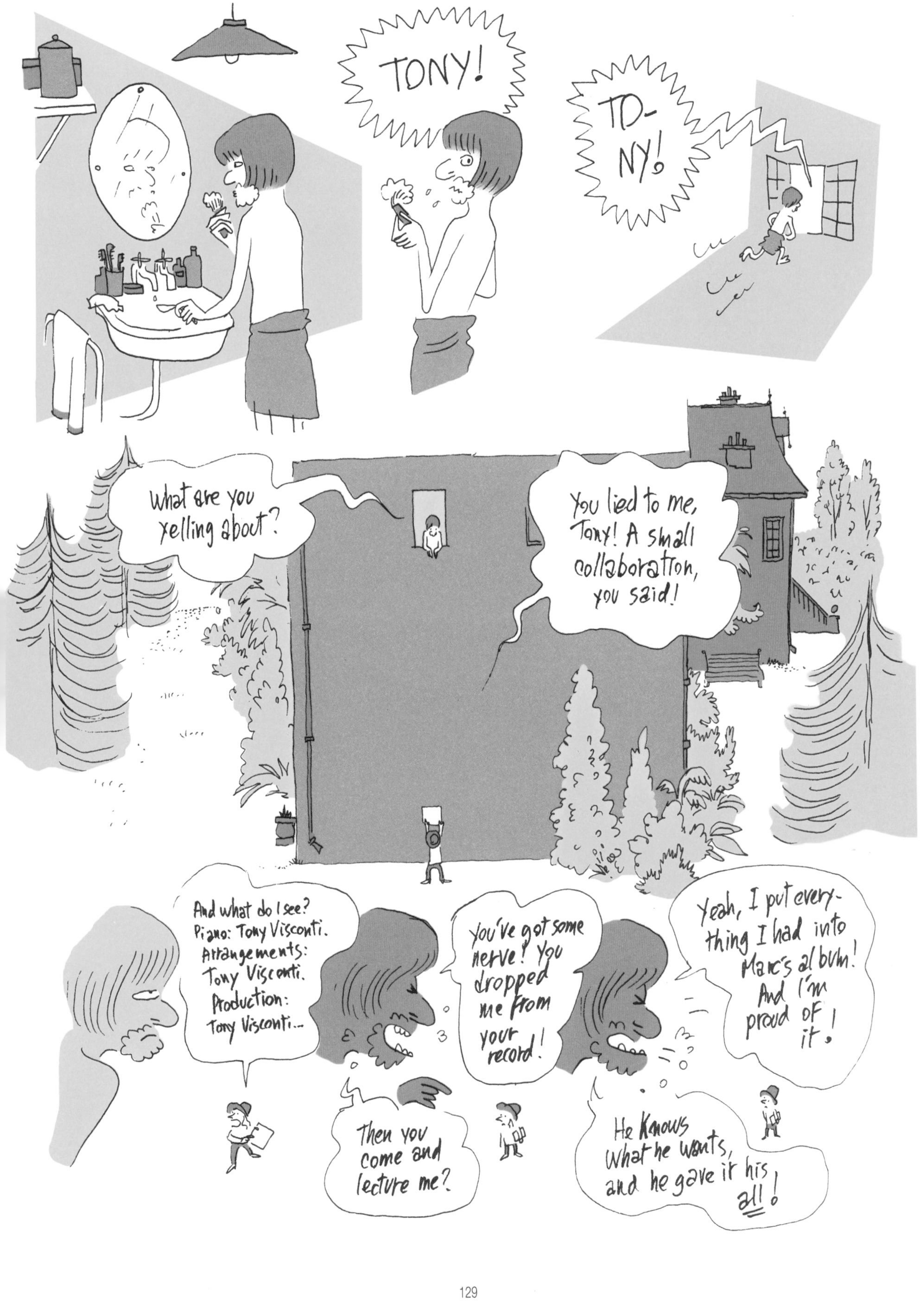
TONY!
TO-NY!
What are you yelling about?
You lied to me, Tony! A small collaboration, you said!
And what do I see? Piano: Tony Visconti. Arrangements: Tony Visconti. Production: Tony Visconti...
You've got some nerve! You dropped me from your record!
Then you come and lecture me?
Yeah, I put everything I had into Marc's album! And I'm proud of it!
He knows what he wants, and he gave it his all!

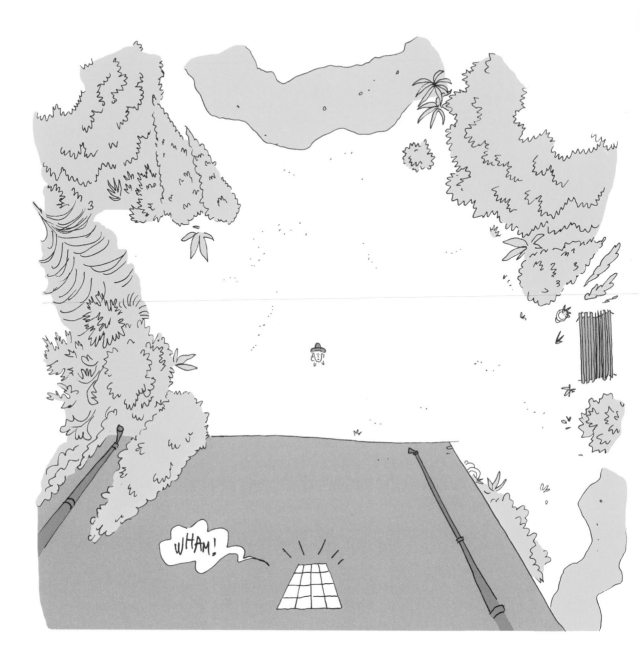

And so it came time for Tony and Liz to leave the house.
Several years would go by before David saw
his friend again.

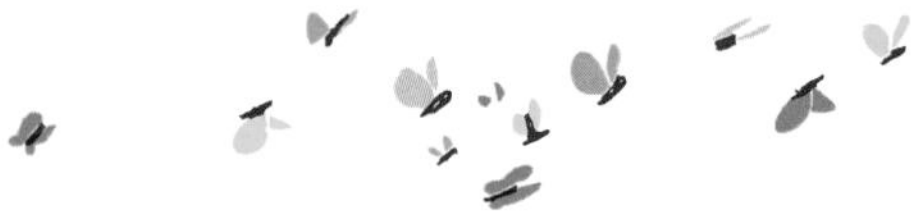

And the months went by . . .

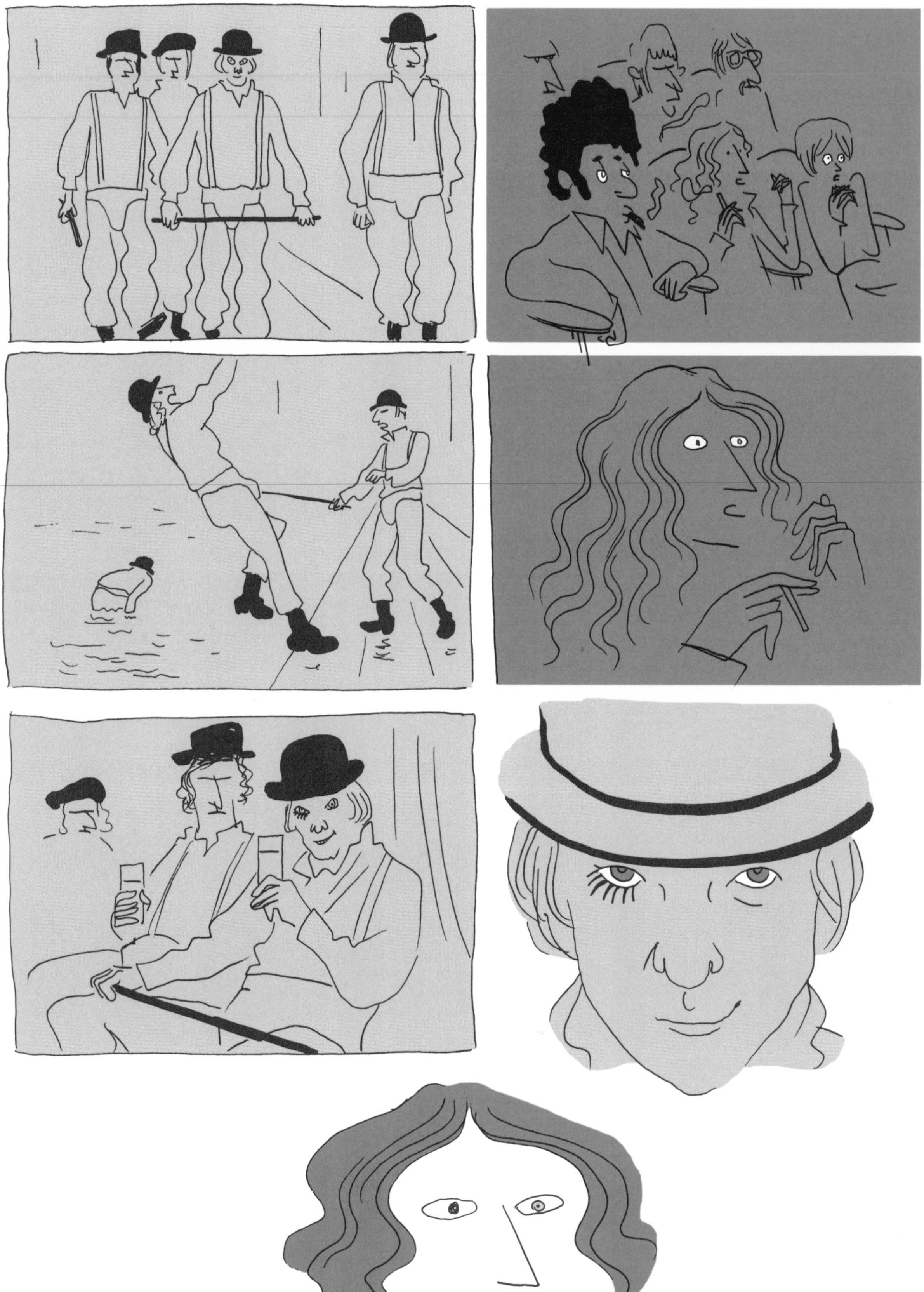

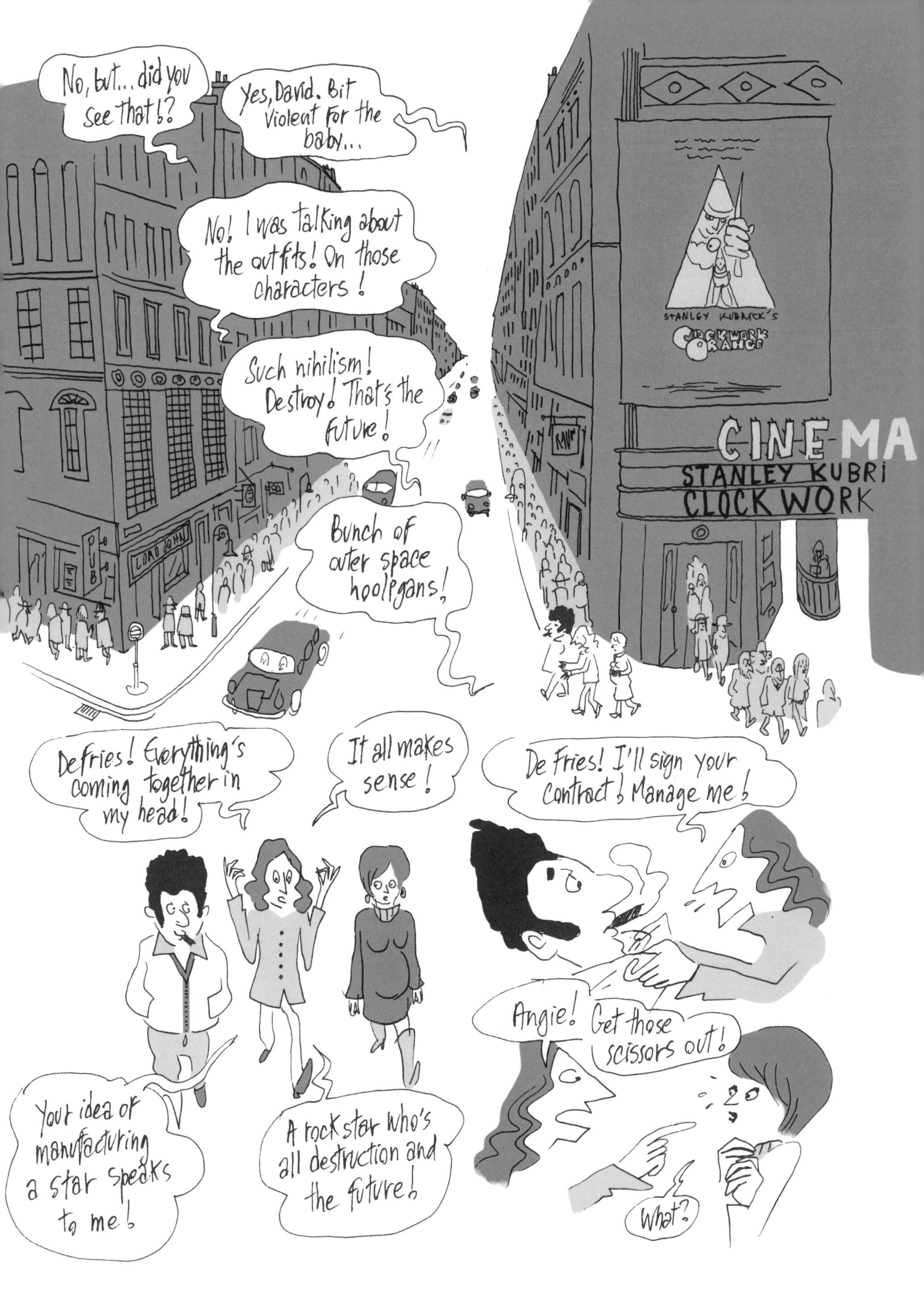
No, but... did you see that!?
Yes, David. Bit violent for the baby...
No! I was talking about the outfits! On those characters!
Such nihilism! Destroy! That's the future!
Bunch of outer space hooligans!
STANLEY KUBRICK'S
CLOCKWORK ORANGE
CINEMA
STANLEY KUBRI
CLOCKWORK
LORD JOHN
PUB
Defries! Everything's coming together in my head!
It all makes sense!
Your idea of manufacturing a star speaks to me!
A rock star who's all destruction and the future!
De Fries! I'll sign your contract! Manage me!
Angie! Get those scissors out!
What?

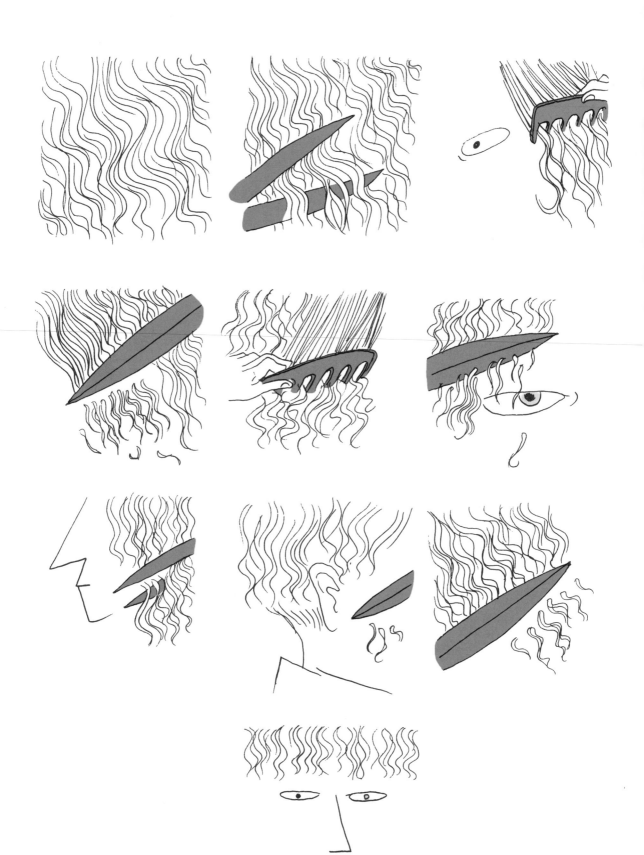

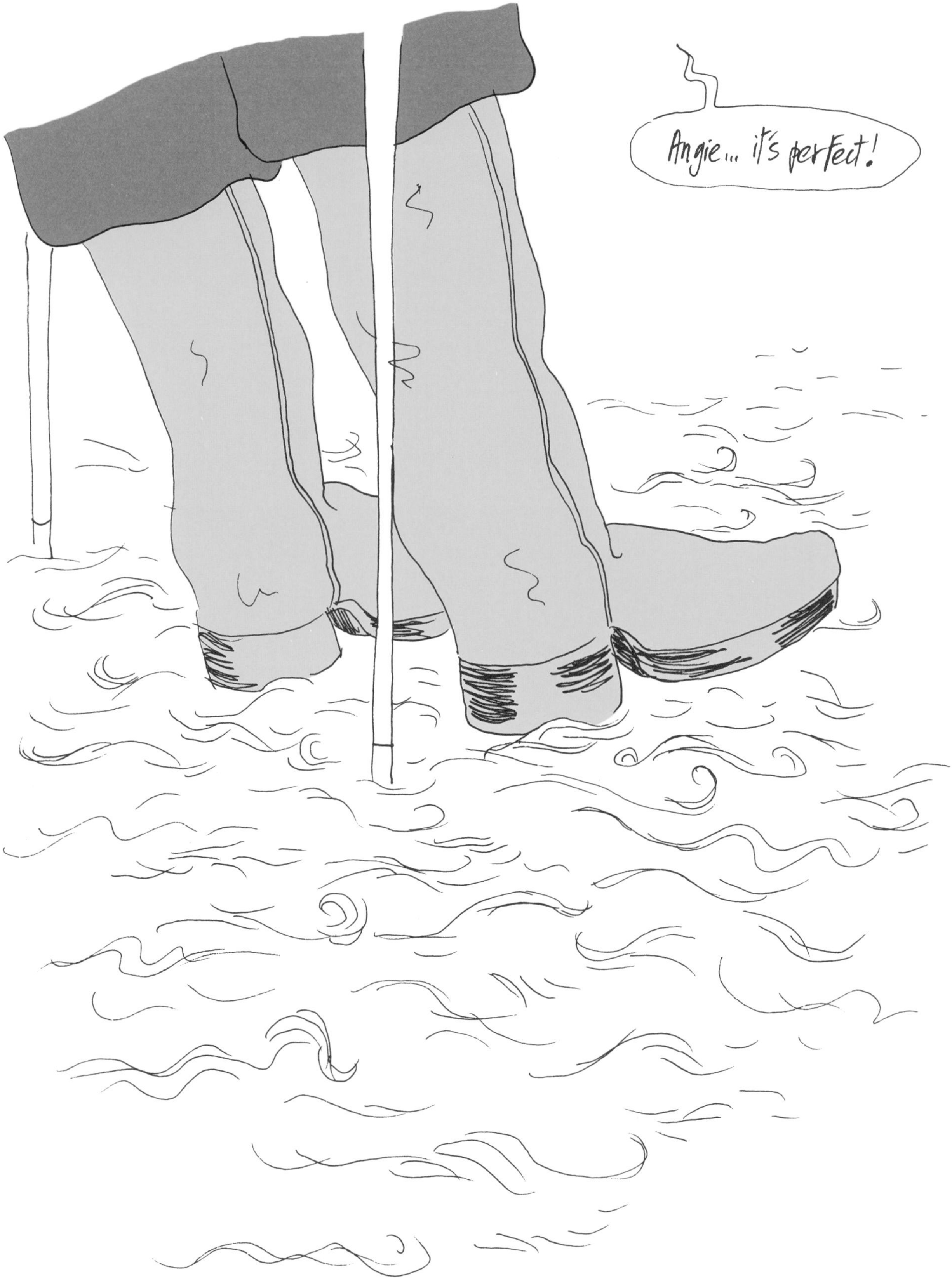
Angie... it's perfect!

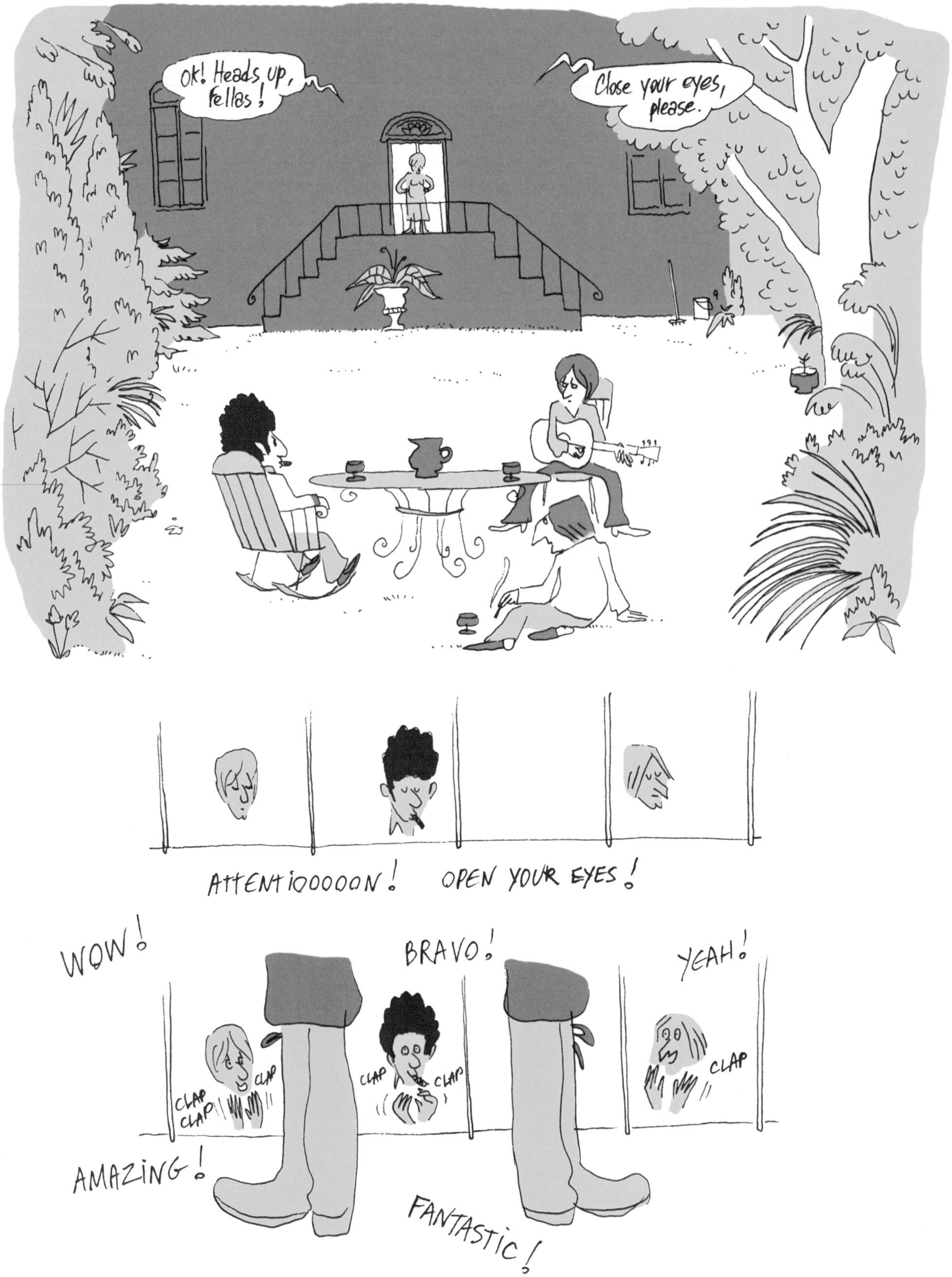
Ok! Heads up, fellas!
Close your eyes, please.
ATTENTIOOOOON! OPEN YOUR EYES!
WOW!
BRAVO!
YEAH!
CLAP CLAP
CLAP
CLAP
CLAP
CLAP
AMAZING!
FANTASTIC!

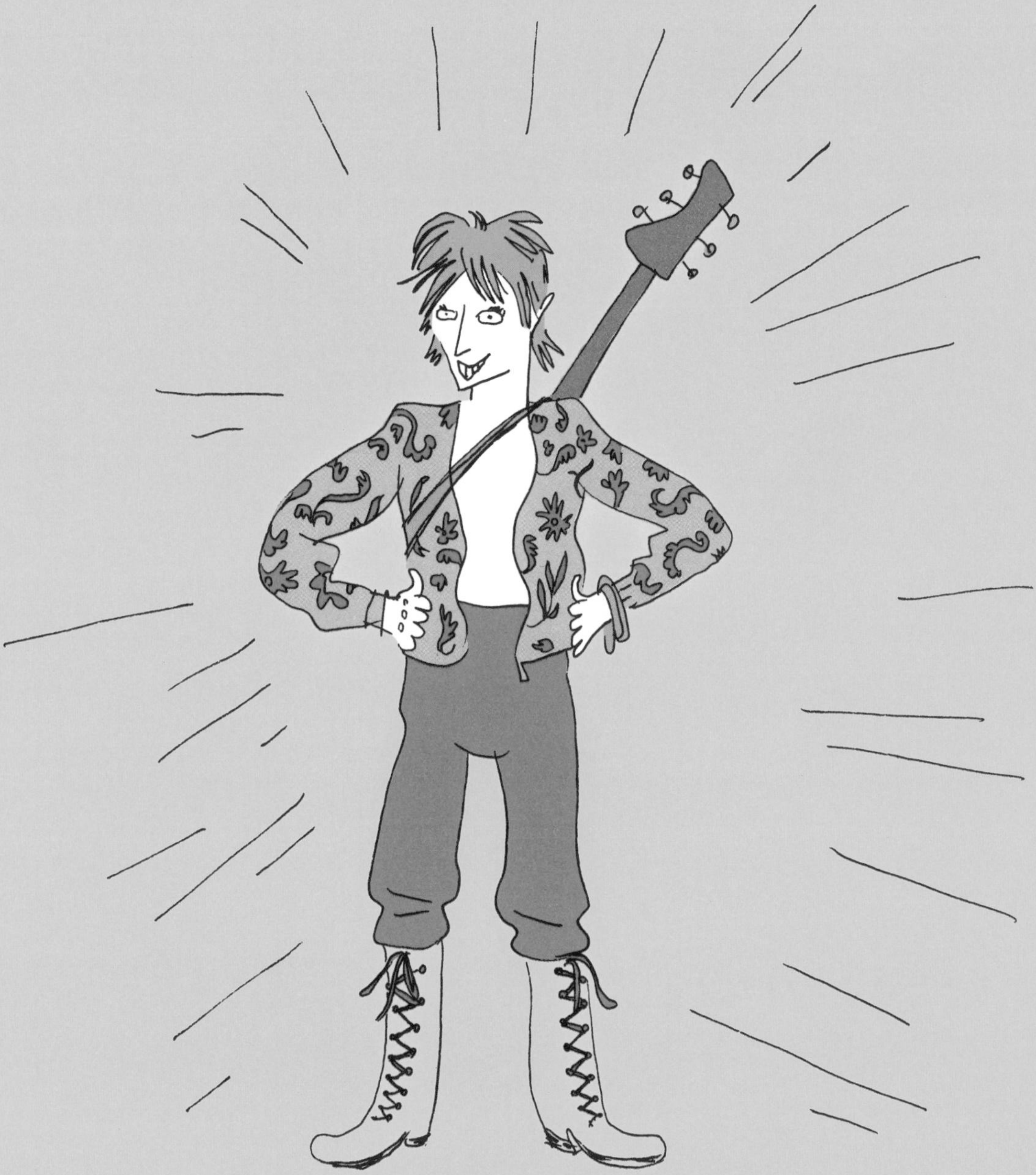

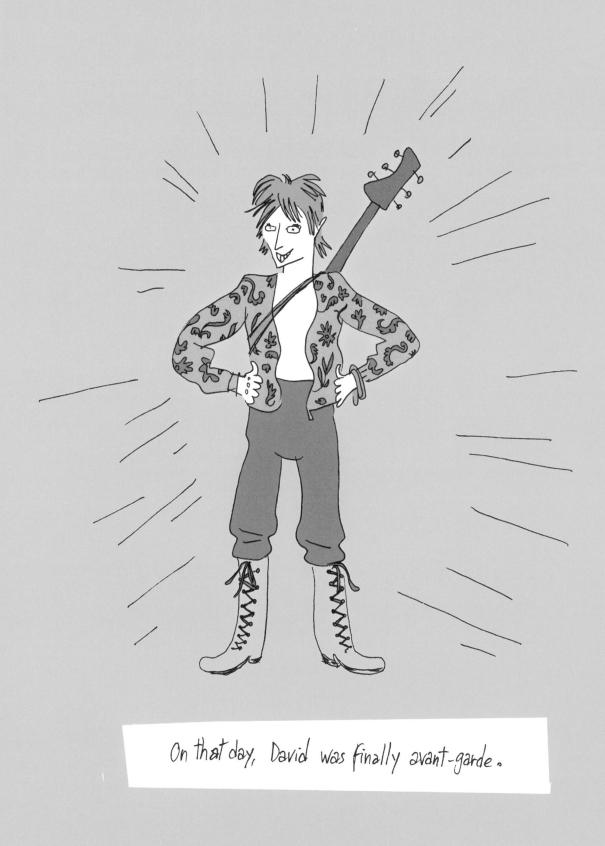

On that day, David was finally avant-garde.

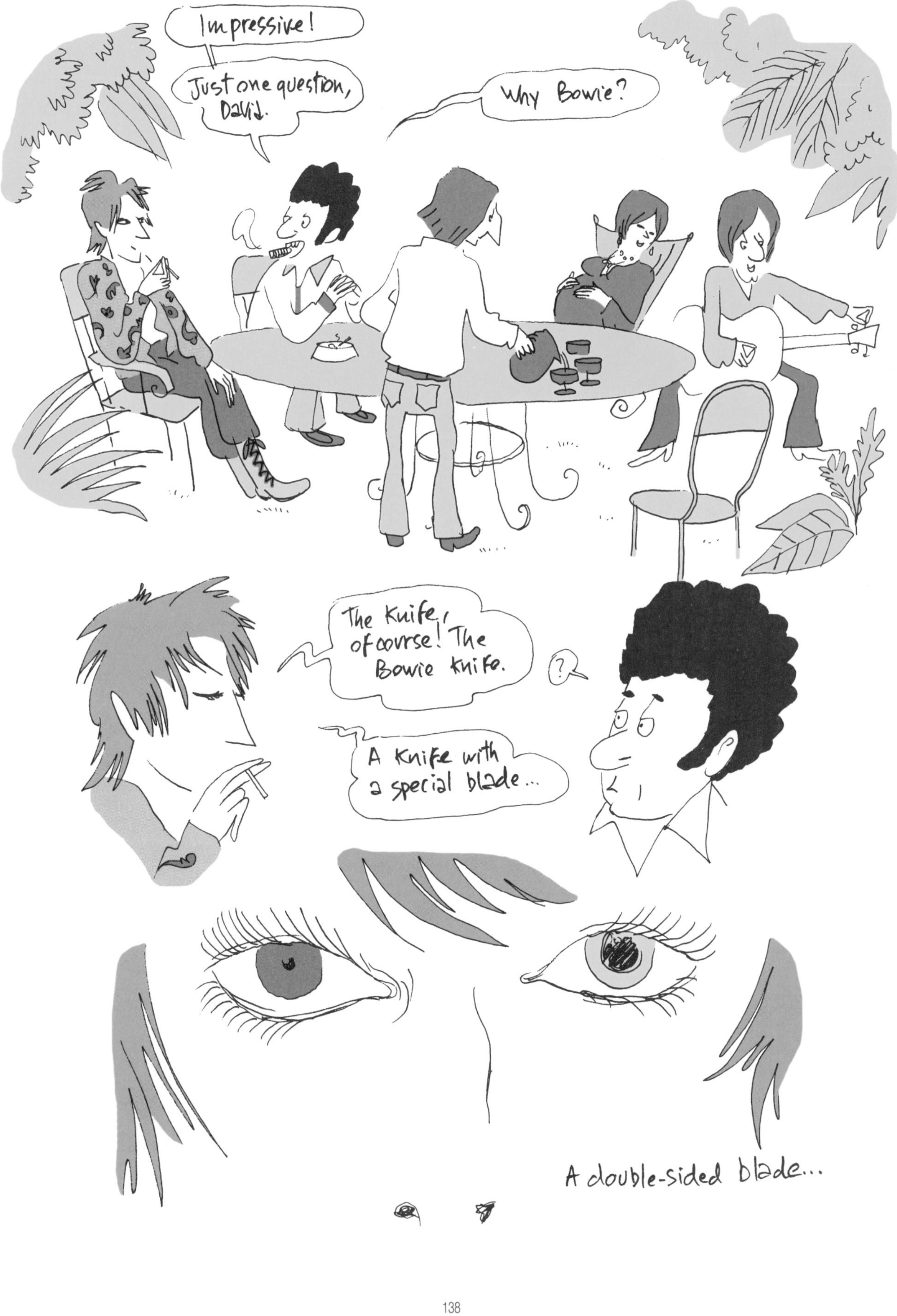

Impressive!
Just one question, David.
Why Bowie?
The knife, of course! The Bowie knife.
?
A knife with a special blade...
A double-sided blade...

It only took David a few months to embrace
success and conquer the world.

In the end, this enchanted interlude in my peaceful
life as a house lasted for only two springs...

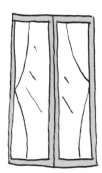

... but not a day goes by that I don't think
back on them fondly.

David, Augie and the others.

My Friends.

Discography.

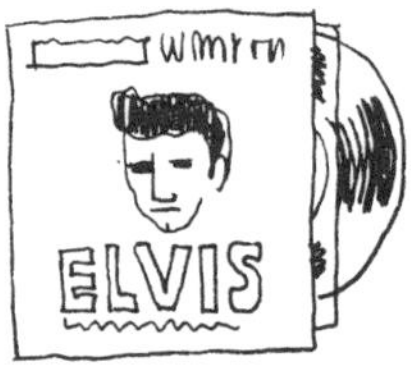
ELVIS

1963

Bowie is still David Jones.
He's 16 and wants to be the next Elvis.

He founds and disbands countless groups and puts out a few singles with no success.
He decides to call himself David Bowie.

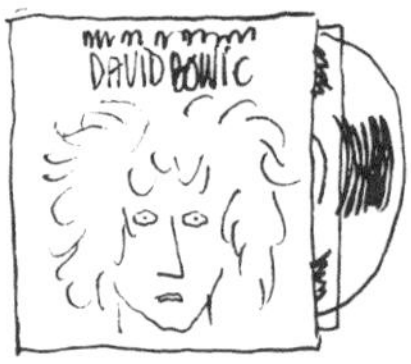
DAVID BOWIE

1969

His single "Space Oddity" is a mini-hit, but his first album, "Man of Words/Man of Music", is a flop.

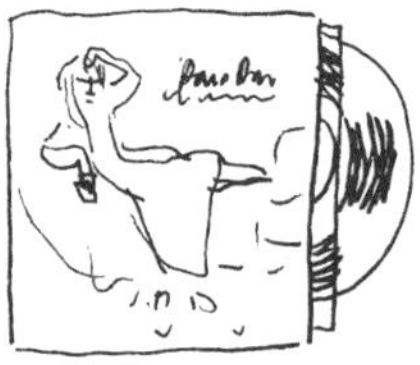

1970

He records his second album, the one our story is about: "The Man Who Sold the World".
A commercial flop, but a critical success.
The Bowie "spirit" is said to begin with this album.

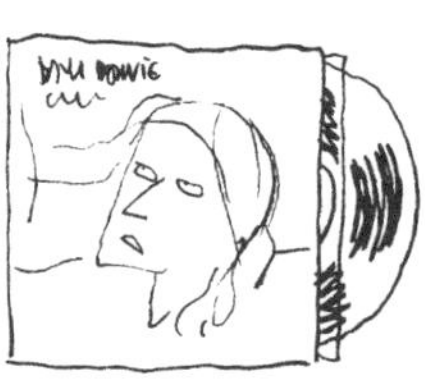

1971

Records, one right after the other, "Hunky Dory" and "The Rise and Fall of Ziggy Stardust and the Spiders from Mars". Critics acclaim the first record; the second is a huge hit.

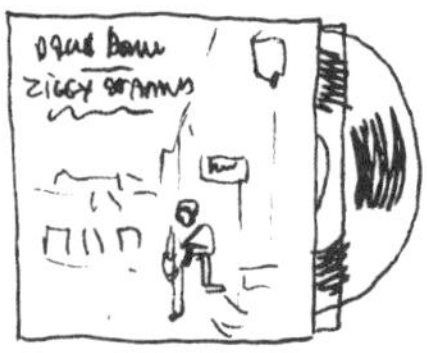

1972

Borne along by his Ziggy Stardust persona, Bowie overtakes his buddy Bolan on the road to success, becoming the biggest phenomenon since The Beatles.

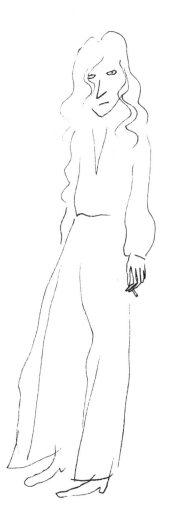

Dedicated to the Man Who Illuminated my Life.

R.I.P.